International
Economics

International Economics
CONCEPTS AND ISSUES

Klaus Friedrich
Associate Professor of Economics
Pennsylvania State University

McGraw-Hill Book Company
New York St. Louis San Francisco Düsseldorf
Johannesburg Kuala Lumpur London Mexico Montreal
New Delhi Panama Paris São Paulo
Singapore Sydney Tokyo Toronto

International Economics:
Concepts and Issues

1234567890KPKP7987654

This book was set in Times Roman by Black Dot, Inc.
The editors were Jack R. Crutchfield, Sonia Sheldon, and Richard S. Laufer;
the cover was designed by Edward A. Butler;
the production supervisor was Thomas J. LoPinto.
The drawings were done by ANCO Technical Services.
Kingsport Press, Inc., was printer and binder.

Library of Congress Cataloging in Publication Data

Friedrich, Klaus.
　　International economics.

　　　1.　International economic relations.　I.　Title.
HF1411.F74　　　382.1　　　73–22444
ISBN 0–07–022435–8

To Matthew, Peter and Pauli

Contents

Preface

The problem with international economics is the large gap between theory and observed reality. One can either expand the theoretical presentation to get away from overly restrictive assumptions, or one can use descriptive material where the theory seems particularly irrelevant. Most texts use one or both of these approaches. The result tends to be highly technical, or voluminous, or both. While students with a solid background in economic principles are well served in this way, beginners are not.

This book attempts to introduce students with a relatively minimal economics background to the field of international economics. Its premise is that a few basic theoretical concepts can go a long way toward helping to interpret international economic relations. These concepts are presented in some detail: Chapters 1, 2, and 3 develop the conventional diagrammatic trade model. Chapters 8 and 9 introduce the concept of the balance of payments in relation to the foreign exchange market. Chapter 12 presents Keynesian income determination for the open economy. All other material is based more or less directly on these concepts.

In terms of institutional coverage, the book is, of course, far less than complete. The material is issue-oriented and reflects the author's opinion on what is and what is not an important issue at a time when issues in international trade and finance seem to change more rapidly than ever. The book has been kept brief enough, however, to allow for introduction of supplementary material by the individual instructor.

I am greatly indebted to the following reviewers for their valuable suggestions: Professor John Letiche, University of California at Berkeley; Professor Ingo Walter, New York University; Professor Dennis Ray Appleyard, University of North Carolina; Professor Percy Warner, University of Connecticut; and Professor Harold Williams, Kent State University. My colleague Richard Rosenberg applied his usual tough but constructive criticism to Chapters 6 and 7. Will E. Mason, also at Penn State, gave his qualified blessings to Chapters 14 and 15. The custom of absolving all reviewers from any share in the remaining errors and omissions contains great wisdom and is eagerly followed here.

Klaus Friedrich

The Principle of Trading

America's reason to engage in international trade with Britain and Mr. Smith's reason to trade with his neighbor Jones are basically the same. Nations as well as individuals trade with each other because gains can be had from trading. Let us look at trade between two individuals in order to develop some of the principles underlying all trading.

In order to appreciate the importance of trading, we need only to imagine a world in which no trading of any kind takes place. No buying or selling would occur. Each individual would have to produce by himself whatever he wanted to consume. Such a situation of self-sufficiency or autarky would obviously mean a drastic decline in our economic welfare.

The following paragraphs will examine the apparent relationship between trade and economic welfare.

THE PRINCIPLE OF DIVISION OF LABOR

People tend to have different skills. Smith may have those of a farmer and Jones may have those of a weaver. Because of these differences in skills, Smith may be relatively good at producing food, and Jones may be good at producing cloth. But both individuals need to consume food as well as cloth. While man does not live by bread alone, he would also find it difficult to live by cloth alone. In autarky, therefore, Smith would have to produce some clothing along with food, and Jones would have to produce some food besides clothing. Each man would waste some time producing a good for which his talents are relatively ill suited, because each man needs both goods in consumption but is relatively skilled at producing only one good.

If we now introduce the principle of division of labor, Smith will produce only food, and Jones will produce only clothing. In this way they would divide the labor of feeding and clothing themselves in accordance with their different skills. It is easy to see that Smith's and Jones's combined production of food and clothing is higher with division of labor than it is in a state of autarky. All production of food is now in the hands of Smith, the skilled farmer, and all production of clothing is done by Jones, the skilled weaver. No farming skills are wasted on the production of clothing, and no weaving skills are wasted on the production of food.

If division of labor increases the amount of food and clothing available *jointly* to both individuals, it must be possible to make *each* individual better off. This improvement is realized through trade. Smith will gain by trading some of his food for clothing, and Jones will gain by trading some of his clothing for food. We can therefore formulate our first principle as follows: Division of labor according to different endowments can improve the economic standard of living of both parties. This principle is very much at work in today's economic world. In modern industrial society nobody lives in autarky. Specialization has reached unprecedented degrees, as has the economic standard of living. The famous English economist of the eighteenth century, Adam Smith, used pin making in his celebrated exposition of the principle of division of labor.[1]

[1]Adam Smith, *An Inquiry into the Nature and Causes of the Wealth of Nations*, The Modern Library, New York, 1937, chaps. 1 and 2. These two short chapters contain the most famous discussion of division of labor to this day.

Specialization here leads to larger output, because each worker is assigned a single task, repeating it again and again. The special skill in this case need not be inborn but is acquired by practice. Division of labor and technological progress thus became related concepts. Henry Ford's innovative production techniques more than a century later represent a further development of this particular aspect of specialization.

INTERDEPENDENCE

Having formulated the basic principle of division of labor, we must now have a closer look at its implications.

One such implication is the interdependence between trading partners. Jones must be able to rely on Smith's willingness to perform his specialty, and vice versa. Should Smith prefer autarky (against his economic interest) to specialization, Jones would be forced into autarky. Division of labor, therefore, requires a certain amount of cooperation which is based on the incentive of economic gain for each party. The interdependence which results from such cooperation has, on occasion, been viewed as a burden. In a modern economy the extremely high degree of interdependence due to specialization is matched by the complexity of the economic system. Very complex economic systems tend to be subject to economic fluctuations which require remedial action by the government.[2] Of course, the benefits derived from division of labor in terms of living standards far outweigh the burdens of interdependence. No one has yet suggested our return to autarky in order to avoid the problems of the complex modern economy and been taken very seriously.

Another burden of specialization involves repetitiveness and dullness of many industrial tasks. The very same principle of specialization, on the other hand, gives the artist the freedom to pursue his vocation without having to worry about actually producing food and shelter. On balance, there seems to be no apparent reason why people should be unhappy doing only one thing and happy doing several things as long as a free enterprise system gives each individual the freedom to choose his specialty.

[2]Any introductory economics textbook can be consulted on this important point. See, for example, Paul A. Samuelson, *Economics*, 8th ed., McGraw-Hill Book Company, New York, 1970, chaps. 8, 9, and 18.

TRADE

A further implication of the principle of division of labor is, of course, trade. To go back once more to Smith and Jones, it is easy to see that they must trade in order to enjoy the benefits from division of labor. Since each of them specializes in only one good, but needs to consume both goods, part of each man's output must reach the other man. Smith exchanges that amount of food which he does not consume himself for that amount of clothing which Jones does not consume himself. This process of exchange must be viewed as the ultimate consummation of the principle of division of labor.

In today's modern economy division of labor has gone so far that the producer rarely consumes more than an insignificant part of his own product. If imports (i.e., goods produced by others) as a percentage of an individual's consumption are used as an index of interdependence (or dependence on trade), this interdependence is very close to 100 percent between individuals in a modern economy. Between nations the dependence on international trade is usually much lower than that.

THE TERMS OF TRADE

The more dependent on trade the individual becomes, the more important are the terms at which he can exchange his product for other products. These so-called terms of trade, in our simple example, are expressed by the ratio in which food exchanges for clothing between Smith and Jones. The determination of this ratio will be subject to bargaining between Smith and Jones; the more clothing Smith can get for a given amount of food, the better off will Smith be and the worse off will Jones be. The precise outcome of this bargaining process is difficult to predict, but we can use what we already know about the principle of division of labor to predict the range into which the outcome must fall: The terms of trade must be such that both Smith and Jones are better off specializing and trading than they would be in autarky. If this were not the case, our basic principle of division of labor, according to which both parties must benefit, would be violated. This conclusion is in agreement with a commonsense observation about trade: If two parties choose freely to trade with each other, i.e., no party can exert any kind of force other than the incentive of gain over the other party, the reason why trade occurs must be that both parties stand to gain from such trade.

THE BASIC CASE FOR FREE TRADE

Our discussion so far contains the ingredients of a strong argument in favor of free trade as opposed to trade which is restricted by official interventionism. With the help of our example the free-trade argument is made easily enough, but we must be careful to note just how far it goes. The volume of trade between Smith and Jones reaches a certain level consistent with each man's output of his specialty product and each man's tastes for both goods. Now let us assume that some outside authority directs that the volume of trade between Smith and Jones is reduced by 50 percent. This decrease does not affect the production potential or the tastes of either individual. It simply forbids Smith, for example, to exchange as much food as he wants to exchange for cloth. If Smith now remains completely specialized in food production, he will have to consume more food and less cloth than suits his taste, and he will be worse off. The same argument holds for Jones.

Smith may now decide to produce some clothing himself, and Jones may decide to produce some food himself. But in this case some clothing and some food are being produced less efficiently than with complete specialization. Total joint production will be less than under free trade, and Smith and Jones together will be worse off. This is the basic case for free trade. Note that it is argued as a joint case for Smith and Jones. As we shall see later, trade restriction may be beneficial for one party if it succeeds in restricting the amount of its own product to be exchanged per unit of the other party's product. The restricting party, by shifting the terms of trade in its own favor, will thereby increase its share of the total gains to be had from trade.

MONEY—A DIGRESSION

Before we proceed to discuss the principle of division of labor in somewhat greater detail, let us note one more implication, which will be taken up in greater detail later on.[3] In our example so far, trade has been conducted in barter terms. Although this is suitable for discussing the underlying principles, we know that in the real world money is used in trading. A barter system is theoretically possible, but it would be extremely impractical, especially where many individuals are involved

---

[3]Chapters 8 and 9.

in trade. Examples of how absurd a barter system would be in our
real-world economy come to mind readily. (The farmer would pay for a
cup of coffee with 2.5 large potatoes, etc. . . .) This is mentioned here
because the need for money as a medium of exchange is an implication of
trade and therefore of division of labor. The existence of money,
however, does not alter our previous conclusions about trade. Rather, it
makes trade more efficient by making barter unnecessary. For the time
being we will proceed with this understanding and continue our discussion in barter terms.

So far we have covered considerable ground on only a few pages.
This was possible because the discussion has remained on a rather
superficial level. Let us now proceed in a somewhat more rigorous
manner. The following numerical example should provide a test for most
of our previous conclusions. At the same time we are now prepared for
the general direction in which the following analysis takes us since it
covers once more the principle of division of labor.

DIVISION OF LABOR—A NUMERICAL EXAMPLE

Since the reader has by now acquired some feeling for the basic issues
involved in trading, the next example is set up in terms of nations and
international trade. Table 1-1 describes the production potentials of two
nations, America and Britain. Using all of her resources with maximum
efficiency, America is able to produce 50 bushels of wheat *or* 30 yards of
cloth per day. Britain can produce either 20 bushels of wheat or 60 yards
of cloth per day. Compared with Britain, therefore, America can produce
more wheat and less cloth. Compared with America, Britain can produce
more cloth and less wheat. The differences in production capacities may
be explained by differences in endowments. Relative to Britain, America
may have more land suitable for wheat production. Britain may have
more labor suitable for cloth production relative to America. The
information of Table 1-1 is used again in Figures 1-1 and 1-2.

Table 1-1

	America	Britain
Bushels of wheat per day	50	20
Yards of cloth per day	30	60

Figure 1-1, for example, shows that America could produce 50 bushels of wheat and no cloth at all or 30 yards of cloth and no wheat at all. In addition, the figure shows all the combinations of wheat and cloth which America could produce. Each of these combinations, such as 25 wheat and 15 cloth, represents one point on the downward sloping line which connects the value of 50 on the vertical (wheat) axis with the value of 30 on the horizontal (cloth) axis. This line is called America's *production possibilities curve.* The fact that this curve is a straight line has the following significance: It tells us that whenever we want to change the wheat-cloth combination produced, we must give up wheat for cloth or vice versa at a constant rate.[4] Consider, for example, a move from point *A* to point *B* in Figure 1-1. At point *A*, America produces 25 bushels of wheat and 15 yards of cloth. Now we would like more cloth, and we know that this must mean less wheat. How much more cloth can we get for how much less wheat? The answer can be read off the production possibilities curve: we must give up 5 bushels of wheat in order to gain 3 yards of cloth.

This relationship can be expressed in a number of different ways: (1) Producing 3 more yards of cloth has cost us the opportunity of producing 5 bushels of wheat. In this sense, the opportunity cost of 3 yards of cloth is 5 bushels of wheat. (2) Moving from a combination of more wheat and less cloth to a combination of less wheat and more cloth amounts to transforming wheat into cloth. The ratio 5/3 can be called the rate at which this transformation is possible, or, in short, the rate of transformation. (3) The ratio 5/3, in geometric terms, is the slope of America's production possibilities curve.

An important observation follows immediately from the above. Since the slope of the production possibilities curve in Figures 1-1 and 1-2 is constant, the rate of transformation and the opportunity costs are also constant. This means that regardless of how much cloth (wheat) we are already producing, a certain additional amount of cloth (wheat) will always cost the same amount of wheat (cloth). A straight-line production possibilities curve is therefore often called a constant-cost production possibilities curve.

Let us proceed now with our numerical example and assume that in autarky each country will choose to produce and consume a certain combination of both goods. We will assume that America's autarky point is point *A* in Figure 1-1, with 25 bushels of wheat and 15 yards of cloth.

---

[4]We shall consider nonlinear production possibilities curves in the next chapter.

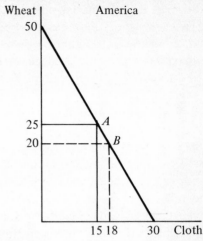

Figure 1-1

Britain will be assumed to have chosen point A in Figure 1-2, i.e., 10 bushels of wheat and 30 yards of cloth.

Case 1: Trade at Britain's Rate of Transformation

We already know that the American and the British rates of transformation are 50/30 and 20/60, respectively. For purposes of comparison let us use a common denominator and write $t_A = 10/6$ and $t_B = 2/6$, where t is the rate of transformation and the subscript refers to the country in question.

The terms of trade, as discussed above, refer to the ratio at which a country's exports exchange for a country's imports. These terms of trade must obviously be the same for both countries, just as any price is the same for both buyer and seller. In our first numerical example of trade, let us assume a terms of trade ratio of 2/6. This means that the terms of trade are equal to Britain's domestic rate of transformation. Let us look at this trade from America's point of view first. We notice that in terms of wheat, cloth is much cheaper in Britain than it is in America. In America, after all, it takes a sacrifice of 10 bushels of wheat to obtain 6 more yards of cloth. In Britain, on the other hand, those 6 yards of cloth can be "bought" for only 2 bushels of wheat.

In order to utilize this potential as fully as possible, America will now produce all the wheat she can, keep what she needs for domestic consumption, and exchange the rest for cheap British cloth. This means

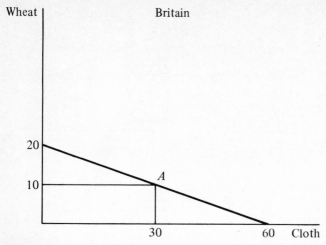

Figure 1-2

that America will produce 50 bushels of wheat. If we assume that she wishes to retain 40 bushels for domestic consumption, this leaves 10 bushels for exporting. At a ratio of 2/6, these 10 bushels of wheat exports will bring 30 yards of cloth imports.[5] Table 1-2 shows that America will consequently be able to consume 40 bushels of wheat and 30 yards of cloth, a clear improvement over the 25 bushels of wheat and 15 yards of cloth which were consumed in autarky.

Figure 1-3 shows this result in diagrammatic form. From her autarky point A, America moves to her production point P, which indicates complete specialization in wheat. As she now begins to trade off wheat for cloth, she moves along the line PC, because this trade occurs at the rate

[5]$30 = {}^6\!/_2 \times 10$.

Table 1-2   Trade at $tt = t_B = {}^2\!/_6$

	America		Britain	
	Wheat	**Cloth**	**Wheat**	**Cloth**
Production	50			60
Exports	10			30
Imports		30	10	
Consumption	40	30	10	30
Gains	15	15		

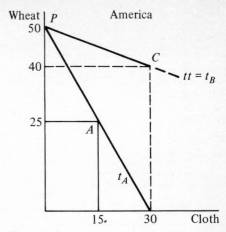

Figure 1-3

2/6 rather than 10/6.[6] Since we have assumed that America wishes to export 10 bushels, she will travel along the line PC until point C is reached. This point, then, is the consumption point after trade; its coordinates are 40 bushels of wheat and 30 yards of cloth.[7] When comparing points A and C, it is visually apparent in Figure 1-3 that America gains from trade.

But how about Britain in this trading situation? Table 1-2 shows that exports of 30 yards of cloth and imports of 10 bushels of wheat leave her with 30 yards of cloth and imports of 10 bushels of wheat to consume, if she specializes completely in cloth production.

Figure 1-4 illustrates Britain's position. Starting from autarky point A, Britain moves to complete specialization in cloth at production point P. Now she exports 30 yards of cloth (at the rate of 2/6) for 10 bushels of wheat. She will therefore move along the line PC to point C, which is her posttrade consumption point.[8] We notice that Britain does not gain from this trade because her posttrade consumption point C is exactly equal to her autarky point A.

---

[6]The slope of the line PC is equal to 2/6, while that of the line PA is equal to 10/6.

[7]Any point along PC is within America's reach through trade at the ratio 2/6. But note that America can hardly import more cloth from Britain than Britain is capable of producing. Britain is not likely to agree to trade which does not leave her with enough cloth for domestic consumption.

[8]Note that the slopes of line PC in Figure 1-3 and line PC in Figure 1-4 are equal. They must be, because their common slope reflects their common terms of trade. These terms of trade, in this case, happen to be equal to Britain's domestic rate of transformation.

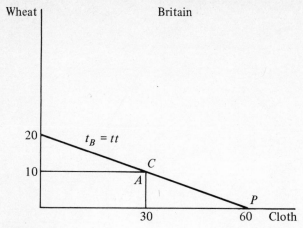

Figure 1-4

We conclude that all of the gains from trade go to America because the terms of trade were equal to Britain's domestic rate of transformation. The case described in Table 1-2 is therefore not realistic because it violates our premise that trade must benefit both parties.

Case 2: Trade at America's Rate of Transformation

Let us assume now that the terms of trade are 10/6, i.e., equal to the American rate of transformation. From Britain's point of view, this ratio is highly profitable. While 6 yards of cloth "buy" only 2 bushels of wheat domestically, they buy 10 bushels in America. Let Britain, therefore, specialize completely in cloth production and export cloth for wheat at 6

Table 1-3   Trade at $tt = t_A = {}^{10}/_6$

	America		Britain	
	Wheat	Cloth	Wheat	Cloth
Production	50			60
Exports	25			15
Imports		15	25	
Consumption	25	15	25	45
Gains			15	15

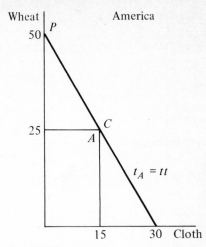

Figure 1-5

yards for every 10 bushels. If we assume that 45 yards of cloth are kept for domestic consumption, this leaves 15 yards for exporting, bringing 25 bushels of wheat imports in exchange.[9] Table 1-3 shows that Britain gains from this trade. She has 15 more bushels of wheat and 15 more yards of cloth to consume than in her original autarky position.

In Figure 1-6, Britain moves to production point P from her original autarky point A. As she now sells cloth for wheat at the rate of 10/6, she moves along the line PC until point C is reached, which is her posttrade consumption point.

America's part in this trade is summarized in Table 1-3 and Figure 1-5. Complete specialization in wheat will send her from autarky point A to production point P in Figure 1-5. She now begins to export wheat, but the amount of cloth she receives per bushel of wheat is no more (and no less) than what she could have produced by herself. This is why America travels back along her own production possibilities curve to point C. She does not gain from trade because point C, her posttrade consumption point, is identical to point A, her initial autarky point.[10]

We conclude that all the gains from trade go to Britain in this case,

---

[9] $25 = {}^{10}/_6 \times 15$.

[10] Note that PC in Figure 1-5 and PC in Figure 1-6 have the same slope, i.e. 10/6. Note also that the distance between points P and C is the same in both diagrams. This follows from the fact that America's exports (imports) must be identical to Britain's imports (exports).

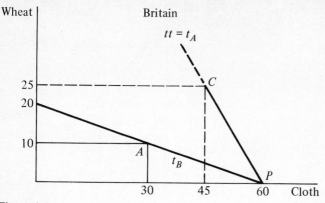

Figure 1-6

because she was able to trade at America's domestic rate of transformation.

Case 3: Trade at Intermediate Terms

We have seen above that Britain has little interest in trading at 2/6 and that America can do without trade at 10/6. Let us therefore try an intermediate ratio—for example, 6/6. It appears that in this case both countries can gain from trading.

Consider Table 1-4. America specializes in wheat and, we assume, exports 20 bushels. This will mean 20 yards of cloth imports at a ratio of 6/6. If we compare the resulting consumption with consumption in autarky, we find that America has gained 5 bushels of wheat and 5 yards of cloth.

Table 1-4   Trade at $tt = {}^6/_6$

	America		Britain	
	Wheat	Cloth	Wheat	Cloth
Production	50			60
Exports	20			20
Imports		20	20	
Consumption	30	20	20	40
Gains	5	5	10	10

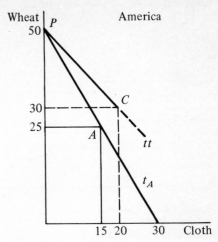

Figure 1-7

Britain, by trading at the same terms of trade, i.e., 6/6, will end up gaining 10 bushels of wheat and 10 yards of cloth. Figures 1-7 and 1-8 demonstrate this trading situation.[11]

We conclude that the terms of trade must fall somewhere between the two countries' rates of transformation, if trade is to benefit both parties.

THE PRODUCTION GAINS FROM TRADE

It was observed earlier that division of labor and specialization would increase total production jointly available for consumption by both parties. Table 1-5 shows that these production gains in our example are 15 bushels of wheat and 15 yards of cloth. The distribution of total gains between the parties depends on the terms of trade. At $tt = 2/6$ all the gains go to America. At $tt = 10/6$ all the gains go to Britain. At the intermediate ratio $tt = 6/6$ the gains are shared by both countries.[12]

---

[11]Note again that the slope of *PC* is the same in both diagrams. But this time this slope no longer equals the domestic rate of transformation of either country. This reflects the fact that the terms of trade in the present case are intermediate, i.e., flatter than America's rate of transformation and steeper than Britain's rate of transformation.

[12]The reader should convince himself that ratios such as 3/6 or 9/6 would also lead to gains for both countries.

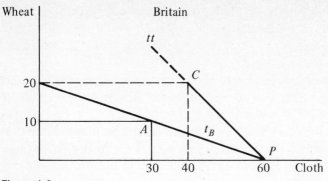

Figure 1-8

THE TERMS OF TRADE

We have defined the terms of trade as the ratio in which exports and imports exchange for each other. It is obvious, furthermore, that the terms of trade must be the same for both trading partners. If America buys 6 yards of cloth for 2 bushels of wheat, Britain sells 6 yards of cloth for 2 bushels of wheat. It follows that the terms of trade must be acceptable to both trading partners. The ratio 2/6, for example, is certainly acceptable to America, because it means the sacrifice of only 2 rather than 10 (according to its domestic rate of transformation) bushels of wheat for 6 additional yards of cloth. But for Britain the ratio 2/6 represents no improvement over autarky conditions. Britain can always obtain 6 more yards of cloth for 2 bushels of wheat by moving along her own production possibilities curve. She does not need to trade for this purpose.

America would be better off yet if she could trade at 1/6. Her imports (cloth) would now be even cheaper. But Britain would now actually lose.

Table 1-5 Production Gains and Their Distribution

	Production in autarky		Production with trade		Gains from trade at 2/6		Gains from trade at 10/6		Gains from trade at 6/6	
	Wheat	Cloth	Wheat	Cloth	Wheat	Cloth	Wheat	Cloth	Wheat	Cloth
America	25	15	50		15	15			5	5
Britain	10	30		60			15	15	10	10
Total	35	45	50	60	15	15	15	15	15	15

She would sell 6 yards of cloth for 1 bushel of wheat, while the opportunity cost of producing 6 yards of cloth would be 2 bushels of wheat. Britain, therefore, would sell cloth below cost. She would not agree to such trade.

We may conclude that any terms of trade lower than 10/6 are beneficial and therefore acceptable to America. Britain, however, will not accept a ratio of 2/6 or lower.

Britain, on the other hand, is interested in terms of trade higher than 2/6. A ratio of 10/6, for example, is quite acceptable to Britain, but now we run into objections by America, who does not need to trade in order to obtain a ratio of 10/6. Furthermore, a ratio of, say, 9/6 would be even more acceptable to Britain, but it would mean a loss for America.

Evidently, then, the terms of trade must fall between the two rates of transformation in order to be acceptable to both parties. Figure 1-9 shows this range of ratios which would benefit both countries.

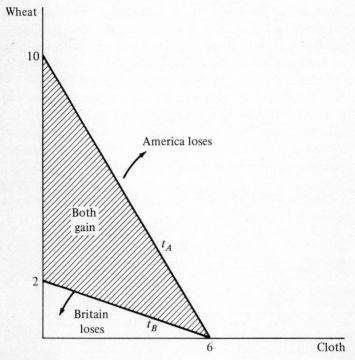

Figure 1-9

COMPARATIVE ADVANTAGE

At this point it may be useful to summarize and generalize the knowledge gained from our numerical example. The basic principle under discussion has been the principle of division of labor. As applied to international trade, this principle leads to the so-called *law of comparative advantage*. Our example was a case of trade according to this law. The meaning of comparative advantage is readily explained with the tools we have already assembled: Consider the production possibilities of our two countries in Table 1-1 and Figures 1-1 and 1-2. What is it that leads to trade between the two countries? Trade is possible because their production possibilities curves have different slopes, which reflects different opportunity costs or different domestic rates of transformation. As long as the price of wheat in terms of cloth or vice versa differs between the two countries, mutually beneficial trade is possible. Assume, as we have, that there are only two goods and two countries, and think of the different ways in which one could express the following: "Cloth is cheap in Britain compared with America." You could say: "Wheat is relatively expensive in Britain"; or "Wheat is relatively cheap in America"; or "Cloth is relatively expensive in America." All these statements are neatly expressed by an American production possibilities curve which is steeper than the British curve. Suppose we change Table 1-1 as follows:

Table 1-6

	America	Britain
Wheat	50	2
Cloth	30	6

Now America can produce more wheat *and* more cloth than Britain. America is said to have the *absolute advantage* in both goods. Does this mean that trade with gains for both countries is impossible? No, since for each bushel of wheat America can still get more cloth from Britain than it can get domestically, and for each yard of cloth Britain can still get more wheat from America than it can get domestically. Of course, since the volume of trade will be much smaller in the case of Table 1-6 than in the case of Table 1-1, the gains will be smaller. But both countries can still gain from trade.

It should now be clear that in the following case trade would not occur:

Table 1-7

	America	Britain
Wheat	50	5
Cloth	30	3

Even though America retains the absolute advantage, trade ceases because no comparative advantage exists. The production possibilities curves, although greatly different in length, are equal in slope, which is what matters for trade.

We conclude that while absolute advantage may occur, the basis of trade will always be comparative advantage. The law of comparative advantage states that a country can benefit from trade whenever its domestic rate of transformation differs from its terms of trade.

THE TRADE PATTERN

In our examples above, America exported wheat and imported cloth. This trade pattern resulted from the fact that America's comparative advantage was in wheat. What are the chances of a reversal in the trade pattern, i.e., a situation in which America would export cloth and import wheat? We know that this would happen if America could obtain more wheat per unit of cloth abroad than according to her domestic rate of transformation. In trade with Britain this is obviously not possible.

Let us therefore drop our assumption of a two-country world and simply look at America's trade pattern in response to a variety of possible terms of trade. We may view these terms of trade as different world market prices for wheat and cloth, to which America reacts by exporting either wheat or cloth. If America's rate of transformation remains $t_A = 10/6$, it is easy to see that she would export cloth whenever the terms of trade are higher than that and export wheat whenever they are lower.

Consider Figure 1-10, where tt_1 is flatter (lower) than t_A and where tt_2 is steeper (higher) than t_A. This means that according to tt_1, America's comparative advantage is in wheat; she will specialize in wheat produc-

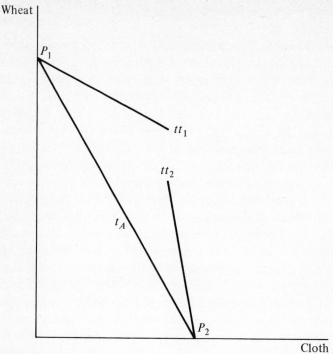

Figure 1-10

tion at point P_1 and trade down along tt_1. If the terms of trade are tt_2, on the other hand, America's comparative advantage is in cloth. In this case she would move to point P_2, specializing in cloth production, and trade up along tt_2. Both cases would lead to gains from trade.

We conclude that a country can always gain from trade as long as a difference exists between its domestic rate of transformation and the terms of trade. Whether or not the terms of trade are larger or smaller (steeper or flatter) than the rate of transformation affects the trade pattern but not the basic reason for trading.

THE GAINS FROM TRADE

Let us focus once more on the gains from trade. In Figure 1-11 the country's production possibilities curve is labeled pp and its terms-of-trade line tt. We know that the country in question, by specializing in wheat, can reach any point on the *tt* line. Which point will it choose, if its autarky point is point *A*?

What we are asking is: Which of the many wheat-cloth combinations along line *tt* will make the country better off than the combination of point *A*? Consider the triangle formed by points *A*, *B*, and *C*. Any point within this triangle must be preferable to point *A* because any such point would represent a wheat-cloth combination with both more wheat and more cloth or more wheat and no less cloth (if the point lies on line *AB*) or more cloth and no less wheat (if the point lies on line *AC*). Points to the left of line *AB* and below line *AC* are difficult to judge even though they could be above the country's production possibilities curve. Such points would involve more of one good, but less of the other good than at point *A*. We shall analyze this difficult judgment later in Chapter 2. For the time being, we conclude that the country in question is clearly better off, if trade enables it to reach any point within triangle *ABC*. Given the terms of trade *tt* in Figure 1-11, the country might move from point *A* to point *C*, if it wishes to consume the same amount of wheat before and after trade, thus taking all of its gains from trade in terms of cloth. Moving from point *A* to point *B*, similarly, would put all of the gains from trade into wheat. A movement to a point such as *D* means that the gains are taken partly in wheat and partly in cloth.

TRADE RESTRICTION AND THE GAINS FROM TRADE

Before concluding this chapter let us consider once more the impact of trade restriction. Suppose America in Figure 1-12 faces terms of trade which lead to exports of cotton and imports of crude oil. Such trade could be illustrated in the familiar way by a move from autarky point *A* to posttrade consumption point C_1 via production point P_1.

As we know, this trade situation involves complete specialization in cotton production. Suppose America now insists on producing at least some oil herself for reasons of national security, support for domestic oil interests, or a combination of both. If the amount of oil produced domestically is equal to *OB* in Figure 1-12, the new production point becomes P_2. Instead of moving all the way from point *A* to point P_1, in other words, America specializes incompletely at P_2. Starting at P_2, she now trades up along *tt*, reaching a posttrade consumption point such as C_2.

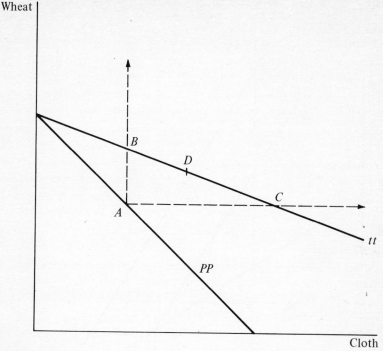

Figure 1-11

It is clear that the gains from trade at C_2 are smaller than they would have been at C_1. The country forgoes the additional cotton *and* oil, which would have been available for consumption under conditions of free trade. This loss must be viewed as the cost of national security or support for domestic oil interests, whatever the case may be.

SUMMARY

The basis for trade is the principle of division of labor. Division of labor increases total production and consumption.

Two parties will trade with each other if each party stands to gain from such trade.

By reducing the volume of trade, trade restrictions tend to reduce the gains from trade.

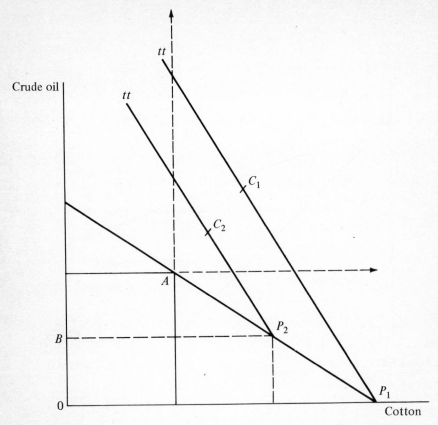

Figure 1-12

A numerical example of trade in a two-country, two-product world led to the following conclusions: If the terms of trade are equal to country A's rate of transformation, country B will reap all the gains from trade. If the terms of trade fall between both countries' rates of transformation, both countries will gain from trade.

The law of comparative advantage states that a country can gain from trade as long as a difference exists between its rate of transformation and its terms of trade.

Whether or not the terms of trade are higher or lower than the rate of transformation affects the trade pattern, but not the basic reason for trading.

The gains from trade may be taken in terms of the export good, the import good, or a combination of both.

If a country does not specialize completely in that product in which it has the comparative advantage, it forgoes potential gains from trade.

SUGGESTED FURTHER READINGS

The classic case for division of labor is made by Adam Smith, *An Inquiry into the Nature and Causes of the Wealth of Nations*, The Modern Library, New York, 1937, chaps. 1 and 2. Comparative advantage was developed by David Ricardo, *On the Principles of Political Economy and Taxation*, Cambridge University Press, London, 1966, chap. 7. For a useful modern review of this material, see P. T. Ellsworth, *The International Economy*, Macmillan, London, 1965, 3d ed., chap. 4.

Chapter 2

Supply, Demand, and Trade

One of the basic conclusions in the foregoing chapter was that in order to maximize the gains from trade, each country must specialize completely in that product in which it has the comparative advantage. Complete specialization means that nothing of the imported good is also produced at home. It is evident, however, that in the real world there are many cases where some amount of a particular product is imported and some amount of it is produced domestically. In this situation, the consumer has the choice between good x produced domestically and good x produced abroad.

INCREASING COST

We can explain this more realistic pattern of trade by continuing to use the principle of division of labor in a slightly altered form. The qualification we will introduce concerns the shape of the production possibilities curve. In the previous chapter all production possibilities curves were linear. This reflected constant opportunity costs or constant rates of transformation. Constant opportunity costs in terms of our previous example meant that regardless of how much wheat (cloth) a country wished to produce, the cost of obtaining one more bushel of wheat (cloth) was always the same in terms of cloth (wheat).

Let us use the American production possibilities curve and explain why it may be concave to the origin rather than a straight line. We know that both land and labor are required for the production of wheat or cloth.[1] We also know that America is endowed with both land and labor and can, therefore, produce both wheat and cloth. But all of America's land is not equally well suited to wheat production, and all of her labor resources are not equally skilled in the production of wheat. Take point A in Figure 1-2, for example. At this point all land and all labor, regardless of suitability, are employed in wheat production. As we move now to point B, a certain amount of land and labor are released from wheat production. The released land is likely to be the least fertile, and the released labor is likely to be the least skilled in wheat production. The barren land, however, may be a perfect site for a textile plant, just as the freed labor may be skilled in cloth production. In this way resources which have been almost useless in wheat production are transferred to cloth production, where they are more useful. For a relatively small sacrifice of wheat, therefore, the country obtains a relatively large amount of cloth. Moving down along America's production possibilities curve, this situation changes. As wheat production is reduced more and more, first-class farm hands must eventually go to work in textile plants which have been built on top-grade wheat soil. The opportunity cost of more cloth is the sacrifice of more and more wheat.

If a and b in Figure 2-1 are equal amounts of cloth, let us say 1 yard, a' and b' are the amounts of wheat which must be sacrificed for 1 yard of cloth. It follows from the shape of the production possibilities curve that the amount of wheat which must be given up for one additional yard of cloth depends on how much cloth is already being produced. The more we specialize in cloth, the more wheat do we have to give up for one additional yard of cloth. Similarly, the closer we move to specialization in

---

[1]Wheat requires relatively more land, however, which is why America with her abundant land endowment had the comparative advantage in wheat in our previous example.

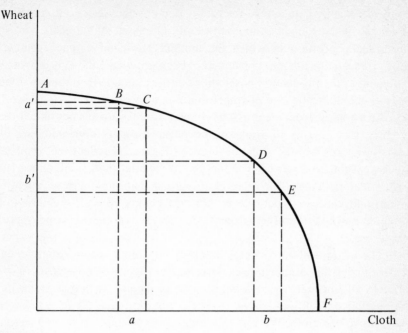

Figure 2-1

wheat (now moving up along the curve), the smaller becomes the amount of wheat gained by the sacrifice of 1 yard of cloth. Figure 2-1, therefore, shows a production possibilities curve with increasing cost or an increasing rate of transformation between wheat and cloth.

It is now no longer possible to describe a country's production possibilities curve by a set of two numbers as we have done in Chapter 1. Nor can we speak of a given domestic rate of transformation regardless of where along the curve a country chooses to be. Since the domestic rate of transformation is equal to the slope of the production possibilities curve, the rate will be different for each point on the curve.

TRADE AND INCREASING COSTS

These alterations of our previous example do not present insurmountable obstacles for the analysis of trade, as we continue to use the diagrammatic approach. In Figure 2-2, for example, we assume that America wishes to

consume *Oe* of wheat. Given the production possibilities curve, it is easy
to find the corresponding amount of cloth *Ob*. Point *A*, therefore, shows
the autarky position in which the amount produced of each product
always equals the amount consumed of each product. Line t_A is drawn as
a tangent to the production possibilities curve at point *A*, so that its slope
reflects the domestic rate of transformation at point *A*.

As we know from the previous chapter, trade is always possible if the
country faces terms of trade which differ from its domestic rate of
transformation. Let the slope of line *tt* in Figure 2-2 reflect the terms of
trade available to America. The fact that *tt* is flatter than t_A indicates that
less wheat exchanges for more cloth abroad than in America. Wheat is
cheap and cloth is expensive in America compared with the terms of
trade. We would, therefore, expect America to export wheat and import
cloth.

The next question concerns precisely how much wheat America will
export under the circumstances described in Figure 2-2. Suppose, in the
process of specializing in wheat, America begins to move along the
production possibilities curve from her autarky point *A* toward more
wheat and less cloth. We are now faced with an implication of increasing (rather than constant) cost: As America moves upward along her

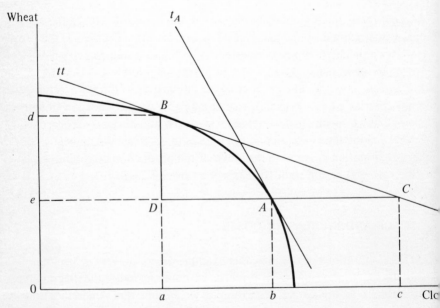

Figure 2-2

Table 2-1

	Production		Consumption		Exports		Imports		Gains from trade	
	Wheat	Cloth	Wheat	Cloth	Wheat	Cloth	Wheat	Cloth	Wheat	Cloth
Before trade	Oe	Ob	Oe	Ob						
After trade	Od	Oa	Oe	Oc	ed			ac		bc

production possibilities curve, she finds her export good wheat, which at *A* is relatively cheap, becoming more and more expensive in terms of cloth. Eventually, at point *B*, the domestic rate of transformation or opportunity cost has reached the level indicated by the line *tt*. If America continues specializing in wheat beyond point *B*, she will produce her wheat more expensively in terms of cloth than she will be able to sell wheat according to her terms of trade *tt*. Increasing costs, therefore, preclude complete specialization in this case. How far, then, should America specialize in wheat? At any point between *A* and *B* production costs of wheat (in terms of cloth) are lower than revenues (in terms of cloth) from exporting wheat. America should, therefore, continue specializing as long as this cost advantage exists, i.e., she should move no further than point *B*. If she moves further than point *B*, her costs (in terms of cloth) will be higher than her revenue (in terms of cloth). If she remains somewhere between *A* and *B*, she will lose the opportunity of selling some more bushels of wheat at a revenue (in terms of cloth) which is higher than their cost (in terms of cloth).

Having shifted her production point from *A* to *B*, America can now choose her consumption point along the line *tt*. We may assume that she wishes to consume the same amount of wheat after trade as before trade. In this case, point *C* will be her consumption point after trade, and her gains from trade will be *bc* of cloth, where *bc* simply measures the horizontal distance between the pretrade consumption point *A* and the posttrade consumption point *C*.

After trade, America produces at *B* and consumes at *C*. Her exports are the amount by which wheat production exceeds wheat consumption, or *ed* in Figure 2-2. Her imports accordingly must be the amount of cloth by which her consumption exceeds her production, or *ac* in Figure 2-2. Note that

$$\frac{ed}{ac} = tt$$

i.e., the terms of trade are the ratio at which exports exchange for imports.

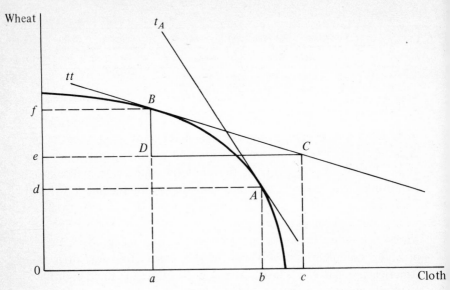

Figure 2-3

The triangle *BCD*, showing exports, imports, and the terms of trade, is called the trading triangle.

In summary, Figure 2-2 introduces increasing cost into our analysis of trade and leads us to conclude that with increasing cost we may find trade with incomplete specialization.

As far as the gains from trade are concerned, our conclusions of Chapter 1 continue to hold. The student should be able to interpret Figure 2-3 without reading any further.

Figure 2-3 repeats the situation of Figure 2-2 with one exception. America chooses her posttrade consumption point *C* in such a way as to consume more cloth and more wheat rather than to consume only more cloth. The gains from trade are still measured by the distance between the pretrade consumption point *A* and the posttrade consumption point *C*.

Table 2-2

	Production		Consumption		Exports		Imports		Gains from trade	
	Wheat	Cloth	Wheat	Cloth	Wheat	Cloth	Wheat	Cloth	Wheat	Cloth
Before trade	Od	Ob	Od	Ob						
After trade	Of	Oa	Oe	Oc	ef			ac	de	bc

But this distance now has a vertical part, *de* of wheat, and a horizontal part, *bc* of cloth. Note that in this more general case point *A* no longer lies on one side of the trading triangle *BCD*.

A TWO-COUNTRY CASE WITH INCREASING COST

Let us construct a simple trade model in which two countries trade with each other, both of which have increasing cost production possibilities curves. Figures 2-4 and 2-5 show production possibilities curves for America and Britain which are concave to the origin. The difference in shape between the curves is explained by our assumption that America has more land, which is relatively important in wheat production, and that Britain has more labor, which is relatively important in cloth production. America is therefore capable, in complete specialization, of producing more wheat than Britain, while Britain can produce more cloth. This assumption was made in Chapter 1 already. What is different now is the fact that each country's points of complete specialization are no longer connected by a straight line (reflecting constant cost), but by a concave curve (reflecting increasing cost).

In autarky each country chooses a point on its production possibilities curve at which it will produce and consume. With regard to the choice of this autarky point, we assume that both countries always wish to consume wheat and cloth in a 1/1 ratio. Each country, in other words, wants to consume exactly one bushel of wheat for every yard of cloth. Given its production possibilities curve, we can therefore find each country's autarky point by drawing a 45-degree line through the origin and marking its intersection with the production possibilities curve.

America's autarky point *A*, for example, indicates production and consumption of *Od* wheat and *Ob* cloth. *Od* is equal to *Ob*, because line *AC* slopes at a 45-degree angle. Britain's autarky point *E* in Figure 2-5 similarly shows equal amounts of wheat (*O'l*) and cloth (*O'g*).

As we can see, the domestic rates of transformation t_A and t_B differ. In America wheat is relatively cheaper and cloth is relatively more expensive than in Britain, as indicated by the fact that t_A is steeper than t_B. This was to be expected for the following reason: Both countries wish to consume wheat and cloth in the same proportion (1/1). While, in this sense, their preferences can be described as similar, their production

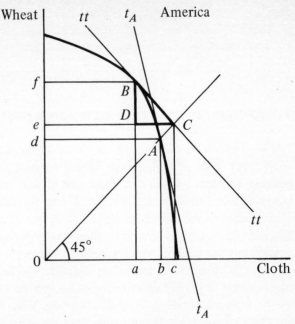

Figure 2-4

possibilities remain different. America can produce relatively more wheat and less cloth than Britain. We would consequently expect that with similar preferences but different production possibilities, wheat would be cheaper and cloth more expensive in America.

As we know from Chapter 1, the terms at which the two countries trade must fall somewhere between t_A and t_B in order to make gains from trade available to each country. The terms of trade (*tt*) are, therefore, flatter than t_A and steeper than t_B. After drawing a line *tt* as a tangent to each country's production possibilities curve, we observe that the tangency points *B* and *F* fall on different sides of the autarky points *A* and *E* in each diagram. Reflecting the fact that America will specialize in wheat, in Figure 2-4 *B* falls to the left of *A*. Britain, on the other hand, finds it more profitable to move toward more cloth production from point *E* to point *F* in Figure 2-5.

America now trades along *tt*, moving her consumption point to *C*, since she continues to consume wheat and cloth in the same ratio (1/1) as before trade. She exports *ef* of wheat for *ac* of cloth. Her trading triangle is *BCD*. Britain exports *hi* of cloth for *km* of wheat, and her trading

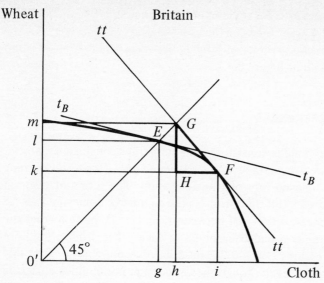

Figure 2-5

triangle is *FGH*.[2] Table 2-3 summarizes these results. Note that the composition of the gains from trade depends on our particular assumption with regard to preferences. Since we assume that each country continues to desire wheat and cloth in the same (1/1) ratio as before trade, each

[2]Note that America's exports (*ef*) should be equal to Britain's imports (*km*), and that America's imports (*ac*) should be equal to Britain's exports (*hi*). Diagrammatically, these equalities can be achieved by giving *tt* exactly the proper slope. This, however, means that the slope of *tt* is uniquely determined (by the condition that it must equate *ef* to *km* and *ac* to *hi*). So far, however, rather than determining *tt* uniquely, we have allowed them to fall within a range between the two domestic rates of transformation. If the terms of trade are drawn in such a way as to equate a country's exports to the other country's imports, they not only fall in the proper range but also represent the *equilibrium* terms of trade. Equating *ef* to *km* and *ac* to *hi* therefore constitutes a (diagrammatically awkward) method of finding the exact equilibrium terms of trade. A simpler method will be developed in in Chapter 3.

Table 2-3

	Production		Consumption		Exports		Imports		Gains from trade	
	Wheat	Cloth	Wheat	Cloth	Wheat	Cloth	Wheat	Cloth	Wheat	Cloth
America Before trade	*Od*	*Ob*	*Od*	*Ob*						
Britain Before trade	*O'l*	*O'g*	*O'l*	*O'g*						
America After trade	*Of*	*Oa*	*Oe*	*Oc*	*ef*			*ac*	*de*	*bc*
Britain After trade	*O'k*	*O'i*	*O'm*	*O'h*		*hi*	*km*		*lm*	*gh*

country takes its gains from trade in equal amounts of wheat and cloth. Since in Figure 2-4 point *C* lies on the same 45-degree line as does *A*, *de* is equal to *bc*. The same relationship holds between points *E* and *G*, and distances *lm* and *gh* in Figure 2-5.

TRADE AND PREFERENCES

The foregoing example is consistent with our earlier conclusion, namely, that a country can always trade with gains *if and only if* the terms of trade differ from its domestic rate of transformation. The terms of trade in Figures 2-4 and 2-5 differed from each country's domestic rate of transformation because they fell between t_A and t_B. If the two domestic rates of transformation had been equal to each other, trade would not have occurred. Figures 2-6 and 2-7 describe this possibility. Note that trade does not occur even though the production possibilities curves in Figures 2-6 and 2-7 differ from each other in the same way as they do in Figures 2-4 and 2-5. What differs now is our assumption concerning preferences: If we make no specific assumption—as we have done in Figures 2-4 and 2-5—about how each country chooses its autarky point, a

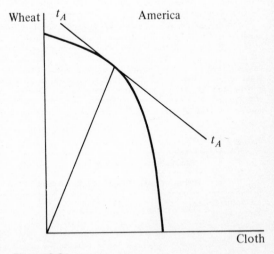

Figure 2-6

situation may arise in which the domestic rates of transformation are equal even though the production possibilities curves are not.[3]

The situation in Figures 2-6 and 2-7 can be described as follows: Even though America can produce more wheat than Britain, the price of wheat is not lower in America than it is in Britain because America also wishes to consume more wheat than does Britain. Similarly, cloth is not cheaper in Britain, because although it is more abundant in supply, it is also more highly demanded in Britain than it is in America. The case described in Figures 2-6 and 2-7 is, of course, a very special one in which the difference in preferences exactly cancels the difference in production possibilities with the result of equal domestic rates of transformation.

The more general conclusion to be drawn is that production possibilities alone do not indicate the pattern of trade; we must also know the relative preferences.

It is quite possible, for example, to construct a case in which America exports cloth and Britain exports wheat even though the production possibilities remain those of Figures 2-4 and 2-5. All we have to do is to

[3]This holds for nonlinear production possibilities curves, but not for linear ones. It is easy to see that with constant cost production possibilities curves, the domestic rates of transformation are constant no matter where the autarky point falls. With constant cost in both countries, trade will therefore occur whenever the (linear) production possibilities curves have different slopes.

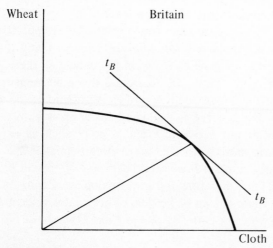

Figure 2-7

assume American preferences extremely biased toward wheat and British preferences extremely biased toward cloth. Diagrammatically, this is done in such a way that t_A is flatter than t_B. The terms of trade, now steeper than t_A and flatter than t_B, will cause America to specialize in cloth and Britain to specialize in wheat. The student should produce the proper two diagrams himself.

INDIFFERENCE CURVES—A DIGRESSION

At this point it becomes necessary to develop some tools of demand analysis, since what we have said above amounts to the proposition that trade may be based on different preferences (demand) as well as on different production possibilities (supply). This proposition is easy to picture in the following way. Suppose America and Britain have identical production possibilities curves. On the supply side, therefore, there is no basis for trade. But now suppose also that each country chooses a different autarky point on its production possibilities curve, because each country has different preferences. The result will be different rates of transformation and, consequently, a basis for trade.

The basic tool of demand analysis is the indifference curve.[4] Starting from any randomly chosen point in Figure 2-8, such as P, let us ask the following question: Which points in the neighborhood of P are likely to represent wheat-cloth combinations which give a level of well-being or satisfaction exactly equal to that derived from point P? To put it differently, a country or an individual may be *indifferent* between being at point P and being at certain other points. We want to connect all these points by a so-called indifference curve. In Figure 2-8 this indifference curve is downward-sloping and convex with regard to the origin.

The downward slope of the curve is explained easily enough: We could not possibly be indifferent between P and a point such as A, because at A we would have more wheat and more cloth than at P. We would be better off. Similarly, at point B we would be worse off than at P. The indifference curve cannot therefore be upward-sloping. Common sense also tells us that the curve cannot be vertical or horizontal, since at points such as C and E we would be better off and at F and D we would be worse off than at P.

[4]Indifference curves are covered in most basic economics textbooks. See, for example, Paul A. Samuelson, *Economics*, 8th ed., McGraw-Hill Book Company, New York, 1970. chap. 22 appendix.

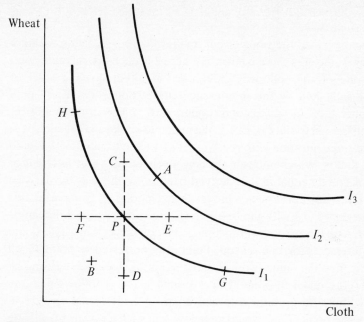

Figure 2-8

The convex curvature of the indifference curve has the following explanation: If we move from point P to point G along an indifference curve, we are choosing more cloth and less wheat in such a way as to always retain a constant level of satisfaction. At what rate are we willing to give up wheat for cloth? Should that rate be constant regardless of how much wheat or cloth we have to begin with? Or are we likely to be willing to give up smaller and smaller amounts of wheat for each unit of cloth as we acquire more and more cloth? As we acquire more and more cloth (and less wheat), additional units of cloth become less useful to us compared to wheat.

The rate at which we are willing to sacrifice wheat for cloth and vice versa in such a way as to retain a constant level of satisfaction may be called the *marginal rate of substitution*. This rate is reflected by the slope of the indifference curve. Where the indifference curve is very steep (at point H), we will need considerable additional wheat to compensate us for the loss of relatively little cloth (while keeping our level of satisfaction constant). This is so because at point H we have relatively much wheat and little cloth to begin with. At point G the curve is very flat and the situation is reversed.

Having explained the slope of our indifference curve, let us consider the meaning of the curve as a whole. In Figure 2-8, each conceivable point falls into one of the following categories: It either gives a level of satisfaction indicated by the indifference curve (points G, H, P), or it gives a higher level of satisfaction (points A, C, E), or it gives a lower level of satisfaction (points B, D, F). We might now take a point such as A and ask the same question with regard to it as we have asked with regard to point P, that is: Which points in the neighborhood of A give us levels of satisfaction exactly equal to that derived from A? In this way we derive a second indifference curve which passes through point A. Comparing this indifference curve (I_2) with the first one (I_1), we observe the following:

Both I_1 and I_2 are downward-sloping and convex to the origin. I_1 and I_2 cannot intersect, for this reason: Point A is preferred to point P. All points on I_1 give the same level of satisfaction as does point P, and all points on I_2 are equal to point A in the same sense. It follows that any point on I_2 must be preferable to any point on I_1. If I_1 and I_2 were to intersect, some points on I_2 would be below I_1 in such a way as to indicate less cloth and less wheat—which indicates a lower lever of satisfaction than I_1.

The preference map shown in Figure 2-8 consists of any number of indifference curves. Each higher indifference curve indicates a higher level of satisfaction.

INDIFFERENCE CURVES AND TRADE

The use of indifference curves helps us to answer two important questions which were evaded in our previous discussion by way of making specific assumptions.

The first question we can now answer is which point on its production possibilities curve a country chooses as its autarky point. If the country wishes to maximize its satisfaction, it will try to reach the highest possible of its indifference curves. Consider Figure 2-9, which shows four indifference curves of a country's preference map and its production possibilities curve. We know that the country is able to produce wheat-cloth combinations A, B, and C. It will choose C over A and B because C

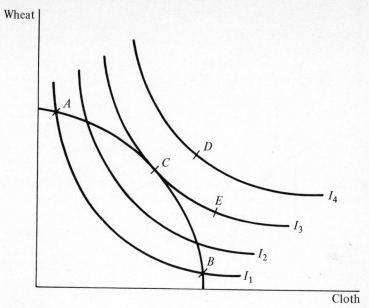

Figure 2-9

lies on a higher indifference curve than A and B. Although D would be preferred to C, the country is unable to reach the indifference curve I_4, given its production possibilities.

With regard to points D and E, we observe the following: Both points are out of reach in terms of production possibilities. But a level of satisfaction equal to that at E can be achieved by moving to C, since C and E are on the same indifference curve. A level of satisfaction equal to that at D cannot be achieved, since I_4 cannot be reached at any point with the given production possibilities.

Finally, consider once more points A and B. For any point of intersection (rather than tangency) between an indifference curve and the production possibilities curve, there must be a point on a higher indifference curve within reach of the same production possibilities curve. Point C, therefore, represents the highest level of satisfaction the country is able to reach under the constraint of its production possibilities.

The second question we are able to answer with the help of indifference curves concerns the gains from trade. Given a country's preference map, we can now determine which point along the terms of trade line it will choose in a trading situation. Figure 2-10 shows a country

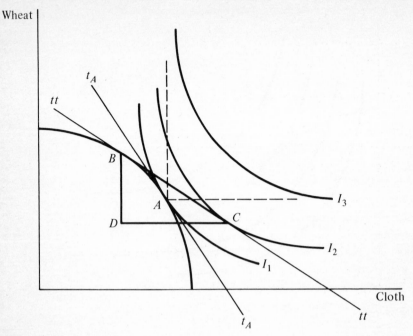

Figure 2-10

which specializes in wheat production in response to terms of trade *tt* which differ from its domestic rate of transformation t_A. We know, from our previous analysis, that the country may now choose any point along the terms-of-trade line as its consumption point after trade. Given its preference map, the country will move to the highest possible indifference curve at point *C*. Note that point *C* lies outside the rectangle above *A*, which we have used previously to delineate possible gains from trade.

The country, in other words, consumes less wheat but more cloth after trade than before and still considers itself better off.[5] It is entirely plausible that the country should be better off with less wheat, as long as it receives enough additional cloth to outweigh this loss of wheat.

The introduction of indifference curves has enabled us to generalize

[5]To obtain gains from trade in both goods, simply draw *tt* in such a way that it touches some higher indifference curve, such as I_3, *within* the rectangle above *A*.

our conclusions about possible gains from trade beyond the previous examples: A country gains from trade whenever trade enables it to reach a higher indifference curve.[6]

IDENTICAL SUPPLY—DIFFERENT DEMAND

Let us turn now to a case in which two countries have identical production possibilities curves and different preference maps. In Figures 2-11 and 2-12 we find identical production possibilities curves for America and Britain. By the shape of the preference maps, however, we recognize that relative to Britain, America wishes to consume more wheat. In autarky, consequently, America chooses point A in Figure 2-11 and Britain chooses point E in Figure 2-12. The resulting rates of transformation are t_A for America and t_B for Britain. By comparing these rates we can determine the trading pattern. Since t_A is flatter than t_B, wheat is relatively cheap in Britain and cloth is relatively cheap in America. Britain will therefore export wheat and America will export cloth.

The terms of trade tt are the same in both diagrams, steeper than t_A and flatter than t_B. Both countries should consequently be able to gain from trade. America moves along her production possibilities curve from autarky point A to production point B. She then trades up along tt, which enables her to reach posttrade consumption point C. America's trading triangle, showing exports, imports, and the terms of trade, is BCD in Figure 2-11. Comparing points A and C, we note that America gains from this trade.

Britain moves from E to F and trades down along tt until she reaches her posttrade consumption point G. Her trading triangle is FGH, and a comparison of points E and G shows Britain's gains from trade. Table 2-4

---

[6]A note of caution is in order when dealing with indifference curves in trade theory. The problem lies in our implicit premise that the preference map is a valid description of group behavior. A country's indifference curve is a "social" or "community" indifference curve and as such not necessarily the same concept as an individual's indifference curve. Take, for example, the choice between points P and G in Figure 2-8. An individual with certain notions about the usefulness of wheat versus cloth can be expected to declare himself indifferent between those two points. A group of individuals, however, is not likely to agree on this. Wheat lovers may feel worse off at G than at P, and cloth lovers may prefer G to P. Only by resorting to some fairly complex methods of weighing the preferences of wheat lovers and cloth lovers against each other can we justify the use of social indifference curves. For a compact exposition of social indifference curves, see H. Robert Heller, *International Trade—Theory and Empirical Evidence*, Prentice-Hall, Englewood Cliffs, N.J., 1968, pp. 45–51.

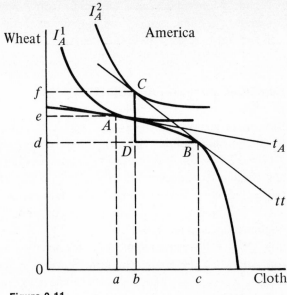

Figure 2-11

summarizes the results of Figures 2-11 and 2-12. Note that the gains from trade in both cases are taken in terms of wheat and cloth. Note also that the production points of both countries are exactly the same after trade, i.e., the tangency points between identical production possibilities curves and identical terms of trade. Trade, in other words, is not based on differences in production and supply, but on differences in demand. The posttrade consumption points C and G certainly differ between the two countries.

Table 2-4

	Production		Consumption		Exports		Imports		Gains from trade	
	Wheat	Cloth	Wheat	Cloth	Wheat	Cloth	Wheat	Cloth	Wheat	Cloth
America Before trade	Oe	Oa	Oe	Oa						
Britain Before trade	$O'k$	$O'h$	$O'k$	$O'h$						
America After trade	Od	Oc	Of	Ob		bc	df		ef	ab
Britain After trade	$O'm$	$O'g$	$O'l$	$O'i$	lm			gi	kl	hi

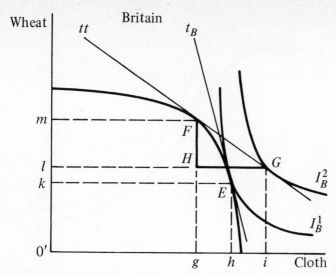

Figure 2-12

IDENTICAL DEMAND—DIFFERENT SUPPLY

We can reverse the situation and assume identical preference maps in both countries, but different production possibilities. Points A and D in Figures 2-13 and 2-14 show the autarky position of each country. According to the rates of transformation, t_A and t_B, wheat is cheaper in America and cloth is cheaper in Britain. This was to be expected, since America's production possibilities are biased toward wheat and Britain's toward cloth, while demand is the same in both countries. America, specializing (incompletely) in wheat production, moves to point B and reaches its consumption point C trading along tt.

Britain specializes (incompletely) in cloth at production point F and exports cloth for wheat along tt until she reaches point E, where her gains from trade are maximized.

Table 2-5 summarizes these results. The reader might test his understanding of the approach used here by working out the details of hypothetical situations, for example: (1) Two countries have different preferences and different supply structures;[7] (2) two countries have identical preferences and identical supply structures.

[7]In a special case of this situation the result may be no trade. Recall Figures 2-6 and 2-7.

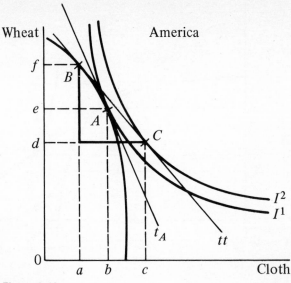

Figure 2-13

Table 2-5

	Production		Consumption		Exports		Imports		Gains and losses (+) (−)	
	Wheat	Cloth	Wheat	Cloth	Wheat	Cloth	Wheat	Cloth	Wheat	Cloth
America before trade	Oe	Ob	Oe	Ob						
Britain before trade	O'l	O'h	O'l	O'h						
America after trade	Of	Oa	Od	Oc	df			ac	de (−)	bc (+)
Britain after trade	O'k	O'i	O'm	O'g		gi	mk		lm (+)	gh (−)

SUMMARY

The production possibilities curve will be concave to the origin if all resources used in producing a particular good are not equally suitable to this purpose. The production possibilities curve in this case shows increasing opportunity cost.

A country with increasing costs is likely to specialize less than completely in a trading situation.

Two countries, each of which has increasing costs, will trade with each other provided their domestic rates of transformation differ.

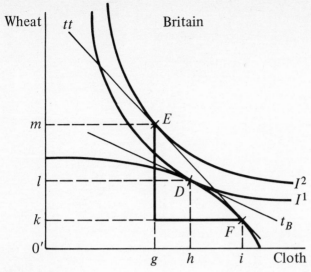

Figure 2-14

Indifference curves are useful in determining a country's autarky position and its gains from trade. A country gains from trade whenever trade enables it to move onto a higher indifference curve.

Given its terms of trade, a country's trading pattern depends on the interaction between its domestic supply and demand structures.

Trade between two countries is possible if they have identical demand, but different supply structures; if they have identical supply, but different demand structures; or if they have different supply and demand structures.

SUGGESTED FURTHER READINGS

About concave production possibilities curves and trade, see Gottfried Haberler, *The Theory of International Trade* (Macmillan, New York, 1950), chap. 10, and his "Some Problems in the Pure Theory of International Trade," *Economic Journal*, June 1950. Also of interest will be Abba P. Lerner, "The Diagrammatical Presentation of Cost Conditions in International Trade," *Economica*, August 1932. For a modern diagrammatical treatment which is more advanced, yet compact, see H. Robert Heller, *International Trade—Theory and Empirical Evidence* (Prentice-Hall, Englewood Cliffs, N.J., 1968), chap. 3. Further references to the pure theory of trade are given at the end of Chapter 3.

Chapter 3

The Terms of Trade

In the two preceding chapters, we have explained why nations trade, how they gain from trading, and how the trading pattern depends on supply and demand conditions. What has been missing from our discussion so far is the determination of the ratio at which a country's exports exchange for its imports, i.e., the terms of trade.

Let us continue to assume a two-country, two-product world in which both countries produce both goods. Let us further assume that we know the trading pattern, that is, that Britain exports cloth and America exports wheat. How many bushels of wheat per yard of cloth will be the mutually agreeable terms of trade? We already know that this ratio must be such as to make it possible for both countries to gain from trade. But this provides us with a range of possibilities rather than with one specific solution.

THE OFFER CURVE

Figure 3-1 attacks this problem from Britain's point of view by recording all those wheat-cloth combinations which Britain considers acceptable in trade. At point *A* Britain is willing to accept only 3 bushels of wheat for 10 yards of cloth. As the cloth exports are doubled, however, this ratio changes. Rather than trading 20 yards of cloth for 6 bushels of wheat, at point *B* Britain now requires 10 bushels of wheat for her 20 yards of cloth. Moving to point *C*, the wheat price per unit of cloth offered rises further. In other words, as Britain increases her exports of cloth, the amount of wheat imports per yard of cloth exports considered acceptable rises. Or, to put this proposition in reverse, Britain will accept increasing wheat imports only in exchange for decreasing amounts of cloth per bushel of wheat.

How can we explain the shape of this so-called *offer curve*? The offer curve drawn in Figure 3-1 is a cloth supply curve in the sense that additional units of cloth will be offered only at an increasing (wheat) price. This is a plausible proposition if we assume that Britain has an increasing cost production possibilities curve. As more cloth is produced for export, its cost in terms of wheat must rise.

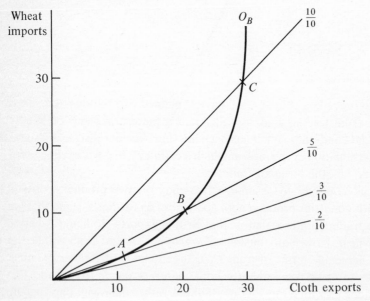

Figure 3-1

We may also look at Figure 3-1 in terms of a demand curve for wheat. The lower the (cloth) price per bushel of wheat, the more wheat will Britain buy.[1]

The offer curve, then, is defined as the locus of all wheat-cloth combination points which Britain finds acceptable in trade. We conclude that its shape is derived from both supply and demand conditions in Britain.

It is now easy to find the terms of trade associated with any wheat-cloth combination traced by the offer curve. We need only to choose a point on the offer curve and connect it to the origin. The slope of the resulting line reflects the terms of trade for the chosen wheat-cloth combination.[2] At point A, for example, Britain is willing to offer 10 yards of cloth for 3 bushels of wheat, the terms of trade being 3/10. At point B, where 20 yards of cloth are offered for 10 bushels of wheat, the terms of trade are 5/10. Alternately, this can be expressed as follows: If the terms of trade are 5/10, for example, Britain is willing to offer 20 yards of cloth. If the rate improved to 10/10, she would offer 30 yards of cloth, and so on.

We may summarize that the volume of trade is a function of the terms of trade, and that the nature of this function depends on supply and demand conditions.

Finally, one terms-of-trade ratio has special significance. The line in Figure 3-1 with the slope of 2/10 reflects Britain's domestic rate of transformation, or that terms-of-trade ratio at which Britain ceases to trade. This line represents the slope of the offer curve at the origin. Beginning with this slope, steeper and steeper lines reflect improving terms of trade for Britain.

America's offer curve may be derived in similar fashion. The amount of cloth required per bushel of wheat exported will increase as wheat exports rise. Or, to put it another way, the amount of wheat offered per yard of cloth imported declines as cloth imports rise. As we move along America's offer curve in Figure 3-2 from point E via point D to point C, therefore, America's terms of trade improve in the sense that the amount of wheat offered per yard of cloth declines. The ratio 30/10 represents America's domestic rate of transformation.

---

[1]Technically, the offer curve is drawn neither as a supply nor as a demand curve but as a total revenue curve, since both axes measure quantity units. Supply or demand diagrams measure price per quantity unit on one axis and quantity units on the other. In Figure 3-1 price per quantity unit is measured by the slopes of the rotating lines drawn through the origin.

[2]We already are familiar with the representation of terms of trade as slopes. In this case, we simply use a positive rather than a negative slope as we did in Chapter 2.

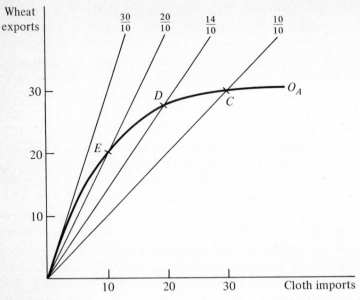

Figure 3-2

THE EQUILIBRIUM TERMS OF TRADE

Let us review the information contained in Figures 3-1 and 3-2. For each country we now know all those wheat-cloth combinations which represent acceptable trading situations. If one point out of these two sets of points should be acceptable to both countries, we will have found the solution to our problem. We need only superimpose Figures 3-1 and 3-2 in order to find this point.

This is done in Figure 3-3, where both countries' offer curves are superimposed. Point P emerges as equilibrium, with the corresponding equilibrium terms of trade tt_o. We can test this equilibrium in the following way: Suppose the terms of trade were shown by tt' in Figure 3-3. At this ratio Britain would be willing to offer or supply OM yards of cloth, while America would want to buy ON yards of cloth. At the terms of trade tt', therefore, we have MN excess demand for cloth. This excess demand will tend to drive the price of cloth (in terms of wheat) upward until the quantity supplied is equal to the quantity demanded. The terms-of-trade line will consequently rotate to the left until it reaches the position tt_o. The reader may wish to test the equilibrium at point P once again by drawing a terms-of-trade line into Figure 3-3 which is steeper than tt_o. In this case, excess supply of cloth will drive its price back to its equilibrium level.[3]

With the discussion leading up to Figure 3-3, we have reached the formal conclusion of our trade model. We now have explained the reasons for trade, the pattern of trade, the gains from trade, and, finally, the terms of trade. The remainder of this chapter will be largely devoted to elaborations of this model.

THE OFFER CURVE AND CHANGES IN DEMAND

In order to enhance our understanding of Figure 3-3 and its implications, let us trace the effect of a sudden increase in British demand for cloth.[4] In Figure 3-4 this is reflected by the shift of the British offer curve from position O_B into position O'_B. The explanation of this shift follows directly from our derivation of the offer curve. Since cloth is now more in

[3]It might be useful to the reader, furthermore, to test the equilibrium in Figure 3-3 by showing excess supply and demand of wheat and their effect on the terms of trade.

[4]As the reason behind this increase in demand, we will assume something unrelated to the price of cloth, such as a hard British winter. This is done to distinguish between a movement along the offer curve, which is not contemplated here, and a shift of the whole curve.

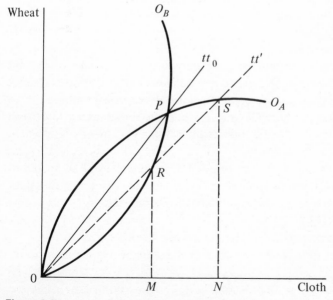

Figure 3-3

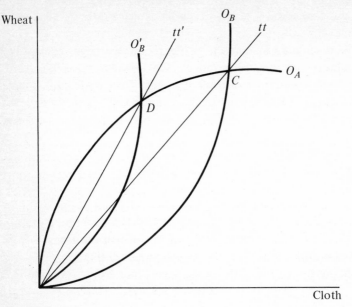

Figure 3-4

demand in Britain, it will take more wheat imports to make the British part with any given amount of cloth. Or, what amounts to the same thing, the British will now be willing to offer less cloth exports for any given amount of wheat imports.

The effect of this change in British demand for cloth can easily be seen in Figure 3-4. The volume of trade will decline as less wheat and cloth are traded at point D than had originally been traded at point C. This result was to be expected by common sense. Britain, after all, desires to keep more of her cloth production for herself, thus making less cloth available for exports. Less cloth exports, however, means less wheat imports.[5]

Britain's terms of trade (tt') at point D have improved compared to the terms of trade (tt) at point C. This, too, is plausible. Britain now values her export good (cloth) more highly and, therefore, requires more wheat per unit of cloth.

We might ask ourselves whether or not all this leaves Britain in a better overall position. The question whether an improvement in its terms

---

[5]We can see from Figure 3-4 that this result depends on the shape of America's offer curve between points C and D. If O_A were horizontal, for example, less cloth exports could go together with unchanged wheat imports. If O_A were even downward-sloping between C and D, decreased cloth exports could mean increased wheat imports.

of trade also improves the welfare of a country can be quite complex, and we shall deal with it on several future occasions. At this time our interest in this question leads us to an instructive review of the different elements of our trade model.

Recalling, for example, the indifference curve analysis of the previous chapter, we may use the indifference map as a welfare index. A country is better off as it reaches a higher indifference curve of the same map.

In our present example, then, we must ask the following question: Will the increase in Britain's demand for cloth and the resulting improvement in her terms of trade enable her to reach a higher indifference curve? Figure 3-5 demonstrates why this question cannot be answered.[6] We start at point A in the original autarky position. Trading now at the terms tt, Britain would move to point B in production and C in consumption.[7] This involves cloth exports, wheat imports, and the gains from trade associated with the move onto the higher indifference curve I_2.

Now we introduce the change in Britain's demand structure by way of a new indifference map represented by Γ_1 and Γ_2. The autarky point consequently shifts to D. Since we know from Figure 3-4 that the terms of trade improve as a consequence of the change in demand, we must now consider trade at tt'. Britain's production point will be E, and her consumption point will be F.[8]

We can see now that our question cannot be answered, because it involves comparing point C in Figure 3-5 with point F. We cannot tell which of these points indicates the higher level of welfare, because each point lies on an indifference map of its own.

We may conclude that it is impossible to judge the effects of a change in terms of trade on the welfare of a country whenever such a change is caused by a shift in its demand structure.

The logic of this result is easy to see. Each demand structure serves as one measuring rod in comparing levels of welfare. To compare two levels by using two different measuring rods amounts to measuring one level in inches and the other in centimeters, while lacking the formula for converting inches into centimeters.

Before we go on to discuss supply changes, it may be useful to list the effects of several demand changes on the offer curves.

Britain's offer curve will shift to the left if British demand for cloth

---

[6]For the technical background of Figure 3-5, the reader may wish to refer back to Figure 2-10 in the previous chapter.

[7]tt represents the original equilibrium terms of trade determined in Figure 3-4 at point C.

[8]The terms of trade tt' in Figure 3-5 may be viewed as equivalent to tt' in Figure 3-4.

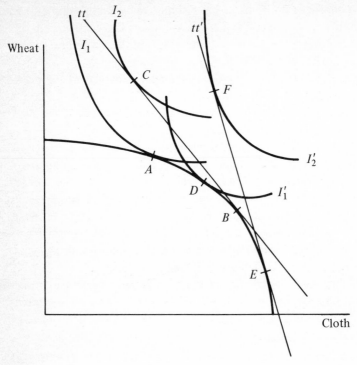

Figure 3-5

rises or British demand for wheat falls. It will shift to the right if British demand for cloth falls or British demand for wheat rises.

America's offer curve will shift to the right if American demand for wheat rises or American demand for cloth falls. It will shift to the left if American demand for wheat falls or American demand for cloth rises.

Each of these shifts may be verified by a quick experiment with the appropriate offer curve.

THE OFFER CURVE AND CHANGES IN SUPPLY

Let us assume now that, due to an advance in agricultural technology, the American supply of wheat increases. This change will shift the American offer curve from position O_A in Figure 3-6 to position O'_A. The shift is explained by America's ability to offer more wheat for each yard of cloth, or, conversely, her willingness to accept less cloth for any given amount of wheat.

At the new equilibrium point in Figure 3-6, the volume of trade has risen as America uses some of her increased wheat production to buy additional cloth from Britain. But the terms of trade at which this additional cloth can be obtained deteriorate for America, since the British, according to their offer curve, require increasing amounts of wheat per unit of cloth as trade expands.

This raises once more the interesting question of whether or not this country has gained from the change in its terms of trade. If America were not involved in international trade, the answer would be simple enough. Technological improvement means that more of a product (in this case wheat) can be produced using a given amount of resources. Translated into the production possibilities framework of the last chapter, this means that more wheat can be produced without the sacrifice of any additional cloth.

In Figure 3-7 the curves AB and AC reflect America's production possibilities before and after the technological advance in wheat produc-

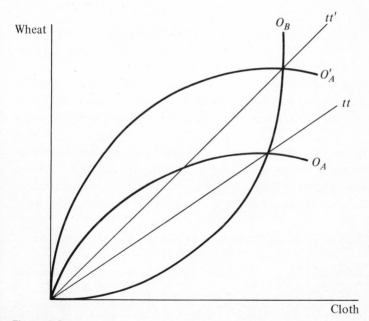

Figure 3-6

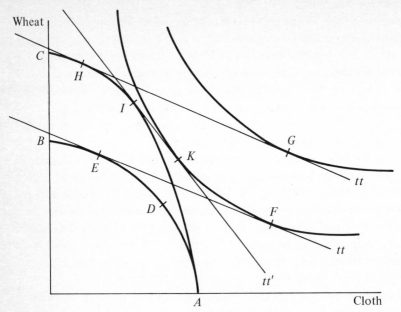

Figure 3-7

tion. Suppose the country is originally in autarky equilibrium at point *D*, where the production possibilities curve *AB* just touches one curve (not drawn) of the indifference map. It is immediately evident that the move to the higher production possibilities curve *AC* will put the autarky point on a higher indifference curve. There is certainly nothing startling about our conclusion that an increase in its production potential will make a country better off.

The existence of trade, however, may upset this conclusion. What if the production gain is eaten up by the deterioration of the terms of trade we have demonstrated in Figure 3-6? America, in other words, may have to use up all of her additional wheat production to buy enough cloth at the increased price.[9]

Let us look once more at Figure 3-7. Point *D*, as already mentioned, is

[9]An argument of this type, but strictly in domestic terms, has been used by American farmers who claimed that their standard of living declined in spite of impressive productivity advances. Prices of industrial products, according to this argument, have risen much faster than those of farm products. In order to be able to buy the industrial products they need, the farmers must, therefore, produce more and more farm products. We may view the farmer's call for "parity" price programs as a call for the maintenance of agriculture's terms of trade.

the equilibrium point before trade and before technological improvement. Now trade at the terms *tt* is introduced.[10] The country moves to point *E* in production and *F* in consumption. It gains from trade because *F* lies on a higher indifference curve than *D*. If the country could trade after technological advance at the old terms of trade *tt*, it could move to point *H* in production and *G* in consumption, thereby clearly benefiting from its technological advance.

But we know from Figure 3-6 that the terms of trade will decline. In Figure 3-7, this is reflected by the application of *tt'* to the new production possibilities curve. According to these terms of trade, production will take place at *I* and consumption at *K*. Figure 3-7 is drawn in such a way that the country is equally well off before and after technological advance, since points *F* and *K* happen to fall on the same indifference curve. This is, of course, a special case. It is easy to see that the outcome depends on the extent to which the terms of trade deteriorate. If *tt'* is drawn flatter than in Figure 3-7, the country will gain from its technological advance; if *tt'* is drawn steeper, it will lose.

This section concludes with a list of potential supply changes and their effects on the offer curves.

The American offer curve will shift to the left if American supply of wheat increases or if American supply of cloth decreases. It will shift to the right if American supply of wheat decreases or American supply of cloth increases.

Britain's offer curve will shift to the right if British supply of cloth increases or if British supply of wheat decreases. It will shift to the left if British supply of cloth decreases or if British supply of wheat increases.

PRICE TAKERS AND PRICE MAKERS

The analysis of the terms of trade by means of offer curves sheds new light on our trade model. In the previous two chapters we had assumed the existence of some terms of trade within the range of the two countries' domestic rates of transformation. We had, furthermore, assumed that a country can trade as much as it wants at the going terms of trade.[11] This assumption has now been dropped, since offer curve

---

[10]These terms of trade may be found in Figure 3-6 as *tt*.
[11]It could trade, in other words, until it reached the highest possible indifference curve by moving along the given terms-of-trade line.

analysis has shown that the terms of trade change with the volume of trade.

In fact, we concluded just above that any shift in a country's offer curve will .change its terms of trade. This means, simply, that a country cannot alter its export offers and import requirements without also altering the ratio at which the two exchange. A supplier of wheat on the world market, for example, cannot expect to increase his wheat sales without suffering a decline in the price of wheat. Similarly, a seller of cloth will be able to increase the price of cloth if he withholds a larger part of his cloth production from the world market.

In general, the ability of buyers and sellers to affect the price depends on their relative importance in the world market. Our offer curve analysis so far has accorded about equal importance to each country because we have assumed a world consisting of two countries of roughly equal size.

Let us now assume that the British economy is minutely small relative to America. What is a large change in exports and imports for Britain remains insignificant for America. Compared with America, the British offer curve is so small that it intersects the American offer curve very close to the origin. Shifts in her offer curve, therefore, which may be important to Britain will not produce a noticeable change in the terms of trade. The terms of trade will always remain very close to the American domestic rate of transformation. Britain, in other words, will be a price taker in the sense that she can trade all she wants at constant (and in this case, most favorable) terms of trade.

In the real world, with many countries of all sizes, this important consideration takes two forms. First, a country may be relatively small, and its offer curve compared with the combined offer curve of its trading partners may be of insignificant dimensions.

Secondly, we must remind ourselves of the vast variety of goods and services that enter international trade. A country's terms of trade actually consist of an average of its export prices relative to an average of its import prices. What matters here is not so much the size of the country, but the share of the products it trades in the world market. Colombia, for example, may be a small country, but her share of world coffee sales is relatively large.

Whether or not it is a price maker or taker in the world market is obviously an important question for a country. Our example above of the small country which is able to trade all it wants at constant terms of trade should not lead us to optimistic conclusions about price takers in general.[12] Price takers must accept whatever terms of trade are determined on the world market. If those terms of trade deteriorate, price takers can do little about it. Their share of the world market is so small that changes in their supply or demand of the product in question will not affect its price.[13]

Price takers, therefore, have on occasion banded together and formed so-called *commodity agreements*. A number of sugar-producing countries, for example, who as individual sellers have insignificant shares of the world market, would join forces. They would typically agree to withhold part of their combined supply from the market in order to raise the sugar price and thus improve the terms of trade of sugar-exporting countries.

FACTOR PROPORTIONS

Before we go on to discuss more applications of our trade model in the following chapter, let us probe somewhat more deeply into this model.

Basically, our model explains trade as a consequence of differences in domestic supply-and-demand conditions. Much analytical attention has been concentrated on the supply side of this model. What, it was asked, is the reason behind different supply conditions between two countries? The answer was put in terms of different factor endowments. Let us see how the argument goes.

The key concept is factors of production. A factor of production is a basic ingredient or input necessary for producing a good or a service. Producing, then, is the activity of combining various factors in such a way as to obtain the desired product.

In practice, it is extremely difficult to define a factor of production. Most inputs, such as materials, plant, equipment, and even skills of various degrees, have themselves gone through some production process. In this sense, therefore, a factor of production must be something which has not been produced beforehand, something, in other words, which

[12]The reader with some background in elementary price theory will recognize the price taker as the perfect competitor and the price maker as an imperfect competitor—monopolist, oligopolist, etc. If no single country in any one product on the world market could affect its terms of trade by changing its offer curve, international trade would follow the outline of the competitive model of price theory. The very introduction of offer curve analysis, of course, discards this assumption.

[13]A price taker, himself having a normal offer curve of the type pictured in Figure 3-1, faces an offer curve which is a straight line going through the origin. The reader can quickly convince himself that no shift of the price taker's offer curve will change the terms of trade in this case.

reflects a country's basic economic endowment. It is customary to list labor, land, and capital as the major components of a country's factor endowment.

The factor proportions theorem explains differences in production possibilities by pointing to differences in the proportions between various factors with which countries are endowed: The production of certain goods requires factors in certain proportions. Automobile production requires more capital relative to land than does the production of cotton. Textile production requires more labor relative to capital than does oil refining. A country, therefore, in which the labor-capital ratio is high relative to other countries should produce textiles and leave most of the oil refining to countries which are more abundantly endowed with capital. A country will consequently have a comparative advantage in that product which uses relatively much of its relatively abundant factor of production.

Proportionate, comparative, relative. . . . Is it necessary to explain trade in such seemingly confusing terms? First of all, trade itself is inherently a relative proposition. What matters, for the ability of a country to export its goods, is its costs of production relative to those in other countries, and not some absolute standard which has to be met.

Secondly, the relativistic approach is essential in avoiding some of the most common fallacies about international trade. Take, for example, that most dreaded of situations, cheap foreign labor. The argument may be summarized as follows: It is patently unfair to subject the highly paid domestic working man to the competition of foreign labor which subsists on a handful of rice per day. Imports of goods, therefore, which are produced by cheap foreign labor should be restricted to protect domestic jobs.

This is the absolute way of looking at trade. It could be extended in the following absurd way: If all trade is based on the cheapness of labor, then there would be no possibility for the country with high domestic wages to export anything. Such exports would have to be produced by domestic workers who are for some reason willing to subsist on even less than a handful of rice.

This is, of course, nonsense, and the comparative approach provides the answer. Labor abroad is comparatively abundant in the sense that the labor-capital endowment proportion is higher abroad than at home. This means that the foreign country is better suited to the production of those goods in which labor is a relatively important factor. Cheap labor will be of little significance, for example, in generating hydroelectric power because labor is only a very small part of total production cost. The cheap-labor fallacy fails to see that different products require different factor proportions. The low-wage country's advantage in labor-intensive goods is comparative, not absolute. Comparative advantage, however, implies by definition the existence of comparative disadvantage. If labor is relatively abundant abroad and scarce at home, it follows, by definition, that capital is relatively abundant at home and scarce abroad. The home country should import goods in which the labor proportion is high and export goods in which the capital proportion is high.

To protect domestic jobs by import restriction in this situation means to insist on an inefficient allocation of resources because too much of the scarce domestic labor factor is used in production of labor-intensive goods. The availability of such goods in the form of cheap imports should serve as a signal to shift domestic labor into more capital-intensive products rather than as a rationale for import restriction.

TECHNOLOGY AND FACTOR SUBSTITUTION

The factor proportions theorem is based on linking certain factor proportions with certain products. In other words, it is based on observing how each good is produced—that is, briefly, its technology. Strictly speaking, the factor proportions theorem must assume that for any given product the same technology is used everywhere. If our theorem, for example, is to be useful in predicting the trade pattern between America and Britain, wheat must be land-intensive and cloth labor-intensive in *both* countries. Only if this assumption of equal technologies holds can we expect land-rich America to export wheat and labor-rich Britain to export cloth.

It is easy to see that our theorem would no longer be helpful if Britain decided to produce wheat by labor-intensive methods or cloth by land-intensive methods. In this case, both countries would use their abundant factor intensively in the same product, i.e. wheat, and factor endowment could no longer predict the trade pattern.[14]

Although the example above is somewhat extreme, it is always possible to substitute between factors of production to some extent. Some jobs which are typically mechanized in America may still be done

---

[14]Trade is still likely to occur because the production possibilities curves are still likely to differ. But this difference can no longer be based on different factor endowments.

by hand in other countries. Capital can be substituted for land by raising cattle in feed lots rather than using the range. Dams have been built by armies of workers moving the earth in baskets and stamping it into place with their bare feet.

The assumption, therefore, that any given product is subject to the same technology regardless of where it is produced must be considered as a serious restriction of the factor proportions theorem. Differences in technology, in fact, emerge from the discussion above as yet another basis for trade. Two countries can have identical factor endowments and identical tastes and still trade because the use of different technologies leads to differences in domestic rates of transformation.

FACTOR PRICE EQUALIZATION

This chapter concludes by discussing an extention of the factor proportions theorem which is in some ways related to our earlier discussion of the cheap-labor fallacy. If trade is based on factor endowments and factor costs, what is the effect of trade on factor costs or factor prices?

Let us return to our old two-country, two-product, two-factor model. Britain exports cloth because she is more abundantly endowed with labor, which is intensively used in cloth production. America exports wheat because she is more abundantly endowed with land, which is intensively used in wheat production. Since labor is abundant in Britain relative to land, and since in America the reverse is true, wages compared with land rents are lower in Britain than in America.

Now let the two countries begin to trade. Britain produces more cloth and less wheat. Keeping in mind that cloth production uses relatively more labor, this means that labor is released from the declining wheat industry in insufficient amounts to produce the additional cloth. Labor, in other words, which originally was abundant and cheap now becomes less abundant, and wages rise. Land, on the other hand, is released in greater quantities from the declining wheat industry than it can be absorbed by the expanding cloth industry. Land rents will therefore fall.

In America, which started with high wages and low rents, the effect will be the opposite. Increased wheat production will require the two factors in a proportion different from that in which they are released by the declining cloth industry. Land will become less abundant, causing rents to rise, and labor will become less scarce, causing wages to fall.

Trade, in short, will lead toward factor price equalization in the sense that in each country the expensive factor becomes cheaper and the cheap factor becomes more expensive.

The tendency toward factor price equalization becomes plausible on reflection. It is evident, for example, that the prices of the traded *products* must move toward equality. International product prices are equalized because products move across national borders. But how about factors which are not internationally mobile in our model? Factors are mobile in the sense that they are embodied in products. A product, after all, is nothing but a particular combination of factors of production. If land is scarce in Britain, for example, this scarcity will surely be alleviated by the import of wheat, which heavily embodies land as a factor of production.

TRADE AND INCOME DISTRIBUTION

Factor prices are, of course, incomes. If trade affects relative factor prices, it affects the distribution of income. For example, in a capital-rich country which imports labor-intensive goods wages must fall relative to capital incomes according to the factor price equalization theorem.

This brings to mind the cheap-labor argument from above. It turns out that relatively abundant (and therefore cheap) foreign labor is indeed reason for concern by domestic labor. But this concern is not properly placed in terms of competition with cheap foreign labor. Rather, it must be put in terms of income distribution. The wage share of national income tends to decline under the circumstances assumed here.

Let us not forget the gains from trade at this point. National income will rise as a consequence of trade. Domestic labor appears to have an option. It can call for trade restriction, thereby protecting its share of a constant national income. Or it can accept free trade. This would mean a declining wage share of a rising national income.

The effect of trade on income distribution will be taken up again in the next chapter, which discusses trade restrictions.

SUMMARY

The offer curve is the locus of all wheat-cloth combinations which are acceptable to a country in trade.

The shape of the offer curve is based on supply considerations in the sense that export offers rise as their price in terms of imports rises.

Demand conditions also explain the shape of the offer curve since imports demanded rise as their price in terms of exports falls.

The offer curve shows for each possible terms of trade what quantities of exports a country is willing to exchange for what quantities of imports.

The equilibrium terms of trade are determined by the intersection of two countries' offer curves.

Shifts in a country's domestic supply or demand conditions can be translated into shifts of its offer curve, which normally result in a change of the equilibrium terms of trade.

Improvement in a country's terms of trade does not necessarily imply a higher level of welfare. The shift causing the improvement must be carefully investigated in order to determine whether or not welfare has increased.

The ability of a country to affect its terms of trade depends on the size of its share in the world market for its exports and imports.

The factor proportions theorem explains differences in production possibilities in terms of differences in factor endowments. It predicts that a country will export that product in which its abundant factor is intensively used.

The factor proportions theorem assumes equal technologies between countries. Differences in technologies may serve as an additional basis for trade.

Trade tends to equalize factor prices by reducing the price of the scarce factor and raising the price of the abundant factor in each country.

Trade affects the relative share in national income of each factor of production.

SUGGESTED FURTHER READINGS

The classical basis of offer-curve analysis was provided by John Stuart Mill in his *The Principles of Political Economy*, Longmans, Green and Co., London, 1923, chap. 18. An advanced diagrammatic derivation of the offer curve was pioneered by James E. Meade, *A Geometry of International Trade*, George Allen & Unwin, London, 1952, chaps. 1–3. A description of the development from classical to modern trade theory may be found in Richard E. Caves. *Trade and Economic Structure* (Harvard University Press, Cambridge, Mass., 1960), chap. 2.

Trade Restriction

The model developed in the last three chapters makes a powerful case for free trade among nations. This case rests basically on the productivity gains to be derived from international division of labor. Free international exchange is the vehicle by which these productivity gains are realized in terms of the ultimate measure of well-being, i.e., consumption. The logic of the proposition, then, that free trade maximizes the well-being of all concerned is powerful because it is quite simple.

Yet in the world today, free trade remains at best a controversial blueprint of international organizations, and at worst the naive ideal of the theoreticians. Virtually every country is surrounded by a maze of trade restrictions. It is difficult to think of a single product in international trade which is not subject to some type of trading restriction. A list of the various restrictive devices and their uses, purposes, and effects would fill volumes and go far beyond the scope of our discussion.[1]

---

[1]To get an impression of existing trade restrictions, the reader may wish to leaf through any recent volume of *Annual Reports—Exchange Restrictions*, published by the International Monetary Fund (Washington). These reports are about 700 pages long and list only the general rules and regulations of IMF member countries.

But this does not absolve us from the need to come to grips with the obvious contradiction between our free trade model and observed practice. Does the abundance of trade restrictions prove that the practitioners are blind to the compelling logic of our model? Or have the theoreticians constructed a model which simply does not do justice to the complexities of the real world?

THE TARIFF

By trade restriction we mean anything which interferes with the free flow of international trade. More specifically, we mean that part of a nation's commercial policy which is concerned with tariffs, quotas, duties, embargoes, prohibitions, etc. In our discussion, we will use the tariff as our example of trade restriction. A tariff is a tax imposed on imports as they enter the country. An *ad valorem* tariff, much like a sales tax, is a percentage charge against the value of the imported good. A *specific* tariff is a fixed charge per unit of the commodity in question.

The most obvious result of a tariff is revenue for the government. Tariffs imposed for just this purpose, that is *revenue* tariffs, have become increasingly rare as governments have found other and better ways to collect revenues.

Today most tariffs are intended to reduce the volume of imports. It is easy to see how both an *ad valorem* tariff and a specific tariff achieve this purpose. Both types of tariffs raise the price of the imported commodity to the domestic consumer. If demand depends on price, less will be bought at the higher price. By adjusting either the *ad valorem* percentage or the amount of the specific tariff, the government can presumably reduce imports by the amount deemed desirable.[2]

NOMINAL VERSUS EFFECTIVE RATES

Even though these definitions of the tariff are clear enough, the actual protection afforded by a given tariff to the import-competing domestic

---

[2]A quota, which simply specifies the amount of a product allowed to enter the country, could also be used for this purpose. The basic difference is the following: If a tariff is used, every importer can buy as much of a given import good as he pleases, provided he pays the tariff. The revenue from the tariff, of course, goes to the government. If a quota is used, the importer pays no tariff, but now the demand will exceed the quota. Rationing devices, other than price, must be used to allocate the quota among importers. Those importers who end up with part of the quota can now add to their revenue the amount that would have gone to the government under a tariff system. Apart from the difficulty in finding a satisfactory allocative formula, quotas have tended to foster favoritism and corruption.

industry is not so easily determined. It may be wrong to conclude, for example, that a 20 percent tariff on shoe imports gives the domestic shoe industry a protective margin of 20 percent against foreign competition. The key to the problem is imported inputs. The shoe industry, for example, may buy most of its raw hides abroad. How much *effective* protection the tariff on shoes provides will now depend on the tariff on raw hide imports. Suppose, for example, that the tariff on raw hides is reduced. This will reduce the cost of producing shoes, and *effective* protection will have increased even though the *nominal* tariff on shoes has remained unchanged. In general, we may conclude that nominal tariff rates on finished goods understate their protective effect if tariffs on raw material imports are low. If tariffs on raw materials are high, on the other hand, the nominal rate may overstate effective protection.

In Chapter 6 we will encounter a contention by underdeveloped nations that the tariff structure of the developed countries discourages industrialization in the underdeveloped world. It is also claimed, in this context, that the effective protection given their industrial products by developed nations is much higher than one would expect by looking at the nominal tariff rates. The reason for this lies in the tariff *structure* of the developed countries, which generally shows low nominal rates on raw material imports and higher nominal rates on finished products.

Having thus outlined the mechanics of trade restriction, we will devote the present chapter almost entirely to the question of *why* a country should want to impose tariffs. We may divide our approach to this question into two general categories. First, as is most obvious, a country may impose a tariff because it expects to gain from this policy. This approach requires the assumption on our part that a country, much like a single person, has a clear idea as to what does and what does not make it better off.[3]

Secondly, the imposition of a tariff may be the outcome of a conflict between vested interests within a country. In this case the question whether or not the tariff benefits the whole country becomes incidental, and the focus shifts to distribution of income within a country.

TARIFFS AND THE TERMS OF TRADE

Let us deal with the first approach now, assuming that judgments about the welfare of a whole country can indeed be made. We may use the offer

---

[3]This assumption made it possible for us to use indifference curves for the purpose of making such welfare judgments in Chapters 2 and 3.

curves derived in the last chapter to show the implications of a tariff. Britain, in Figure 4-1, imposes a tariff on wheat imports; that is, she declares that she will henceforth require more wheat per unit of cloth and offer less cloth per unit of wheat. If point D in Figure 4-1, for example, reflects the wheat-cloth combination acceptable in trade to the private British sector, then the tariff moves point D to point E. The distance between points D and E would reflect the tariff collected by the British government in terms of wheat. The distance between D and C, similarly, would be the same tariff but collected in the form of cloth.

The tariff, in short, shifts the British offer curve to the left from its original position O_B to position O'_B.[4] The distance between the two British

[4]These tariff-induced shifts of the offer curve are different from the shifts we have discussed in the last chapter, which were caused by changes in domestic demand-and-supply conditions. The tariff shifts the offer curve without changing domestic supply-and-demand conditions. This makes it easier to discuss the gains from trade in this chapter than the last one.

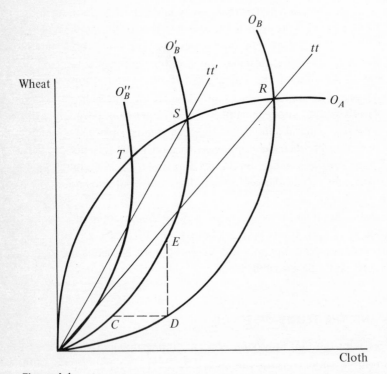

Figure 4-1

offer curves, measured either vertically or horizontally, reflects the interference of the authorities with private trading preferences.

Figure 4-1 shows that Britain's terms of trade improve as a consequence of the tariff. Does this imply an increase in Britain's welfare? Possibly, but not necessarily. We must note that two forces are at work here. One is the improvement in the terms of trade, which, by itself, tends to benefit Britain.

But the second force, clearly visible in Figure 4-1, is the reduction in the volume of trade. By moving from the original equilibrium point R to the new point S, the amounts of wheat and cloth changing hands are both reduced. The combination of these two forces means that Britain sells less exports at higher prices and buys less imports at lower prices. This situation is familiar to any businessman who must strike the proper balance between pricing and sales volume. A price hike will pay off only if he does not lose too much in volume. A price reduction will be profitable only if it leads to a sufficient rise in volume.

Looking back at Figure 4-1, we can therefore conclude as follows: The leftward shift of the British offer curve will make Britain better off as long as the improvement in her terms of trade is not outweighed by the decline in trade volume. But, as the leftward shift continues, a point will be reached where any further shift would reduce the gains from trade because the decline in volume would outweigh the improvement in price.[5] If we assume that this point is T in Figure 4-1, we can summarize that an import tariff will benefit Britain until it shifts her offer curve into position O''_B. Any further increase of the tariff would be detrimental to Britain.

A tariff which shifts the British offer curve exactly into position O''_B may therefore be viewed as the *optimum tariff* from the British point of view.

DISTRIBUTION BETWEEN COUNTRIES

How can our conclusion that a tariff can make a country better off be reconciled with our basic notion that free trade will maximize the welfare of the world community? Even though any tariff is likely to reduce the

---

[5]This can very easily be visualized by continuing to shift the British offer curve in Figure 4-1 to the left until it intersects the American offer curve at the origin. This, obviously, means no trade and no gains from trade (even though Britain's terms of trade have improved as much as possible). We know, therefore, that while Britain's gains from trade may increase for a time as we move from point R along America's offer curve toward the origin, they must begin to decline at some point.

gains from trade to the world community as a whole, an individual country may be able to increase its share of the total gains from trade. Our basic case for maximum overall welfare through free trade says very little about the distribution of this welfare among nations.

The individual country is therefore constantly torn between two possible approaches to trade. On the one hand, it may cast its lot with the free-trade ideal, working toward maximum overall welfare in the expectation that its share in the general bonanza will be satisfactory. We might view the classic free-trade era under the leadership of Great Britain during the latter half of the nineteenth century along these lines.

On the other hand, a country may be dissatisfied with its share in the overall gains from trade. In view of this insufficient share, the road toward increased national welfare may not be found in working toward maximum overall gains through free trade. Rather, the country may impose a tariff, expecting to gain by increasing its share of the reduced overall gains from trade.

RETALIATION

In our discussion so far, we have considered the implications of a tariff from the point of view of a single country. Above all, this involved the assumption that other countries would not retaliate against the imposition of a tariff with tariffs of their own. Let us discuss the likelihood of retaliation with the help of Figure 4-2.

At the original equilibrium point R Britain might see an advantage in imposing an import tariff, which would shift her offer curve into position O'_B. Britain has acted on the assumption that America will not retaliate. This assumption, however, may have been unrealistic. If Britain has gained by moving from R to S, this gain must have been America's loss.

How can America recoup this loss? Obviously, she cannot shift Britain's offer curve back to its original position and thus regain point R. But America can shift her own offer curve by imposing an import tariff of her own. Suppose this tariff shifts the American offer curve into position O'_A. The new equilibrium is now at point U, which is preferable to America over point S.[6] Britain, now confronted with point U, may decide to further increase her tariff; America may once more retaliate, and so on.

---

[6]This assumes that the improvement in the terms of trade was worth the reduction of trade volume. We recall that this question arises with any shift of the offer curve, whether or not it is retaliatory.

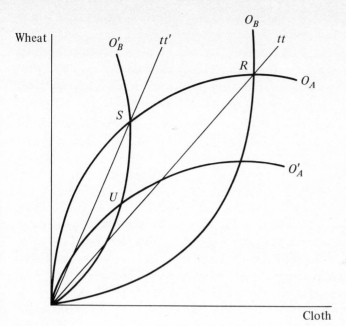

Figure 4-2

We can see how the trade volume may gradually be choked off as the equilibrium point moves ever closer to the origin along a terms-of-trade line which may not differ much from the original terms of trade (*tt*) in Figure 4-2.

Both countries, in other words, emerge as losers from this tariff battle, even though each individual move made by each country may have involved short-lived gains within the options available to the country under the circumstances.[7]

What makes this mutually disagreeable result possible? We can point to each country's disregard for the possibility of retaliation. Britain, for example, might have thought twice before moving to point *S* in Figure 4-2 had she realized that this would eventually mean point *U*. Although fear of retaliation remains a very important obstacle to trade restrictions in today's world, things are far less clearcut than in our example above. In a

---

[7]This becomes clear by reviewing how we proceeded from *R* to *U*. Britain prefers *S* to *R*. America prefers *R* to *S* but cannot go back to *R*. So America goes to *U*, which it prefers to *S*. Britain prefers *S* to *U* but cannot go back to *S*. Both countries end up preferring *R* to *U*, but neither country, by itself, can go back to *R*.

world of many countries and innumerable products, a small country may believe a tariff on one of its imports will go unnoticed. Or, a country may claim that its new tariff retaliates against some type of hidden restriction. American steel producers, for example, have claimed that Japanese steel producers receive subsidies from their government. The American tariff on steel imports is thus seen as retaliatory in a sense—a point of view which is not shared by the Japanese. Disputes of this nature tend to be drawn out over long time periods. In the meantime, tariffs may rise.

TRADE LIBERALIZATION

If Figure 4-2 shows the relative ease with which countries can drift into restrictive situations which benefit no one, it also shows the difficulty involved in reversing this trend. What does it take to move back from point U to point R, a movement which would benefit both countries? Both countries would obviously have to eliminate their tariffs to regain point R. But who is to take the first step? Again we run into the disregard for the possibility of retaliation.[8] America may be unwilling to move from U to S without assurances that Britain will "retaliate" by moving from S to R. Britain, similarly, would lose if she took the initiative and moved her offer curve back from position O'_B to O_B without a move by America from O'_A to O_A.

The last great upsurge of restrictionism occurred during the worldwide Great Depression of the early 1930s, when round after retaliating round of restrictions brought the world close to a virtual standstill in meaningful trade relations. This set the stage for the ensuing climate of trade liberalization. Many institutions and organizations have been involved in this effort. As our discussion above would lead us to expect, the key to trade liberalization is negotiated reciprocity.

The first major piece of U.S. legislation concerned with trade liberalization after the Great Depression was the Reciprocal Trade Agreement Act. According to this act, the U.S. government could negotiate tariff reductions, provided that other countries reciprocated.

Probably the most important institution involved in trade liberalization to this day is the General Agreement on Tariffs and Trade (GATT). Again we find our two crucial ingredients, negotiation and reciprocity,

---

[8]Retaliation of tariff reduction is called *reciprocation*.

very much in evidence. GATT provides a neutral international forum which hosts tariff negotiations on the basis of carefully established ground rules. The well-known Kennedy Round series of wide-ranging tariff reductions, for example, took place under the sponsorship of GATT.

DISTRIBUTION WITHIN A COUNTRY

It is time now to examine more closely an assumption we have used in this chapter which has, indeed, been crucial in the derivation of our basic trade model. This assumption concerns judgments about a country's welfare. Specifically, we have assumed that it is always possible to decide which one of two positions is more beneficial to a country as a whole.

Let us expose the weakness of this assumption by way of a simple example. We want to compare the position of a country before and after trade. Suppose the posttrade position involves more wheat but less cloth than the pretrade position. A single individual may prefer the posttrade position because the additional wheat more than compensates him for the loss of cloth. This is a matter of the individual's taste. A second individual may feel differently. He may find the additional wheat insufficient compensation for the loss of cloth. How are we to decide whether or not a country, which includes both individuals, is better off after trade?

One answer developed by economic theorists uses the following rationale: There must be a way to compare the first individual's gain with the second individual's loss. If individual A, for example, were able to use part of his gain to compensate B for his loss and still retain enough to benefit himself, both would be better off after trade. To employ this approach in practice obviously requires a formula by which the gains from trade must be redistributed by the government. The theorem outlined here, however, evades the practical problem by claiming that the mere possibility (rather than the actuality) of successful compensation is sufficient grounds for judging the posttrade position as superior for the country as a whole.

We need not take sides in this somewhat esoteric debate in order to see its implication for the topic at hand, i.e., trade restriction. With respect to the described trade, compensation or no compensation, individual B may see his fortunes waning. He may therefore resist the opening of trade with all the energy and ingenuity of one whose economic existence is at stake.

With this example, we introduce considerations which are basically different from our earlier approach. No longer does it matter whether or not a country as a whole gains from trade. If anyone within a country stands to lose by trading, there will be some pressures for trade restriction.

A review of our model shows that someone indeed stands to lose in almost any situation. We may recall, for example, the factor price equalization theorem of Chapter 3, according to which the income of the scarce factor will decline with trade. Or, to put it in even simpler terms, recall our basic two-country, two-product case. If each country produces both products, it follows that each country ends up importing one product which it also produces at home. The import-competing industry is threatened in its own domestic market, sometimes with outright extinction. Nothing seems more natural than this industry's insistence on protection, that is, trade restriction.

THE CORN LAWS

An example of how this type of problem relates to the real world is given by one of the most widely debated tariffs of all time, the so-called Corn Laws of eighteenth- and nineteenth-century Great Britain. Before we discuss this tariff specifically, however, let us outline its general background.

Britain, the cradle of the industrial revolution, was beginning to emerge as the world's first industrial power. Inevitably, this process brought with it great changes in the structure of British society. In particular, it brought the rise of a new class of capitalist entrepreneurs, who burst upon the British scene with industrial progress as their vehicle. They found many obstacles in their way. Traditional British society was dominated by its landed aristocracy and the great monopolistic trading companies which were sanctioned by the British government. British society, in short, did not welcome its new industrialist class with open arms.

It was against this background that Adam Smith's celebrated *Inquiry Into the Nature and Causes of the Wealth of Nations* appeared in 1776. Smith's message was division of labor, free domestic exchange, and freedom of international trade from state-sponsored monopolistic giants such as the East India Company. As the title of his book suggests, Smith

was concerned with the wealth (or welfare) of the (Briti
whole.

But how was this wealth to be distributed within tl
were the rising industrialists and the established lande
share those gains from trade promised by Smith so convincingly? These
questions became the great social issues in the wake of Smith's triumph in
the battle for liberal economics.

It is significant that our basic trade model of comparative advantage
grew out of this distributive discussion rather than out of the earlier
debate over economic liberalism in general. In order to show this, we will,
in the following passages, state comparative advantage deliberately as an
advocacy for the industrialists' cause rather than as an abstract "law" of
logic.

The Corn Laws were essentially a structure of tariffs on the import
into Britain of grains from the European Continent. They were designed
to protect the landed interests from foreign competition. The industrialists opposed the Corn Laws on the grounds that the price of grain was an
important factor in the wages of industrial labor. Opening the borders to
cheap foreign grain would not only lower its price but also make industry
less dependent on the annual vagaries of the British harvest alone.

To add to the controversy, British agriculture was, by far, the most
advanced of its day in the world. In fact, an early phase of the industrial
revolution had consisted in the application of new technology to British
agriculture. We can see how this technical superiority raised difficulties
for the spokesmen of either side. The advocate of agriculture could not
very well claim international superiority for British agriculture and insist
on protection in the same breath. The industrialist, on the other hand,
might use this agricultural superiority as an argument against the Corn
Laws, but he would then have to expect Britain to *export* agricultural
products rather than to import them, as the industrialists' interest
required.

It was under these circumstances that David Ricardo, the brilliant
champion of industrialism, developed comparative advantage as an
advocacy for industrial progress. We are technically familiar with his
argument from the preceding chapters: While British agriculture might
have an *absolute* superiority or advantage, the *comparative* advantage
belonged to British industry. Every unit of British resources that was
transferred from agriculture to industry would increase its productivity to
such an extent that more food could be exchanged abroad for the

ustrial output of this resource than it could possibly have produced at nome. Agricultural superiority was thus reconciled with food imports. The landed interests with their Corn Laws were putting artificial obstacles in the way of Britain's industrial development.

The Corn Laws thus became the prime focus in the struggle between the old order and modern industrialism. With Ricardo, himself a member of Parliament, as their most forceful advocate, the industrialists continued to gain strength. Not until 1846, however, twenty-three years after Ricardo's death, were the Corn Laws finally abolished.

What can we learn from this digression into the history of economic thought? The circumstances surrounding its origin give us a perspective on our trade model which is lacking from abstract derivations. Free trade under British sponsorship, although brilliantly based on logic, might never have materialized had it not served the interests of Britain's emerging industrialism. This perspective should caution us against too quickly pointing to tariffs and other trade restrictions as the handiwork of special interests. We have just seen that free trade, too, can be represented as the result of partisan advocacy.

NATIONAL SECURITY

So far we have discussed trade restrictions in very general terms. Let us use the remainder of this chapter to look into some more specific cases for and against tariffs.

Free trade, as observed in Chapter 1, involves economic interdependence between countries. This interdependence may run counter to the political relationships between a country and its neighbors. For the sake of its national security, in other words, a country may wish to maintain the capacity of producing certain goods even though this may be inefficient on purely economic grounds.

Even Adam Smith, for example—whose devotion to free trade we need affirm no further—remained a staunch supporter of the British Navigation Act, which amounted to a prohibition against the import of all foreign shipping services. Shipping and naval power was of such obvious strategic importance to Britain that even the great liberal economists kept it out of their treatises on free trade.

It is easy to see, of course, that the security argument for tariff protection may be abused. The world abounds with examples and we need not belabor the point. In some sense any amount of trade affects national security if this security is identified with the ability of a nation to survive in autarky. The obvious question is where to draw the line. The more products a country protects by tariffs for strategic reasons, the higher the price of national security in terms of the gains from trade forgone.

Finally, it is not inconceivable to challenge the premise that national security depends on a country's ability to survive in autarky. On the contrary, one might argue, the more interdependent two countries have become through trading, the less they can afford to wage war against each other. It may therefore be in the interest of each country's national security to foster interdependence rather than autarky.[9]

PROTECTION FOR INFANT INDUSTRIES

It is no coincidence that this argument for trade restriction emerged at the very time when free trade was advocated by David Ricardo in England. Infant-industry protection, in fact, was the answer from the European Continent and the United States of America to British free trade.

The time element is crucial in the infant-industry argument. Friedrich List, the German economist, and Alexander Hamilton, the American— both approximate contemporaries of Ricardo—argued that British industrial superiority was a matter of time lag between their countries' development and Britain's. Free trade at a time when England was ahead would force Germany and America into specialization in nonindustrial products and thus inhibit industrial development. The infant-industry tariff was designed to give these countries a period of grace in which to develop their industrial potential.

The infant-industry tariff is one of the most widely accepted forms of trade restriction with obvious appeal to any country which considers its industrial potential underdeveloped. It is therefore important that we understand the assumptions on which it must be based.

First, it must be assumed that industrial development is in the interest of the country in question. Our discussion of industrial development in Britain showed a conflict of interests within the country and complicated the judgment of what is and what is not in the national interest.

Even if this problem is resolved in favor of industrial development,

---

[9]The history of France and Germany, for example, is marked by several wars between these two countries. Today, as a result of the European Common Market, their economies are interdependent to an extent which makes war all but technically impossible.

the country must be sure of its long-range potential to develop a comparative advantage in the temporarily protected industries. Ultimately, this goes back to the factor proportions theorem. If the basic factor endowment is not suited (relative to other countries) to the protected industries, the country will end up either with permanent misallocation of its resources or with an experiment doomed to failure. The experiment may be costly in terms of the gains from trade forgone. The consumers of this country, after all, are being asked to buy high-priced and often inferior goods from domestic industries while the infants are growing to maturity.

Finally, an infant-industry tariff, once instituted, is extremely difficult to remove. If the protected industries have indeed achieved the efficiency and size required for international competition, they are not likely to welcome the removal of the extra margin provided by the tariff. If, on the other hand, the experiment remains a failure, removal of the tariff cuts the lifeline of a whole industrial establishment.

We will return to the infant-industry argument in its more modern form in our discussion of developing nations in Chapter 6.

JOB CREATION BY TARIFF

In terms of current sensitivities on the issue of trade restriction, the relationship between tariffs and jobs is certainly at the forefront of the debate. On the surface, the argument for tariffs here is simple: What we do not import, we produce ourselves. Each imported product, therefore, takes away a domestic job opportunity.

The fallacy of this argument is no doubt evident to the reader. If imports reduce jobs, exports increase jobs. This brings to mind the ever-present possibility of retaliation. Suppose an industry threatened with layoffs because of foreign competition succeeds in obtaining tariff protection. If other countries retaliate, some export industry will be affected and possibly have to lay off as many workers as the protected industry has managed to keep employed. As a result, the comparatively inefficient industry keeps operating while the efficient one is set back. Total employment, at the same time, may remain unchanged. This distortion in resource allocation occurs not only in the domestic country but also in the retaliating countries, which now also protect their comparatively inefficient industries.

In the real world, of course, the problem does not appear as simple as that. The threat of Japanese steel, for example, to jobs in the American steel industry is real and certainly well publicized. The *immediate* choice seems to be between a protective tariff and the loss of thousands of jobs. Compared with the urgency of this problem and its focus on one particular industry, the consequences of *potential* retaliation seem distant and diffuse. It is not certain, for one thing, that retaliation will indeed occur. And even if it is expected to occur, there is no certainty as to which export industry will be most heavily affected.

THE BALANCE OF PAYMENTS TARIFF

A tariff, by reducing imports, will tend to improve a country's balance of international payments. In practice, this is an important aspect of the tariff, because a government with a balance of payments problem is more likely than otherwise to lend a sympathetic ear to protectionist interest groups. The most obvious argument against such a tariff is, once more, the likelihood of retaliation. Even without retaliation the question remains whether an improvement in the balance of payments is worth the misallocation of resources due to the tariff. Balance of payments adjustment, as we shall see in later chapters, is properly the task of aggregate or macroeconomic policies rather than the restriction of specific imports.

THE ANTIDUMPING TARIFF

When a country sells its exports abroad at prices below those charged at home for identical products, we have a case of *dumping*. Intermittent dumping could be a part of a country's strategy to drive its competitors out of the world market, establish monopoly, and thereafter raise prices to more profitable levels. This type of commercial aggression obviously has no place in our trade model and will lead to a decline in the overall gains from trade. Permanent dumping may be the result of international price discrimination. Such discrimination consists in charging different prices for the same product according to what different national markets will bear. A Japanese optical company, for example, may have a considerable share of the domestic market, little domestic competition, and (due to tariff protection) little foreign competition. This company will therefore be able to charge domestic consumers a high price for its cameras. On various international markets, however, international competition will have to be met. This may be possible only by reducing price below its domestic level.

One defense against such tactics is a tariff. But clear cases of dumping are difficult to establish. An individual firm may use certain products as loss leaders. This is dumping. A country may exempt all exports from sales taxes or even subsidize certain export industries outright. Considering the fact that all taxes and subsidies have some effect on prices and that no two countries have exactly the same tax systems, cases of this latter type tend to be extremely complex. Dumping is far more often charged than clearly documented. Antidumping tariffs far too often are based on the charge rather than on conclusive evidence.

THE "SCIENTIFIC" TARIFF

Finally, let us consider the following quote concerning the most general of all tariff arguments, the so-called *scientific tariff*.

> Offset the higher expenses of the American producer, put him in the position to meet the foreign competitor without being under a disadvantage, and then let the best man win. Conditions being thus equalized, the competition will become a fair one. . . .[10]

The scientific tariff, in other words, is designed to eliminate all disparities in cost of production. The reader is right in judging this statement as the poorest argument for a tariff we have encountered yet, even though it rings with fairness, equality, and hearty competition. Once more we face the absolute view of trade, which has led us to poor results before.[11] It is evident that the scientific tariff conflicts directly with the logic of comparative advantage and disadvantage. One might well ask just what remains as the basis for trade after all cost differences have been equalized by the tariff. Conditions being "scientifically" equalized, we have good reason to expect most or all trade to cease.

---

[10]F. W. Taussig, *Free Trade, The Tariff, and Reciprocity*, Macmillan, New York, 1920, p. 134. The above quote is part of Taussig's rejection of the scientific tariff.
[11]Compare for example the cheap-labor fallacy in the preceding chapter.

THE CASE OF THE U.S. STEEL INDUSTRY

We could continue listing arguments for and against particular kinds of tariffs for some time without exhausting the literature on the subject. It would perhaps be more useful to look at one particular industry and its position with regard to the tariff question.

The Smoot-Hawley Tariff Act of 1930 had provided the American steel industry (as well as most other American industries) with the highest tariff protection ever. Smoot-Hawley led to worldwide retaliation and contributed to the general climate of protectionism at that time. By 1933 steel tariffs reached their peak with 12 to 45 percent *ad valorem*.[12] But these rates were short-lived, since the Reciprocal Trade Agreement Act of 1934 reversed protectionist trends and ushered in a long period of tariff reduction, which seems to show signs of weakening only at the present time (early 1970s).

Reciprocal tariff reduction under the auspices of GATT and sustained by periodic renewals of the Reciprocal Trade Agreement Act appeared to have been in the interest of the U.S. steel industry for some time. The industry had considerable cost advantage over foreign steel producers. American ore and coking coal was of superior quality. The newest technology was being used in plants of more than sufficient size to take advantage of the economies of scale. During the Great Depression of the early 1930s, when steel producers abroad were struggling to survive, American steel equipped its plants with modern facilities for the continuous-rolling process.[13]

This situation invites a reference to the cheap-labor discussion of the previous chapter. American steel workers were earning higher wages than their foreign counterparts. But this did not mean that American steel was more expensive than foreign steel. Superior efficiency of American steel production resulted in higher output per worker, so that the labor cost per ton of steel could have been lower than abroad.

During the 1950s, as European and Japanese production facilities were being newly rebuilt, American steel began to lose its advantage. Some experts also believe that the oligopolistic structure of the American steel industry, i.e., the lack of domestic competition, had slowed its progressiveness. At about this time, furthermore, tariff reductions were

---

[12]Leonard W. Weiss, *Case Studies in American Industry*, 2d ed., Wiley, New York, 1971, p. 189.
[13]Ibid., p. 190.

stepped up on the basis of the U.S. Trade Expansion Act of 1962, which led to the "Kennedy Round" of negotiations, resulting in major tariff reductions by 1967. The steel industry consequently lost most of its tariff protection just at a time when foreign producers became competitive. In 1968, for example, steel tariffs were down to 3 to 13 percent.[14] During this year about 17 percent of all steel sales in America came from abroad.[15]

Seeing their position thus threatened by imports, American steel producers mounted a well-organized campaign for protection. Several of the arguments discussed above were used. Particular emphasis was placed on the national security aspect, the potential loss of jobs, and antidumping. The Johnson administration, concerned as it was with a balance of payments problem, sought to accommodate the industry while at the same time avoiding possible retaliation. The device used for this purpose was a "voluntary" quota on steel imports. Japanese and European producers were prevailed upon to voluntarily restrict their exports to the United States. This request was backed by the implication that the United States would enact mandatory quotas if steel imports continued to grow.

The apparent success of this voluntary steel quota was not lost on other American industries. Under the Nixon administration, for example, such a "voluntary" quota was negotiated for textiles. The possibility of mandatory quotas was meanwhile kept alive by Congress, which was preparing to consider the Burke-Hartke Bill. This bill, among a number of other restrictive measures, provides for sweeping quotas on all products in order to keep imports at their 1965 to 1969 levels.

SUMMARY

The discussion of trade restriction may be divided into two general areas. First we may view trade restriction as a means by which one country can increase its share of the overall gains from trade. Secondly, we may view trade restriction as a means by which an interest group within a country can increase its share of its country's gains from trade.

The first view requires the assumption that we can make welfare judgments for a country as a whole.

---

[14]Ibid., p. 185.
[15]Ibid., p. 191.

Using this assumption, the following has been concluded: A country can improve its terms of trade by imposing a tariff. This leads to increased welfare if the resulting decline in trade volume does not outweigh the price increase. The optimum tariff is one which maximizes the gains from trade under these conditions. The potential of gaining from a tariff is greatly reduced as soon as the tariff provokes retaliation. The most likely outcome of retaliation and counterretaliation is a decline in trade volume and no decisive change in the terms of trade. Trade liberalization, or the removal of existing tariffs, requires retaliation in removing tariffs, that is, reciprocity.

The second view, which sees trade restriction as the result of conflicting interests within a country, emphasizes the fact that all trade involves redistribution of income within a country. Since almost any international trading situation means losses to someone within each trading country, trade restrictions in the interest of the losing party are to be expected. Whether or not the country as a whole benefits is, in this case, incidental.

The Corn Laws can be used as an example to represent our free-trade model of comparative advantage as a partisan argument on behalf of British industrialism.

A tariff may be justified in the interest of national security on the assumption that the protection of certain strategic industries enhances national security.

The infant-industry tariff justifies protection on the grounds that a country needs time to catch up with other countries' industrial development. A meaningful infant-industry tariff requires factor endowments which are suitable to the eventual development of internationally competitive industries.

A tariff for the protection of jobs must face the possibility of retaliation, which would lead to misallocation rather than protection of jobs.

A tariff for the purpose of reducing imports and thereby improving the balance of international payments faces the possibility of retaliation and misallocation of resources. A better way to adjust the balance of payments is by aggregate economic policy.

A tariff against dumping involves the problem of proving that dumping has indeed occurred. In the absence of such proof, dumping may be used as an excuse to impose a tariff for some other reason.

The "scientific" tariff is designed to eliminate all cost differentials and as such would also remove much of the basis for trade. The appeal of this tariff is in its rhetoric rather than its logic.

SUGGESTED FURTHER READINGS

L. B. Yeager and D. G. Tuerck, *Trade Policy and the Price System* (International Textbook Company, Scranton, Pa., 1966). A survey of the technical literature is provided by R. M. Stern, "Tariffs and Other Measures of Trade Control: A Survey of Recent Developments," *Journal of Economic Literature*, March 1973. This article contains extensive further references. For broad background studies, see Sir William Beveridge, *Tariffs: The Case Examined*, 2d ed. (Longmans, Green & Company, New York, 1932); Asher Isaacs, *International Trade: Tariffs and Commercial Policies* (Richard D. Irwin, Inc., Homewood, Ill., 1948).

Chapter 5

Economic Integration

In the preceding chapter we have touched on the problem of trade liberalization. In retrospect, we can divide the obstacles to trade liberalization into three general areas. First, unilateral trade liberalization may be detrimental to the economic welfare of an individual country. This follows directly from our conclusion that unilateral trade restriction may, under certain conditions, improve the position of an individual country. Secondly, if trade restriction serves special interests within a country, trade liberalization will conflict with such interests. Thirdly, trade liberalization requires reciprocity and therefore negotiation. The complexity of such negotiations depends on the number of countries involved and on their economic, cultural, and ideological differences. This means that trade liberalization on a global scale faces the highest conceivable degree of complexity as far as negotiation and reciprocity are concerned. It is consequently not surprising that progress in worldwide trade liberalization has been slow and sporadic, even though the theoretical case for the economic gains from free worldwide trade is clear-cut.

Trade liberalization on a global scale is not the only approach to free trade. One way, for example, to reduce the problems of reconciliation between different cultures and ideologies is to limit trade liberalization to certain groups of countries, typically on a regional basis. This approach leads us to the concept of economic integration, to which the present chapter is devoted.

THE STAGES OF INTEGRATION

Such regional groupings often go further than establishing free trade. Once it has been decided to promote exchange and interdependence, the ultimate goal may become the complete integration of the region. Free trade, in other words, is only the first step toward economic integration.

A region in which this first step has been taken is called a *free-trade area*. The countries belonging to such an area have agreed to abolish all obstacles to trade among themselves. Each country, however, maintains its own system of trade restriction with regard to the outside world. These individual tariff systems may cause problems for the free-trade area. Suppose two countries within the area continue to maintain greatly different import tariffs on a particular product against the outside world after agreeing to free trade among themselves. Importers in the low-tariff country will then find it profitable to import this product from the outside world only to reexport it to the high-tariff country.[1] Apart from distorting resource allocation in production and transportation, this artificial trading pattern will almost certainly strain relations within the free-trade area.

To avoid this and related problems connected with different levels of outside tariffs, the free-trade area may advance to the stage of *customs union*. This means that free trade inside the area will continue as before, but that all restrictions with regard to the outside world will be equalized. Each member country, in other words, now maintains identical tariffs against nonmembers.

With this uniform policy toward nonmembers, a customs union has integrated several countries into one unit from the point of view of our trade model. For example, we could represent the entire union and its

---

[1] This phenomenon is called *trade deflection* or *transshipment*.

uniform tariff with the help of a single offer curve. The customs union may negotiate as one unit in worldwide trade negotiation, perhaps trying to improve its collective terms of trade. But within the union, the member countries still remain separate entities, even though free trade may lead to increased interdependence. This trade is based, as we know from our model, on differences in factor endowments and tastes.

The next stage of integration is the formation of a *common market*. This stage adds to the concept of customs union the freedom of factors of production to move across national borders within the region. It becomes clear at this point that we are going beyond the framework of our basic trade model, which is based on the mobility between countries of products, but not of factors. The relationship between the members of a common market area is therefore closer than mere interdependence caused by free trade in products. Their economies are beginning to merge into one integrated economic region. Labor is allowed to move anywhere within the area without regard for national borders. Firms may establish themselves wherever they wish, and capital moves without restrictions.

At this stage of common market, integration may have reached the point of no return. If labor, for example, indeed takes advantage of its newly won mobility, national differences in taxation, social security, union laws, etc. will have to be abolished to avoid distortion in the allocation of the labor resource. The same is true for corporate taxation, antitrust laws, and corporate finance arrangements, if the location of corporate enterprises is not to be distorted by national differences in these provisions. The final stage of integration, then, in which all artificial distortions of resource allocation between member countries are abolished, is called *economic union*. Such a union will require the administration of important economic functions by supranational institutions, as more and more aspects of national economic life become subject to the collective decisions of the economic union. The ultimate symbol of economic union may be a common currency, administered by a supranational central bank, which is in charge of the union's monetary policy. In this case the economic union is also a *monetary union*.

ECONOMIC INTEGRATION VERSUS TRADE LIBERALIZATION

The discussion above has shown economic integration as a concept which is applied to the limited context of a particular group of countries. Within this limited context, integration includes trade liberalization as one of its earliest stages. The concept of trade liberalization by itself, on the other hand, has no such limited connotations and refers in general to the reduction of trade restrictions on a worldwide basis. We have already observed that global trade liberalization is an extremely complex problem. It is therefore not surprising that most cases of trade liberalization today occur in the limited context of regional groupings rather than on a worldwide scale. Almost every country today belongs to some type of regional group.[2] Many of these groups have not advanced beyond the planning stage, while others have made more tangible progress. Whatever the actual state of affairs may be, it appears that the world today envisages trade liberalization within the context of regional integration, rather then on a global scale.

This leads us to the following crucial question: Can trade liberalization within the limited context of regional integration be considered progress toward worldwide free trade? Our trade model tells us only that the global gains from trade are maximized by free global trade. It does not tell us that trade liberalization within certain groups of countries will lead to increased global gains from trade. Nor does it even tell us whether or not the gains from trade will increase within the regional group. In order to work our way through these questions, we must analyze regional integration with the help of our basic tools developed in the previous chapters.

Let us begin with a simple example. Suppose the world is composed of ten countries, each of which trades with the other nine, using various degrees of trade restrictions. Now we divide this world into two customs unions of five countries each.[3] Is world trade now freer than it has been before? The two unions might concentrate completely on free internal trade and use the outside tariffs to shut out all imports from the outside world. Trade between the two groups of countries now ceases. Inside each customs union, on the other hand, trade is now liberalized and bound to increase.

In a sense we now have two separate free-trade worlds instead of one

[2]Some examples of such groups are the European Economic Community (EEC), the European Free Trade Association (EFTA), the Latin American Free Trade Association (LAFTA), the Central American Common Market (CACM), and the communist Council for Mutual Economic Assistance (COMECON).
[3]The stage of customs union is frequently chosen as an example of integration, because with its free internal trade and common external tariff it is more easily adapted to trade theory than other stages of integration.

world with trade restrictions. Which is better? Much depends on how the two customs unions were formed to begin with. Let us assume, for example, that they were formed on a regional basis, and that the two regions have approximately identical factor endowments and tastes, while individual countries within each region differ greatly. In this case not much could be gained from trading between the two customs unions, and the effect of free trade within each region will outweigh that of trade restriction between the two regions.

Suppose, on the other hand, that differences in factor endowments and tastes between the two regions leave much scope for trade and that such differences are small between individual countries within each region. In this case not much is gained from free trade within each region, and much is lost by forgoing trade between the two regions. It is perfectly possible, in other words, that a customs union formed for reasons of political alliance, and without regard for its economic potential, may reduce economic welfare within the region and the rest of the world.

THE THEORY OF CUSTOMS UNIONS

The simplistic example above can serve only as an outline of the type of problem with which the theory of customs unions is concerned. Let us take a closer look at this theory.

Free trade among the members of a customs union will bring optimal resource allocation within the region. Before the formation of the union, various producers were protected by tariffs against the competition of more efficient producers elsewhere. Identical goods thus might be produced by high-cost and low-cost producers within the region. From the collective regional point of view this obviously represents a waste of resources. Each good should be supplied by that producer who uses the smallest amount of resources per unit of output. This is precisely what happens as trade is freed within the region, because without tariff protection high-cost producers will be driven out of the market. As production settles at its various low-cost locations without regard for national borders, the volume of products crossing those borders will rise. This process is called the *positive production effect* of a customs union.

Consumers in the region will benefit from this increased efficiency in resource allocation. Before formation of the customs union they were obliged to buy the expensive output of high-cost domestic producers.

Now they have access to the lowest costs and prices in the region. This *positive consumption effect* of a customs union raises the real income of consumers because a given amount of money income will buy more goods as prices decline.

These positive production and consumption effects may be combined under the term of *trade creation*. We can easily see that trade creation is nothing else but the application of our basic free-trade model within the limited context of a customs union.

But it is precisely on account of this limited context that we must look beyond trade creation. We must also think of that trade which takes place between the customs union and the outside world.

Suppose, for example, that before the formation of the customs union a country maintains a tariff on wheat imports in order to protect its relatively inefficient farmers. Let us further assume that wheat is produced at somewhat lower cost in countries which are prospective members of the customs union. But the lowest-cost wheat is produced somewhere in the outside world. Whatever wheat imports our country permits to enter will therefore come from the outside world. As the customs union is formed, our country drops its tariff on wheat imports from member countries but maintains some tariff against the outside world. It is possible now that the member countries' wheat will undersell the low-cost wheat of the outside world on the domestic market. Wheat purchases in this case shift from low-cost producers outside the union to higher-cost producers inside the union. Resource allocation is distorted in favor of inefficient production inside the customs union. We may call this process the *negative production effect* of a customs union.

Again there is a parallel to this production effect in the area of consumption, especially when we think of the equalized outside tariff system which is typical of a customs union. By adopting the unified tariff, some members may have to impose new tariffs on some imports which may have been allowed to enter the country freely before the formation of the customs union. Consumer purchases will thereby be diverted from low-cost outside producers to high-cost producers inside the customs union. This then is the *negative consumption* effect of a customs union. The term *trade diversion*, finally, applies to the combination of negative production and consumption effect.

As far as the gains from trade through customs unions are concerned, we have a number of possibilities, depending on the relative strength of each of the effects described above. Trade creation will always increase the volume of trade and improve the allocation of resources. This should mean an increase in the gains from trade not only for the customs union internally, but also for the outside world, which stands to benefit from the union's increased efficiency.

Trade diversion, on the other hand, could reduce the volume of trade.[4] Perhaps more important is the fact that it tends to distort the trading pattern and lead to misallocation of resources. The gains from trade will therefore be reduced for both the customs union and the outside world.

FACTORS AFFECTING TRADE CREATION AND DIVERSION

We have seen that the prospects for economic viability of a customs union depend on the presence or absence of circumstances conducive to trade creation and diversion.

Trade diversion, for example, becomes obviously less important as the membership of the customs union expands, because the outside world, from which trade is to be diverted, becomes smaller. In the extreme case, where the "customs union" covers the whole world, no trade is left for diversion, and the formation of the customs union becomes equivalent to global trade liberalization, which leaves room only for trade creation.

Another consideration with an obvious bearing on the likelihood of trade creation versus diversion is the degree of restriction prior to the customs union. Let us assume, for example, that the tariffs vis-à-vis prospective union members and the outside world are very high. In this case the introduction of free trade inside the union will bring substantial trade creation, since we are starting from a level of considerable misallocation of resources. Trade diversion, on the other hand, will be relatively unimportant, since high tariffs have already restricted the volume of outside trade before the customs union was formed, and there is consequently little trade to divert. It follows that a low pre-union level of trade restriction will narrow the scope for trade creation and increase the possibility of trade diversion. We may envisage the extreme case, where no trade restriction exists originally. The only effect of the customs union now is trade diversion. This result is not surprising. We have started

[4]Consumers may reduce their purchases of those goods, which must now be bought from high-cost internal producers.

with a freely trading world and formed a customs union which introduced new tariffs. The result must be a decline in the global gains from trade.

Another aspect of trade creation and diversion involves the nature of the economies to be integrated into a customs union. This consideration is based on differences in factor endowments and tastes between prospective union members. Two economies may be said to be competitive if, due to similar endowments and tastes, a similar range of goods is produced in both countries. Complementary economies, on the other hand, have significant differences in their tastes and endowments and therefore less overlapping in the assortment of goods they produce.

Off hand, we would expect a customs union to cause more trade creation between complementary economies than between competitive ones. This follows from our trade model, which bases trade on differences in factor endowments and tastes, rather than on similarities. But we must not overlook the fact that the extent of pre-union trade restriction is likely to have been higher between competitive economies than complementary ones. Competitive economies would have reasons to protect their producers from each other, since they largely produce the same goods. Complementary economies, on the other hand, have little reason to construct tariff walls between themselves, since there is little to protect. As we know from our discussion above, the lower the pre-union tariff levels, the smaller will be the chance for trade creation by the customs union. This leaves us with two forces to consider. A customs union between competitive economies, for example, may not look very promising in view of the similarity of the economies. But this very similarity may have led to high protective tariffs, the abolition of which may be sufficiently beneficial to compensate for the structural similarities.

DYNAMIC EFFECTS

A customs union, or indeed any other stage of integration, offers each individual producer a widely expanded market for his goods. It also makes him subject to entirely new and different forms of competition and rivalry. Integration, in other words, will place the producer in a drastically altered business environment. Where once there may have been the security of tariff-protected monopoly in narrow domestic markets, there is now the challenge of foreign competition and a region-wide market. It is easy to see that these changes in their surroundings will affect the size and methods of operation of the firms themselves. Such changes are the *dynamic effects* of economic integration, while trade creation and diversion are generally considered static effects.

Let us try to visualize just how a given firm might react to the formation of a customs union. We might assume, for example, that our firm has a large share of the domestic market prior to the customs union. It may even dominate the domestic industry if the residual of the market is shared by a number of smaller firms. Or it may be one of a few large firms which share the domestic market. The result in either case tends to be oligopolistic behavior, which usually means that prices charged the consumer are higher than the cost of production. Oligopoly also often means that the industry has a substantial stake in maintaining the status quo. Price competition or rapid expansion by one firm at the expense of its rivals tend to be avoided. Even though our firm may be capable of greater efficiency and expansion, it may prefer the peace of the status quo.[5]

The customs union changes all this. Our firm is forced now to compete on the basis of price with the most efficient producers in the union. If it is unable to improve its own efficiency, it may go under. But while the new foreign competition forces our firm to raise its efficiency, the newly expanded market may provide the opportunity to do just that. No longer will the firm feel reluctant to expand. In fact, expansion may be its only chance for survival if a reduction in cost can be achieved only by adopting large-scale production techniques. Our firm will thus be forced to take advantage of the *economies of scale*, which means the decline in unit costs associated with expansion in output.

This example shows two important dynamic effects of a customs union. First, individual firms are forced to become more efficient. This, of course, affects the economic welfare of the customs union because a given amount of resources will yield an increased amount of goods. Secondly, competition between firms has increased. The customs union has greatly expanded the market in which the individual firm operates. It has created a market, in other words, which is large enough to accommodate a sufficient number of large-scale firms from the point of view of competition.[6] The combination of increased efficiency and competition

---

[5]Suppose our firm could expand and reduce unit costs in the process. But suppose also that it would have to grow so large for this purpose that it would have to supply the whole domestic market by itself. It would have to drive all of its rivals out of the market and become a monopolist. Outright monopoly, however, is likely to lead to government control of its prices, and so on.

[6]The firm in our example above, for instance, exchanges a large share of the pre-union domestic market against a small share of the much larger market of the customs union.

is crucial in the sense that competition ensures that the efficiency gains are passed on to the consumers.

Another important dynamic effect may be expected in the area of capital formation. The newly opened opportunities for expansion could provide new incentives for investment. This may be particularly true for region-wide investment by outside concerns. The customs union, with its discriminatory tariffs against the outside world, may attract foreign capital as a substitute, in a sense, for foreign goods.[7]

In our discussion so far, we have outlined some of the theoretical considerations of economic integration. The conceptual basis has been our trade model as developed in the previous chapters. While this approach points to some of the criteria commonly used in judging the prospects of integration, we need some real-world examples to add perspective to our discussion.

THE UNITED STATES AS AN ECONOMIC UNION

The United States of America, for example, provides a textbook case of economic integration. In the days of the founding fathers, the U.S. economy was far from integrated. Various states maintained their own tariffs and other trade restrictions against both other states of the union and the outside world. Monetary systems were independent along state lines, with considerable variations between some systems.[8]

> Eastern territories, which served as distribution centers and sources of credit for those in the west, exacted levies and tolls and sought to preserve and exploit their favorable position. States responded to economic fluctuations or adverse balances of payments and to local mercantile and producer interests by passing laws favoring now merchants and shipping interests, at another time the debtor or primary producer.[9]

Economic integration was one of the key issues at the Constitutional Convention in 1788. The constitutional provision of giving all tariff authority to the U.S. Congress amounted to the formation of a customs union, since it abolished most internal trade restrictions and established

---

[7]U.S. Investment in the EEC area, for example, has increased sharply after the formation of the EEC.

[8]Virginia, for example, was using pounds and shillings, while most of her neighbors used dollars and cents.

[9]David G. Smith, *The Convention and the Constitution*, St. Martin's, New York, 1965, p. 16.

an equalized external tariff system. The Constitution further provided for monetary union by giving Congress certain monetary authorities. In fact, when reading through the Constitution of the United States, one is very much reminded of a blueprint for economic integration. Here are some excerpts:

> Article I, Section 8, The Congress shall have the power:
>
> 1 To lay and collect taxes, duties, imports and excises, to pay the debts and provide for the common defense and general welfare of the United States; but all duties, imports and excises shall be uniform throughout the United States;
>
> 3 To regulate commerce with foreign nations, and among the several states and with the Indian tribes;
>
> 4 To establish a uniform rule of naturalization, and uniform laws on the subject of bankruptcies throughout the United States;
>
> 5 To coin money, regulate the value thereof, and of foreign coin, and fix the standard of weights and measures.
>
> Article I, Section 10.
>
> 2 No state shall, without the consent of the Congress, lay any imports or duties on imports or exports, except what may be absolutely necessary for executing its inspection laws; and the net produce of all duties and imports laid by any state on imports or exports, shall be for the use of the treasury of the United States; and all such laws shall be subject to the review and control of the Congress.

But the adoption of the Constitution did not integrate the U.S. economy overnight. Many factions saw their interests served best by independence rather than integration. In several instances, involving for example Texas, the Louisiana territory, and California, these independence movements became serious threats of secession from the union. The final and most serious challenge to integration in the United States was the War between the States, which ended eighty years after the adoption of the Constitution.

As far as the agricultural Southern states were concerned, customs union with the industrial North forced them to buy their industrial products in the protected Northern market at high prices. Most of their agricultural production, on the other hand, was sold in the world market at low prices. The effects of trade diversion, therefore, were most heavily felt in the South, while trade creation mostly benefited the North.

Full economic union has not been achieved by the United States until quite recently, even though customs union and monetary union existed by the end of the War between the States. The missing element was actual mobility of the factors of production. This mobility has been insignificant between North and South until World War I. Only for about half a century, therefore, has the American economy been fully integrated.

THE ZOLLVEREIN

Another example of economic integration can be found in the formative years of Germany as a modern nation. What later became Germany consisted of a multitude of kingdoms, dukedoms, and other formally independent domains. Trade in the region was accordingly subject to innumerable restrictions. In 1828 the North, the South, and the Middle of the region formed three independent customs unions, which in turn were combined in the German Zollverein (customs union) of 1833. The Zollverein eventually led to the formation of Germany in 1870 under Prussian leadership.

One of the important consequences of the Zollverein was a high external tariff on grains, which happened to be the principal product from the eastern estates of the Prussian nobility. The industrial west was thus obliged to buy expensive food from the protected east, while steel and other industrial products were sold at low world market prices. In contrast to the American situation, therefore, trade diversion affected mainly the industrial part of the union, while the agricultural east benefited from trade creation.

THE EUROPEAN ECONOMIC COMMUNITY

By far the most ambitious and important project of economic integration in recent times is the European Economic Community (EEC), also referred to as the European Common Market. The EEC today is well on the way toward economic union between France, West Germany, Italy, Belgium, the Netherlands, and Luxembourg.[10] These countries' population is roughly equal to that of the United States, their combined GNP is

---

[10]These are the original six members. Others have joined and are in the process of joining. See below.

about one-half of the GNP of the United States, and the volume of their trade with nonmember countries is about equal to the volume of U.S. foreign trade. The EEC is therefore an important development if only from the point of view of its size.

The EEC has absorbed several schemes of integration which preceded it. Belgium, the Netherlands, and Luxembourg had already formed a customs union (Benelux, 1921) before the EEC was established. Another forerunner of the EEC was the European Coal and Steel Community (ECSC) of 1951, which represents an interesting form of integration. Instead of integrating whole economies, the ECSC concentrated on two key industries and made considerable progress on that limited basis. Finally, there was the European Atomic Energy Community (Euratom), established for the purpose of coordinating the development and uses of atomic energy on a regional basis.

The EEC was formed in 1957 by the Treaty of Rome. The treaty provided a program for gradual integration of the six economies. The organizational structure of the EEC was designed to strike the essential balance between centralized authority and national autonomy. The central administrative agency is the EEC Commission in Brussels, which serves as the executive branch in the normal functioning of the EEC. The Commission would oversee, for example, the gradual liberalization of internal trade and the establishment of uniform outside tariffs. Important decisions involving policy have to be approved by the Council of Ministers, which brings the member countries' governments in direct contact through members of their cabinets.

The Commission's orientation is basically *supranational*, while that of the Council remains *international*. The Commission and its vast bureaucracy are serving the EEC, while members of the Council represent the respective national governments. The Treaty of Rome envisages a gradual transfer of authority from the Council to the Commission, which means a gradual increase of central EEC authority at the expense of national economic autonomy. One important aspect of this process is the manner in which the Commission is to be financed. Initially this was done through contributions by the member countries.[11] Later on the Commission was to have independent sources of its own in the form of tariff revenues.

---

[11]The United Nations provides a good example of the difficulties which tend to be associated with this way of financing an international institution.

The EEC also has a Court of Justice which has jurisdiction over the inevitable disputes arising out of the integration process. Finally there is the European Parliamentary Assembly, composed of one hundred and forty-two delegates from the member countries. This assembly has no real legislative function, but serves mainly as a forum for the debate of integration issues.

The actual implementation of the EEC program proceeded according to a timetable, which was fixed in advance within certain limits. Removal of internal trade restrictions and harmonization of the external tariff system were to be achieved in three stages of four years each. This put the entire adjustment period at roughly twelve years, with certain built-in extensions. By the end of 1969, or 1972 at the latest, full customs union was to come into effect. This goal was reached, for all practical purposes, in 1971.

An interesting device, once more reflecting the delicate problem of national sovereignty, was used in the transition between different stages of the EEC program. Transition from the first to the second stage, which was accomplished in 1962, required the unanimous approval of the Council. The third stage, however, could be entered on the basis of a qualified majority vote in the Council. Once the second stage had begun, therefore, it became possible to overrule national autonomy in certain economic matters by a qualified international majority.

EEC AGRICULTURE

The willingness and relative ease with which the industrial sectors of the six member countries adjusted to the new environment of the EEC removed many doubts about the viability of the EEC and made it possible at several junctures to proceed more rapidly than had initially been anticipated.

Such was decidedly not the case with agriculture. The agricultural problem has been a more or less constant source of discord among EEC members and has on a number of occasions threatened to upset the entire program. A number of factors come into play here, some of which concern the special nature of agriculture as an industry and some of which stem from the substantial differences in agricultural efficiency between members, and between members and the outside world.

Agriculture is a way of life as much as it is an industry. The changes required by the EEC program therefore involve social and political factors more intensely here than in the industrial sectors. In democratic societies the farm sector tends to be a political constituency which can be highly effective in resisting change in general and reallocation of agricultural resources in particular. Agriculture in the EEC is generally less efficient than agriculture elsewhere. This is to say that the lowest-cost producer of almost any given agricultural product is to be found somewhere outside the EEC. To the extent that EEC agriculture remains protected by a uniform external tariff system, this leads to trade diversion. Consumers in the EEC must pay high food prices and suffer a loss of real income.

The problem is compounded by the differences in agricultural efficiency between the member countries. France, for example, whose agriculture is relatively efficient by European standards, wants a level of external tariffs which would give her the EEC market without interference from American, Canadian, or South American producers. Germany, with high-cost agriculture by any standard, would press for very high EEC tariffs. Even that would not protect her from French competition if trade within the EEC were completely liberalized. In short, the debate not only concerns the external EEC tariff on agricultural products, but also internal liberalization of trade in this sector. As a compromise, EEC administrators envisage the harmonization of individual farm support programs with the overall purpose of moving gradually toward an integrated EEC farm sector which is protected from the outside world at a level acceptable to all members. It is easy to see that such a compromise will be difficult to achieve.

THE EEC AND ECONOMIC WELFARE

The EEC today represents economic integration at an advanced stage. Some aspects of what seemed an ambitious experiment in 1957 have become reality. Considering also that this development involves some of the world's more important economies, it is not surprising that the EEC has been widely debated and promises to remain a popular topic for the foreseeable future.

First, there is the question whether or not integration has actually raised the economic welfare in the EEC region. We find the experts unable to agree on a clearcut answer to this question. If we use growth rates of national incomes, for example, as a criterion, it turns out that the growth rate of the combined EEC national incomes was about the same before and after formation of the EEC. This comparison, however, may not be very meaningful. What we really need to know is how fast the six member economies would have grown if the EEC had not been formed. This involves comparing the same time period with and without the EEC, which is obviously difficult. For one thing, such a comparison would have to be based on certain assumptions about the course of events without the EEC. Would all trade restrictions, for example, have remained exactly as they were in 1957? Or would some alternate form of trade liberalization, possibly based on individual countries' initiative, have taken place? Even comparisons between EEC growth rates and growth rates elsewhere remain inconclusive.[12]

If we measured the success of the EEC by the volume of its international trade, we would indeed conclude favorably, since trade accelerated considerably after 1957. But this approach also faces the problem described above.

In addition, our discussion of trade creation and diversion has warned us not to identify gains from trade with volume of trade. The rapid expansion of internal EEC trade thus included trade diversion from low-cost outside suppliers. The pattern of trade, in other words, changed along with the volume of trade, as EEC trade became reoriented toward members and away from nonmembers.[13]

If there is anything approaching consensus on positive economic results of the EEC, it is probably with regard to its dynamic effects. Few experts doubt, for example, that competition among EEC producers (excepting, perhaps, farmers) has increased markedly. Some see this

[12]Real GNP in the EEC grew by 5.7 percent during 1950 to 1958 and by 5.7 percent during 1958 to 1969. Comparable rates for EFTA are 3.6 in 1950 to 1958 and 3.9 in 1958 to 1969. Other European countries grew by 3.2 percent in 1950–1958 and 4.3 percent in 1958 to 1969. Source of data: "Effects of Regional Trade Groups on U.S. Foreign Trade: The EC and EFTA Experiences," *Executive Branch GATT Study No. 4*, Committee on Finance, U.S. Senate (Washington, 1973). Lawrence B. Krause concluded in 1968 that integration had increased the EEC growth rate by 0.2 percent [*European Economic Integration and the United States* (The Brookings Institution, Washington, D.C., 1968)]. The British *National Institute Economic Review* (November, 1970) declared that comparative growth rate studies are inconclusive regarding the effects of integration.

[13]In 1958, 32.1 percent of EEC member countries' total exports went to other EEC countries. By 1970 this figure had increased to 48.9 percent. The corresponding import figures were 34.7 percent in 1958 and 51.0 percent in 1970. This change toward intra-EEC trade was also noticeable in U.S. trade figures; the U.S. share of total imports by the EEC fell from 12.2 percent in 1958 to 9.7 percent in 1969. Most of this decline occurred in those agricultural products which were highly protected by the EEC. It is with regard to these products that the evidence points most clearly to trade diversion. Source of data: Executive Branch GATT Study No. 4.

competitive effect as the most important economic consequence of the EEC. But here again, hard factual evidence is difficult to provide.

THE EEC AND TRADE LIBERALIZATION

Although the effect of the EEC on the economic welfare of its members is certainly an important question, our primary interest remains with the problem of trade liberalization on a global scale. We may ask ourselves whether or not the EEC has contributed to global trade liberalization. What, for example, is the relationship between the EEC and the General Agreement on Tariffs and Trade (GATT), which is concerned with worldwide trade liberalization?

When dealing with the outside world, the EEC negotiates as one unit under GATT rules. For example, the uniform external tariff imposed by the EEC on a particular product may not exceed the arithmetic average of the member countries' pre-union tariff rates. This provision is aimed at preventing an overly protective attitude of a customs union toward the outside world.

The fact that the EEC negotiates as one unit with nonmembers under GATT sponsorship is also significant. We have observed above that the complexity of trade liberalization increases with the number of parties to the negotiation. Customs unions tend to reduce the number of parties to such negotiations. Some of the problems which would otherwise surface during negotiation under GATT are in this way handled within the EEC.

EEC EXPANSION

This leads us to a somewhat related aspect of the EEC, namely the possibility of its extension to additional countries. We could visualize, for example, an EEC including eventually all of Western Europe, negotiating trade liberalization as one unit with the United States. A considerable share of all world trade would in this case be subject to negotiation between just two parties. Such visions, however, are decidedly premature for the time being.

Formally, the EEC is open to any European country willing and able to meet the same requirements which have been met by the six original members. But until very recently (1971) only Greece and Turkey have obtained membership, which was arranged at the associate level.[14] In addition, a special trade agreement was made with Spain. Among non-European countries, the former possessions of France and Belgium in Africa receive preferential treatment by the EEC. Products from these countries enter the EEC without restrictions. Tunisia, Morocco, and Algeria even have permanent associate status. Special arrangements also exist with regard to Israel, Iran, and Lebanon.

Notably absent from this list were important European countries such as Great Britain, the Scandinavian countries, Switzerland, Austria, and Portugal. Rather than joining the EEC, these countries formed the European Free Trade Association. EFTA was essentially a free-trade area, formed in reaction to the EEC, possibly for the purpose of increasing its members' bargaining strength in negotiating entry into the EEC. What is important from our present perspective is that EFTA is not represented at GATT as a single bargaining unit. In terms of economic integration EFTA was not intended to go beyond free internal trade, and even this goal was considerably hampered by agricultural problems.

Britain's entry into the EEC was a lengthy process marked by several sharp setbacks in the form of French vetoes in the Council of Ministers. Again we find agriculture at the heart of the problem. Britain has traditionally imported a much larger share of her food than any of the EEC countries. Tariffs on agricultural products therefore have a direct impact on the cost of living, wage rates, and production costs in Britain. Low tariffs on food items have consequently been an important tradition of British economic life.[15]

This concern with low food prices is also reflected by the British farm support system, which relies on direct income subsidies to low-income farmers rather than price support.[16] Membership in the EEC would

---

[14]The goods of an associate member enter the EEC free of restrictions, while the associate member may maintain restrictions against imports from the EEC for 20 years, after which it becomes a full member. Full membership is open to European countries only.

[15]This tradition can be traced back to David Ricardo, the Corn Law controversy, and comparative advantage itself. The reader may recall our discussion on this subject in Chapter 4.

[16]Assuming that some system of support for agriculture is necessary, a system of direct income support is probably preferable to a price support system on economic grounds. Under a price support system the government may enter the market as a large-scale buyer in order to keep prices high. This results in high food prices for consumers and expensive government stockpiling. Another form of price support guarantees the farmer the difference between the free market price and some higher support price set by the government. The major drawback in both cases is misallocation of resources as farmers overproduce in response to the distorted price signal. In addition, questions of equity arise because price supports, by definition, are given in proportion to output rather than income. The largest and most productive farms will thus receive the highest subsidies.

A system of direct income support for low-income farmers tends to be more efficient because of less distorted production. It also seems better designed to achieve the stated goal of alleviating farm poverty.

require the British to make two major changes in this sensitive area. First, harmonization of EEC farm support programs would oblige the British to adopt some form of price support system, which is in effect on the Continent. Secondly, the unified external tariff on food items would divert British food purchases from other low-cost sources to the EEC. Apart from raising the cost of food to British consumers, this trade diversion would mean a serious loss of trade for some of the Commonwealth countries, to whom Great Britain has special obligations.

The most recent round of negotiations, dealing with the entry into the EEC of Great Britain, Ireland, Denmark, and Norway, resulted in the entry of Great Britain, Denmark, and Ireland. The cases of Norway and Denmark were put to popular referendum in each country in 1972. Norway refused to enter, while Denmark agreed. Once again, the agriculture issue suggests an explanation. Denmark is a relatively efficient agricultural producer with much to gain from free access to the EEC market. In Norway, on the other hand, the possibility of increased food prices may have been an important factor in the negative outcome of the referendum.

SUMMARY

The stages of economic integration are free-trade area, customs union, common market, and economic and monetary union.

Free trade on a regional basis (resulting from economic integration), does not necessarily increase the gains from trade, because the region's trade relations with the outside world may be affected.

Trade creation is the combination of positive production and consumption effects of customs unions. Trade diversion is the combination of negative production and consumption effects of customs unions.

Factors affecting trade creation and diversion are the size of the customs union, the levels of pre-union tariffs, and complementarity versus competitiveness of member economies.

The dynamic effects of customs unions include the economies of scale, increased competition, and increased incentives for capital formation.

The Constitution of the United States contains a blueprint for economic integration. Full economic union in the United States was not achieved until factor mobility between North and South took on significant proportions after World War I.

The German Zollverein, another example of economic integration, laid the basis for the German nation. Trade creation and diversion appear to have benefited the agricultural east at the expense of the industrial west.

The EEC is the most ambitious contemporary integration project. Its institutions reflect a delicate balance between centralized authority and national sovereignty.

Internal trade restrictions were abolished and external tariffs equalized according to a preconceived timetable.

The agriculture sector presents the strongest challenge to EEC administrators. Individual farm support programs must be harmonized, and an external tariff acceptable to all members must be established.

The effect of the EEC on the economic welfare of its members is difficult to measure objectively. Neither income growth rates nor trade growth rates provide entirely satisfactory results.

Membership in the EEC is expanding gradually and with considerable difficulties. Visions of an EEC negotiating at GATT for all of Western Europe are premature.

SUGGESTED FURTHER READINGS

An excellent general treatment of economic integration and the EEC may be found in Ingo Walter, *International Economics, Theory and Policy* (Ronald Press, New York, 1968), chaps. 23–25. These chapters contain extensive references to the literature. See also J. Greenwald, M. S. Wionczek, and M. Carnoy, *Latin American Economic Integration and U.S. Policy* (The Brookings Institution, Washington, D.C., 1972). For a highly theoretical treatment, see R. G. Lipsey, *The Theory of Customs Union: A General Equilibrium Analysis* (Weidenfeld & Nicholson, London, 1970).

Chapter 6

Trade, Growth, and Development

Our basic trade model so far has been decidedly *static* in nature. This is to say that we have assumed given states of factor endowments, technologies, and tastes in each country. But the world does not stand still. We must consequently consider changes over time in both supply and demand conditions. The present chapter analyzes the effects of such changes on trade patterns, terms of trade, and gains from trade.

CHANGES IN TASTES

Let point A in Figure 6-1 represent an initial equilibrium position without trade. The domestic rate of transformation consistent with point A is t_A. At the indicated terms of trade tt, the country will export cloth and import wheat and move to point B after trade. Point B lies on the indifference

105

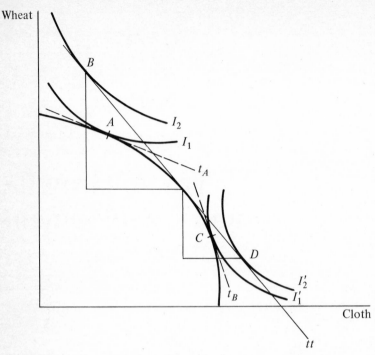

Figure 6-1

curve I_2, which belongs to the same preference map as I_1. By comparing points A and B, we establish that the country gains from trading.

Now we assume that preferences change from the map $I_1 - I_2$ to the map $I'_1 - I'_2$. In autarky, now, our country would produce and consume at point C in accordance with this shift in preferences toward more cloth. Trading at unchanged terms of trade tt, the country moves to point D, importing cloth and exporting wheat. The effect of the change in preferences, therefore, is a reversal of the trading pattern.

It is easy to envisage this reversal. As the demand for cloth rises, cloth becomes more expensive (in terms of wheat), since the production possibilities curve indicates increasing cost. The country finds that cloth, rather than wheat, is cheaper on the world market than at home, so it proceeds to import cloth. Note that it is impossible for us to compare the gains from trade associated with point B with those at point D, since these two positions involve different preference maps.

The procedure used in Figure 6-1 may be called *comparative statics* in the sense that we have compared two static situations, i.e., the situation having the preference map $I_1 - I_2$ with the situation having the preference map $I'_1 - I'_2$. Note that everything in Figure 6-1 has remained static except tastes. Although this is not a very realistic treatment of the passage of time, it does allow us to isolate that particular aspect of change in which we are interested.

Having considered the effect of demand changes on trade, we may now ask ourselves what the reasons underlying such changes might be. In particular, is it possible that trade itself has an effect on tastes? Trade, after all, brings different countries and cultures into contact with each other. It exposes people who might otherwise live in isolation not only to new products, but to completely different lifestyles. There is little doubt, for example, that European tastes have been changed by trade with America and vice versa. Western tastes and consumption patterns, similarly, have made inroads into traditional oriental ways. Trade between industrial and underdeveloped countries is said to have a "demonstration effect," by which consumers in underdeveloped countries become aware of consumption patterns elsewhere and gradually change their own preferences accordingly.

We may therefore conclude that changes in tastes or preferences not only have an effect on trade, but are themselves affected by trade.

CHANGES IN SUPPLY: LABOR

Let us proceed now to use comparative statics in order to analyze changes in factor endowments and technology. In terms of our standard diagram, such changes must somehow be translated into shifts of the production possibilities curve.

Let us assume, for example, a country with two factors of production, capital and labor, and two products, cloth and steel. Let us assume further that, relatively speaking, labor is intensively used in cloth production, while capital is intensively used in steel production. What effect would, say, an increase in the labor force have on this country's production possibilities curve? Obviously, more of both products could now be produced, because labor is used in both cloth and steel production. But since labor is more important in cloth production, the potential gain in cloth output will be larger than that in steel output. This is shown in Figure 6-2, where the outward shift of the production possibilities curve indicates a bias toward cloth.[1]

The shift in Figure 6-2 could, alternatively, have been caused by a change in technology. In general, technological progress may be labor-saving, capital-saving, or neutral (in the sense that it saves both factors in such as way as to lead to a uniform outward shift of the production possibilities curve). In case of Figure 6-2, we know that the technological advance was labor-saving, since it increased production potential relatively more in that product which is relatively labor-intensive.

What effect does factor growth or technological progress have on trade? Figure 6-3 shows a case in which an increase in the labor factor (or labor-saving technological progress) leads to the expansion of trade volume and the gains from trade. Let us note that in this case factor growth was biased toward the export good. It seems plausible that an increase in production potential in one's export good, without any change

---

[1]Note the use of the term *potential gain*. Actual gain depends on demand. If this country, for example, has a preference structure which is extremely biased toward steel, the actual gain will be small. The country will have had the bad fortune to grow in a factor whose product is not in great demand.

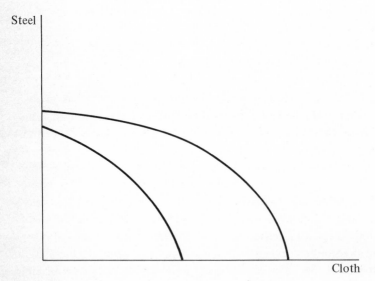

Steel

Cloth

Figure 6-2

in terms of trade or demand, should lead to an increase in exports, imports, and therefore gains from trade.[2]

CHANGES IN SUPPLY: CAPITAL

But what about an increase in capital endowment, or an improvement in capital-saving technology? Let us assume that this increases our country's potential to produce steel, which has been the import good heretofore. Much depends now on the degree of this shift. If it is small, some more domestically produced steel will be substituted for imports, but the country will continue to import some steel. In other words, the volume of trade will decline, and the trade pattern will remain unchanged.

If, however, the production potential increases substantially, domestic steel production will rise enough not only to satisfy all the domestic demand, but also to provide for exports. This would reverse the trading pattern. Point A in Figure 6-4 shows the trading position before factor growth. Since the corresponding production point is D, we know that cloth is the export good and steel is the import good. Now an increase in the capital factor shifts the production possibilities curve upward with a bias toward steel. At point B, the increased capacity to produce steel is used to exactly eliminate all imports. No trade takes place at point B, which, as we can see in Figure 6-4, is both the production and the consumption point.

Moving on now to point C and a further increase in capital (or capital-saving technology), we find the trading pattern reversed. Steel has now become the export good, while cloth is being imported. Point E is the production point, which corresponds to the final consumption point C.

Let us conclude, then, that the effects of factor growth or technological improvement on trade depend on whether the import or the export industry is benefited by these changes. If the export industry benefits, trade is likely to expand within the existing trading pattern. If the import industry is affected to a substantial extent, the trading pattern may be

---

[2]Implicit assumptions about demand are crucial to this result. Consider Figure 6-3. If the higher indifference curve were to touch the expanded production possibilities curve at point E, no trade would take place after growth. The preference map used in Figure 6-3 assumes that the proportions of income spent on steel and cloth remain constant as income rises, but their relative prices remain unchanged. Geometrically, this condition is fulfilled if all successive indifference curves intersected by a ray through the origin have the same slope at the point of this intersection.

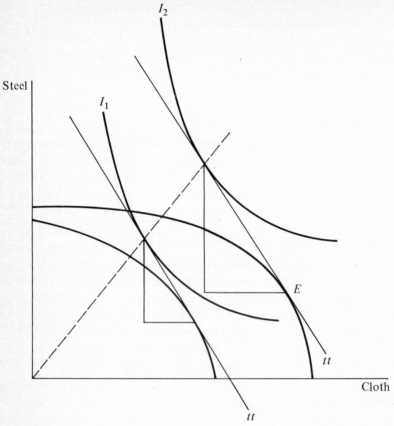

Figure 6-3

reversed. Let us note that we have assumed the shift of the production
possibilities curve to be the only change taking place. Preferences and the
terms of trade have remained constant.[3]

TRADE AND FACTOR GROWTH

Having observed some of the effects of factor growth on trade, we may
now turn the question around and look into the effect of trade on factor
growth or even on economic growth in general. What sort of *causes* come

---

[3]By constant preferences we mean the type of preference map according to which the proportions
of income spent on steel and cloth are constant.

to mind when we see a production possibilities curve shift outward? What is the magic formula by which a country increases its productive capacities? These are very broad questions, the answers to which are rarely the same in any two countries. The labor factor, for example, may grow by a rise in birth rates, a fall in death rates, or by massive immigration. The land factor may grow by pioneering of virgin lands or intensification of present usage. Technology may be developed at home or imported from abroad. There is no end to the list of possible variations, and the study of economic growth is an important separate field of economics.

What interests us particularly at this point is the idea of international trade as a stimulus to economic growth. Let us, for the time being, identify economic growth with industrial growth as observed in the great examples of Western industrial countries and, more recently, Japan.[4] Industrial growth has typically been dependent on large and expanding

[4]Later on we will take up the question of growth in underdeveloped countries.

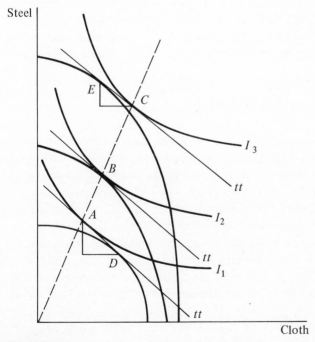

Figure 6-4

markets for the products of industrialization. England, for example, was looking for such markets at home *and abroad* as soon as its industrial revolution was under way. Increased production not only enhances the export industries themselves, but tends to spill over into related domestic industries which may be connected in various ways as suppliers to the export industries. Growing activity in the export-related sector, furthermore, will generate higher incomes, which will be spent throughout the economy with generally stimulating effects. Such export-led growth has often been an important part of industrial growth in general.

In fact, we may go back to the very origins of our static trade model for indications of such dynamic overtones. David Ricardo himself, although he chose to present his theory of comparative advantage in static terms, was fully aware of its dynamic implications. In this connection we must recall that comparative advantage was a powerful argument against the protectionist Corn Laws.[5] It was in the course of this debate that Ricardo rarely failed to point out what free trade (i.e., industrial exports) would mean for England's future as an industrial nation. While the compelling logic of comparative advantage pointed to the immediate and static gains to be derived from exporting industrial products, the dynamic effects of growing export industries did not escape Ricardo's attention.

We may conclude, then, that a two-way relationship exists between trade and economic growth. While growth affects trade in its patterns and gains, trade, in turn, has important implications for economic growth.

TRADE AND ECONOMIC DEVELOPMENT

When in our discussion above we associate the process of economic growth with industrial growth, we are restricting ourselves to growth in the industrialized countries, i.e., essentially the countries bordering the North Atlantic Ocean and Japan. This is a highly selective basis for discussion. In particular, of course, it leaves out the underdeveloped countries of Africa, Asia, and Latin America.

Dynamic economic processes in underdeveloped countries generally come under the heading of economic development. To delve even superficially into the problems of development in general would go beyond our present study. Our concern is only with the relationship

[5]See Chapter 4.

between international trade and development, and we shall view development only from this narrow perspective.

Limited though this perspective may be, it plays a role of considerable importance in the underdeveloped countries' view of their problems. Rather than accepting the orthodoxy of comparative advantage and its implication of export-led economic growth, these countries consider the orthodox model as biased in favor of the industrialized countries. Some go further and challenge this model as largely a rationalization of exploitation of the poor nations by the rich. Let us try to summarize some aspects of this challenge.

COMPARATIVE ADVANTAGE CHALLENGED

We may begin with the indisputable fact that per capita income, i.e., the economic standard of living, is far higher in industrialized countries than in predominantly agricultural countries. With very few exceptions, countries which produce and export primary products (food and raw materials) have been unable to achieve high per capita incomes.[6] Table 6-1 shows the per capita income in a number of selected countries. It bears out the general proposition that industrial countries are rich while nonindustrial countries are poor.

This simple and well-known fact has received a very special interpretation at the hands of those who are skeptical of the orthodox trade model. This interpretation holds the trade pattern between advanced and underdeveloped countries responsible for the poverty of the latter (and, by implication, the affluence of the former). A simplistic version of the argument may be summarized as follows.

Suppose the world consists of two types of countries, advanced and underdeveloped, who produce two types of goods, industrial and primary. According to comparative advantage, the underdeveloped countries will export primary and import industrial products. This trade pattern provides gains from trade for both the underdeveloped and the advanced countries. But rather than looking at these static gains, the skeptics focus on the dynamic implications of this trade pattern. They maintain that exports of primary products do not have the same stimulating effects on general economic growth as do industrial exports. They argue that

---

[6]Notable exceptions are Denmark and New Zealand (see Table 6-1).

Table 6-1   Per Capita GNP of Selected Countries*
(1969) (in U.S. dollars)

United States	4,240	Mexico	580
Sweden	2,920	Chile	510
Switzerland	2,700	Nicaragua	380
Canada	2,650	Brazil	270
France	2,460		
Denmark	2,310	Iran	350
Australia	2,300	Turkey	350
New Zealand	2,230	Jordan	280
Germany, F.R.	2,190		
Norway	2,160	Algeria	260
Belgium	2,010	Kenya	130
Finland	1,980	Uganda	110
United Kingdom	1,890		
Netherlands	1,760	Korea, Rep. of	210
Israel	1,570	Ceylon	190
Japan	1,430	Thailand	160
Italy	1,400	India	110

*Comparisons of GNP between countries are very difficult and of necessity only rough approximations. The table from which the figures above are taken contains 21 countries for which the per capita GNP estimate is below $100.

Source: *Finance and Development*, a publication of the International Monetary Fund and the World Bank Group, March 1972.

primary products pass through relatively few stages of production and fabrication and, therefore, generate few supplementary activities in the exporting country. Under such circumstances even the static gains from trade tend to remain isolated within the export sector without significant spill-overs into the rest of the economy.

Arguments of this nature are offered as explanation of the indisputable fact that countries which export mainly primary products are in general underdeveloped and poor. The critics of comparative advantage, accordingly, see the underdeveloped countries as locked into a trading pattern which has proved sterile with regard to economic growth and development. They see industrialization as the key to higher living standards, a key that is denied them by the grim rule of the law of comparative advantage.

Let us not fail to note that this attack on comparative advantage and its dynamic implications has been put in very simple terms here and remains debatable. First, and most generally, one should not overemphasize the importance of international trade. To associate *all* problems of economic development with international trade patterns may be a politically convenient distraction from domestic inefficiency and mis-management, but it is hardly realistic. The process of development is first and foremost an internal challenge to the underdeveloped country. It may be useful to recall one of our very first and most plausible principles of trade in this respect, according to which countries trade with each other because they gain from so doing. A sovereign nation could presumably refrain from trading, if such trade turns out to be disadvantageous in the dynamic sense.

One might argue that this point is too obvious, perhaps even cynical, and contend that underdeveloped countries often continue to trade because the static gains accrue to certain entrenched interest groups, even though such trade may be disadvantageous for the country as a whole.[7] But in this case the problem rests with the distribution of the gains from trade within a country rather than with the trade pattern.

Secondly, let us recall that we have assumed, for the sake of simplicity, that there are only two types of products, industrial and primary. There are obviously countless categories of products which fall between the extremes of "industrial" (automobiles, for example) and "primary" (say, peanuts). Food and fiber can be processed and fabricated to various semifinished or finished stages. Minerals and crude oil can be processed and refined, and so on. Under the simplistic assumption of only two product categories, it would be plainly impossible for an under-developed country to export anything but primary products, unless, of course, it overtakes its industrial trading partners in terms of industrial-ization and thus reverses the trading pattern on the basis of comparative advantage.

FLEXIBILITY OF TRADE PATTERNS

If the unrealistic assumption of only two product types is relaxed, it becomes possible for underdeveloped countries to export the products of light industry, such as certain textiles and other labor-intensive products, semifinished products, minerals which have been processed to some

---

[7]We should mention at this point the possibility of exploitation which occurs whenever a country is forced into disadvantageous trading patterns. History abounds with examples of such "trade"—from colonial exploitation under various degrees of duress to Nazi Germany's "oil for harmonicas" trade with the Balkan countries. Such practices are presumably rare today. Somewhat related remains the possibility of an export industry which is controlled by foreign interests and which may therefore be indifferent to the gains from trade to the host country.

degree, etc. It is not necessary to reverse the trading pattern to this purpose.

This is true, the skeptic might answer, and the road to development might indeed point in this direction, but there is yet another obstacle to overcome. Industrial countries have tended to discourage such movement into light industry by underdeveloped countries through their tariff structure. Import tariffs are generally much higher on semifinished or finished products than on raw materials.

Table 6-2 shows average tariffs on three categories of products. Unprocessed skins, to take just one example, would fall into the low-duty first category. On leather, which would be listed under semifinished products, the tariff is already up to ten times higher. Shoes, finally, would be charged an even higher import duty by the developed countries.[8]

THE TERMS OF TRADE

In addition to the above-discussed very general critiques of the orthodox trade model, a more specific hypothesis has been formulated regarding the terms of trade between developed and underdeveloped countries. According to this hypothesis the terms of trade have been gradually shifting against primary products. Underdeveloped countries, in other words, are receiving less and less imports per unit of their exports according to this hypothesis. Or, to state it somewhat differently, the advanced countries' share of the global gains from trade has been increasing at the expense of the underdeveloped countries' share.

[8]It may be recalled from Chapter 4 that the *effective* protection of finished products in Table 6-2 may be much higher than the *nominal* duties suggest.

Table 6-2   Average Rates of Import Duties in 1969

	EEC	Japan	U.K.	U.S.
Raw materials	0.8	1.6	1.5	3.6
Semifinished products	8.0	10.1	8.5	8.3
Finished products	11.7	14.6	18.0	20.8

Source: World Economic Survey, 1969–1970, United Nations, New York, 1971, p. 158.

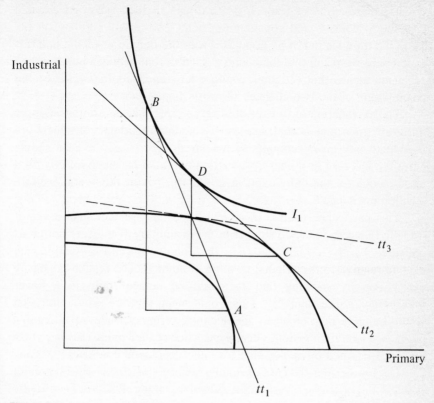

Figure 6-5

Before we discuss the pros and cons of this hypothesis, let us restate it by using a diagram. In Figure 6-5 we show an underdeveloped country which has achieved an increase in its capacity to produce primary goods, but which experiences a deterioration of its terms of trade at the same time. Initially the country trades at the terms of trade tt_1, which results in production point A and consumption point B. The country exports primary products and imports industrial products. Now we introduce two changes. First, the production possibilities curve shifts in such a way as to reflect an increase in production potential biased strongly toward primary goods.[9] Secondly, the terms of trade become flatter, i.e., they deteriorate from our country's point of view.

[9]Compare Figure 6-3.

The new terms of trade (tt_2) are drawn in such a way as to yield production point C and consumption point D, the latter falling on the same indifference curve as point B. From the definition of the indifference curve we recall that the country is indifferent between points B and D, which means that economic welfare has remained unaffected by the combination of the two changes shown in Figure 6-5.

The explanation of this result is very simple. The deterioration of the terms of trade means that increasing amounts of primary products are needed to buy given amounts of industrial imports. In the case shown here, the increase in primary production potential has been exactly used up in paying for the more expensive imports, leaving the overall welfare position unchanged.

This particular result is of course a special case. The final terms of trade in Figure 6-5 may be steeper or flatter than tt_2. If they are flatter, as indicated by the dotted line (tt_3), the country's welfare position will decline relative to the original position at point B. The reader can easily verify this by showing that tt_3 could be tangent only to a lower indifference curve than I_1.[10] This would mean that the production gain would be more than offset by the declining terms of trade, resulting in a decreased welfare position. This case has been called *immiserizing growth* and is often cited by spokesmen for underdeveloped countries.

Let us consider the case of immiserizing growth in somewhat greater detail with particular regard to the gains from trade. Position D in Figure 6-6 is clearly inferior to position B. Does this mean that position D involves no gains from trade? The answer is no. We must compare point D with C. Point D lies on an indifference curve which could not be reached without trade, because it does not touch or intersect the production possibilities curve anywhere. Once the production possibilities curve has shifted outward, therefore, it still pays to trade (even at deteriorated terms of trade) rather than not to trade.[11]

DECLINING RELATIVE PRICES OF PRIMARY GOODS

So far we have treated the growth in primary production possibilities and the deterioration of the terms of trade as events which occur in-

---

[10]Terms of trade steeper than tt_3 in Figure 6-5 would improve the country's welfare position.

[11]The reader can make further observations using Figure 6-6. If, for example, no growth were to take place, but the terms of trade were to deteriorate anyway, the resulting welfare position would be inferior to point B. If, on the other hand, growth were to take place and the terms of trade remained unchanged, point F could be reached.

dependently of each other. What if the shift of the production possibilities curve actually *causes* the decline of the terms of trade? In this case the movement in Figure 6-6 from point *B* to *D* becomes the inescapable consequence of growth in the production capacity of primary goods, and the gains from expanding output may indeed turn into losses.[12]

This is precisely the contention of many underdeveloped countries. The argument may be summarized as follows: One basic difference between primary and industrial goods is the way in which demand reacts to gradually rising world income. While the proportion of income spent on industrial goods rises, the proportion spent on primary products falls.[13] Demand for primary products, therefore, declines relatively to the demand for industrial products. This relative decline in demand is reflected in the decline of relative prices, i.e., the terms of trade.[14]

Of course, a change in relative demand alone will not necessarily result in changed price ratios. Prices are determined by supply as well as demand. For example, if increases in productivity and supply of industrial goods were to exceed those of primary goods, the terms of trade might not necessarily move against primary goods, in spite of a decline in relative demand for them. But the underdeveloped countries have an answer for this case too. They argue that what is relevant on the supply side is not so much productivity, but the market power of the seller. They claim that the degree of competition among sellers of primary products is higher than among sellers of industrial products. This means that productivity gains in primary production are largely passed on to the buyers by way of lower prices, while industrial producers, by virtue of their market power, are able to retain much of their productivity gains in the form of higher profits and wages.

A NOTE OF CAUTION

Let us remind ourselves at this point that we are summarizing a controversial issue, rather than presenting a generally accepted analysis. The various aspects of the challenge to the orthodox trade model are very

[12]This outcome depends, as we have seen, on the extent to which the terms of trade decline.

[13]The observed tendency of the proportion spent on food to fall with rising family income is often seen as analogous in this context.

[14]A number of exceptions come to mind readily. Oil and natural gas, for example, cannot be viewed in this way. It appears that demand for these products has increased very rapidly with rising incomes. The terms of trade of oil-producing countries, accordingly, have held up very well, and there are indications that they will improve in the 1970s. Another primary product for which demand has increased recently is gold. This has been basically a monetary phenomenon. Some aspects of it will be taken up in later chapters.

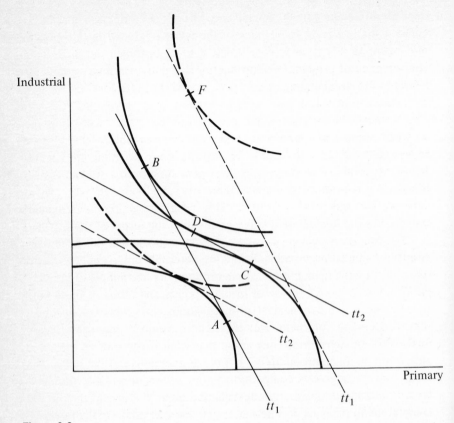

Figure 6-6

difficult to demonstrate conclusively. However, all of the orthodox countercontentions must not necessarily be taken at face value either. While no one, for example, has yet conclusively shown that sellers of primary goods, on a worldwide scale, are more competitive than sellers of industrial goods, a definitive denial of this contention has not emerged either.

Even with regard to the central claim of deteriorating terms of trade, no definite conclusion can yet be drawn. This is not only due to the immensity of the research task involved but also to conceptual problems. How shall individual commodities be weighted in order to calculate a single terms-of-trade index for all commodities? How meaningful is the concept of commodity terms of trade, i.e., the ratio between certain quantities of imports and exports? A country's welfare level can increase in spite of a deterioration of the commodity terms of trade if productivity in its exports increases.[15] Would it make better sense to use so-called *factoral terms of trade*, which measure the imports obtained per unit of product of a given factor of production? The list of problems could be continued for some time.

Furthermore, whatever makes "proof" for the challenge to the orthodox system hard to come by usually makes empirical proof of the orthodox model equally difficult. In view of this inability of either side to demonstrate its case conclusively, it would appear inappropriate to adhere to any single one-sided conclusion. But this is a position which those who are actively involved in the conduct of trade and development can ill afford to take. Policy makers must make decisions, which usually are based on their notions of how trade and development interact. Our discussion above suggests that such notions are likely to depend in large measure on where the burden of proof is placed—on the challenge or on the orthodoxy.

SOME POLICY ISSUES

It should not surprise us that the different attitudes toward trade discussed above have their counterpart in different approaches to policy questions involving trade. Consider, for example, the question of trade liberalization, which was discussed in Chapter 4. Completely free world trade would of course constitute the ultimate triumph of the law of comparative advantage. While the advanced countries have many practical problems in achieving this goal, they recognize, at least in principle, that such a state of affairs would maximize the global gains from trade.

The underdeveloped countries, being skeptical of comparative advantage in the first place, take a different attitude. They fear that multilateral trade liberalization without fundamental changes in trading patterns would lock them even more tightly into primary production. On the other hand, they cannot afford to disregard the static gains from trade. These two considerations are not entirely consistent with each other and result in a certain degree of ambiguity in the underdeveloped countries' approach to practical trade problems.

---

[15]Recall Figure 6-5, where this result depends on the degree of change in the terms of trade.

PRIMARY EXPORTS

A frequently emphasized need of the underdeveloped countries is improved access to the advanced countries' markets for primary products. While the industrial countries' import tariffs on many primary goods are relatively low, as we have observed above, some qualifications are necessary here. Various primary imports compete with domestic agriculture in industrial countries. Agriculture in these countries, however, tends to be subsidized and protected. Underdeveloped countries have not failed to point to the irony in this. It seems that in some of these areas, where static gains from trade could, indeed, be obtained on the basis of comparative advantage, the industrial countries resort to protection.

One example of this is the Common Agriculture Policy of the EEC, which consists of domestic (intra-EEC) price supports in combination with import levies and export subsidies. Its effects have been a substantial increase in EEC production, intra-EEC trade, and even exports to outside countries. The relatively modest import duties on primary products discussed above apply mainly to those categories which do not compete with EEC agriculture. Even noncompeting products, e.g., coffee or tobacco, are often subject to other levies such as internal consumption taxes, which tend to reduce demand.

COMMODITY AGREEMENTS

Another aspect of the underdeveloped countries' efforts to improve their position under present trade patterns concerns price stability for their exports. It is a generally accepted fact that prices of primary products in the world market tend to fluctuate far more than prices of industrial products. This instability in itself complicates the task of economic development considerably.

In order to achieve greater stability in export prices, *commodity agreements* covering many of the major primary goods (such as sugar, coffee, cocoa, grains, tin, etc.) have been formed. Commodity agreements usually represent an attempt to control supply on the world market. They typically involve acceptance by individual producer countries of certain export quotas which are set by negotiations among all participating producer countries. In this way, by controlling most or all of the supply on the world market, price fluctuations could presumably be held to an acceptable minimum.

In practice, however, these commodity agreements have typically failed to achieve their purpose. One obvious problem is to persuade all producer countries to join (and stick to) the agreement. For example, nothing might suit a nonmember country better than to sell all it can at prices which are stabilized by the member countries. Once this advantage of nonmember status is sought by a sizable group of producers, the commodity agreement becomes ineffective, and its membership erodes.

Another major problem exists with regard to consensus among the member countries on the objectives of the commodity agreement. Some may wish to stabilize export prices, other may wish to stabilize export revenues, while still others may wish to use the commodity agreement to achieve long-term increases in export prices or revenues. Each of these factions may favor a different level of export quotas or buffer stock maintenance under certain circumstances. It appears that a greater degree of cohesion among member countries than has yet been demonstrated will be needed to make commodity agreements work.

THE CASE OF COFFEE

The International Coffee Organization (ICO) presents a good example of the problems faced by commodity agreements. This London-based organization was created in 1963 by an agreement between producer and consumer countries. Its function was to be the stabilization of the price of coffee, which had been falling steadily from a temporary peak in 1953.[16] Under the provisions of the International Coffee Agreement, producer countries were to limit their exports to quotas set by the ICO. Consumer countries agreed to keep their imports from nonmember countries to certain fixed levels. This provision was designed to ensure that only member countries would benefit from expanding world demand for coffee, thus reducing the incentive for producer countries to remain outside the agreement.

The ICO was to determine the export quotas in such a way as to keep the coffee price within certain limits. These quotas were to be adjusted in response to "trigger prices," i.e., prices which had reached the upper or lower limit. It seems that originally the main concern was to prevent a further decline, while the upper limit remained somewhat vague.

The first test came in 1963 as a result of a crop failure in Brazil, which

---

[16]The price fell from 85 cents per pound in 1953 to 35 cents in 1962. *International Financial Statistics*, International Monetary Fund.

accounts for about one-half of the world's coffee output. Supplies became scarce, the price rose, and the ICO promptly proposed to increase export quotas. Votes in the ICO are distributed among member countries in proportion to their importance as buyers or sellers.[17] Consumer countries voted for the proposed increase in quotas, while producer countries voted against it. The line was thus clearly drawn between buyers and sellers, and the situation remained uneasy in spite of the formal decision. Another vote in 1964 went the other way, and quotas were raised slightly.

The next crisis began with the devaluation of the U.S. dollar in December, 1971. Since coffee shipments are commonly paid for in dollars, this devaluation meant a decline in export revenues. As a compensation for these losses, the producer countries sought a price increase of 4 cents per pound. When this suggestion met with the consumer countries' disapproval, the most important producers formed the "Geneva group" in April 1972, vowing to take action independently of the ICO.[18] They planned to set their own quotas and even to establish a buffer stock.

The ability of the Geneva group to achieve an increase in the price of coffee remained doubtful until it was helped by a July frost in the Brazilian province of Parana which killed 32 percent of that nation's output for 1972.[19] The price of coffee consequently rose from about 45 cents per pound to 60 cents during 1972. Although this was considerably in excess of the 4 cent price increase originally sought by the producers, they chose to hold out for even higher prices. An ICO meeting late in 1972 failed to produce agreement. As a result, the ICO was unable to assign any quotas whatsoever for the first time since its establishment.

The outlook for the survival of the ICO was dim as the date for its basic renegotiations, September 1973, approached. Although the International Coffee Agreement was formally extended until September 1975, the basic price and quota adjustment function of the ICO was suspended, thus terminating its price stabilization activities.[20]

It appears that the chief concern of the coffee-producing countries has been to achieve an upward trend in coffee prices (i.e., improving terms of trade), rather than price stabilization. When this was opposed by the consuming countries, the coffee agreement was doomed.

---

[17]The United States, for example, which consumes almost one-half of the world's coffee, has 400 out of 1,000 consumer country votes.

[18]The countries were Brazil, Colombia, Portugal, and Ivory Coast. Their combined share of world coffee production is about 85 percent. They were later joined by 16 other countries, which brought the share represented by the Geneva Group to 90 percent.

[19]*IMF Survey*, International Monetary Fund, Feb. 12, 1973, p. 47.

[20]*IMF Survey*, International Monetary Fund, Apr. 23, 1973.

Once more the producing countries are left to their own devices. Their ability to achieve higher coffee prices will depend on the extent to which supply can be controlled by cooperation among producers. But such cooperation is difficult to achieve, as we have seen above. One London coffee merchant had this comment on the situation: "If roasters in the United States can stay out of the market for a month or two, we'll probably find that the weaker brethren in the producer group would be delighted to get some sales as insurance against an uncertain future."[21]

IMPORT POLICY

While underdeveloped countries favor trade liberalization as far as their access to the markets of advanced countries is concerned, they wish to reserve the right to keep their own imports strictly controlled. Imports, they insist, must be concentrated on those products which are essential for their development plans. Since foreign exchange available for the purchase of imports is notoriously scarce in most underdeveloped countries, it must not be "wasted" on consumer goods in general and luxuries in particular.

Another major reason for import control is the infant-industry argument, encountered in its general form in Chapter 4. If the trade pattern is ever to take on different dimensions from the present primary product—industrial product dichotomy, the underdeveloped countries must protect their emerging industries from foreign competition. The problem here is to identify *in advance* those industries which have the best chance of eventually becoming efficient and competitive on the world market.

This infant-industry approach is connected with the issue of access to the advanced countries' markets to the extent that efficiency involves the economies of large-scale production. Efficiency may require a size of operations in a particular industry which cannot be accommodated by the domestic market alone.

The infant-industry approach remains a thorny problem not suitable to broad generalizations. For example, the idea of modern integrated steel-producing facilities "in the middle of the jungle" without an adequately trained labor force or significant domestic markets for its output, or of an automobile factory in a country without modern roads,

21 *The Wall Street Journal*, Dec. 13, 1972.

has provoked much derision. It is probably true that certain types of "prestigious" heavy industry have been unwisely promoted by some underdeveloped countries. On the other hand, we should now be able to understand the suspicious reaction which meets Western suggestions to stick to primary products consistent with static comparative advantage.

GATT AND UNCTAD

As our discussion above suggests, the underdeveloped countries' participation in reciprocal trade liberalization schemes is less than enthusiastic. The General Agreement on Tariffs and Trade (GATT), for example, has been labeled the "rich man's club" by some. Although GATT has made efforts to modify its provisions and its structure to accommodate underdeveloped countries, the basic idea of multilateral and reciprocal trade liberalization remains difficult to reconcile with the viewpoint of these countries.

Ironically, it may well be that certain advantages could be derived from not being associated with GATT, whose so-called *most-favored nation clause* stipulates that tariff reductions, once they are negotiated between some countries, must be extended to all countries.

Suppose, for example, that Japan exports wristwatches to the United States and the United States exports airplanes to Japan. Now let us assume that GATT-sponsored negotiations between these two countries lead to tariff reductions on wristwatches and airplanes. The most-favored nation clause now stipulates that Japan must apply the reduced tariff on airplanes to all airplane imports regardless of the country of origin. The United States, similarly, must apply the reduced tariff to all imports of wristwatches.

This would appear to benefit exporters of wristwatches and airplanes elsewhere, who receive tariff concessions without having to reciprocate with tariff reductions of their own. Underdeveloped countries have been quick to observe, however, that such GATT agreements in practice rarely involve those products which they most commonly export, i.e., primary products.[22] Only if an underdeveloped country has an exportable indus-

---

[22]A very important and comprehensive series of multilateral tariff negotiations sponsored by GATT was the Kennedy Round (concluded in mid-1967). Temperate farm products, i.e., the developed countries' own agricultural products, were exempted altogether from the negotiations. Tariffs on machinery and equipment were reduced by 44 percent, and on other manufactured products by 31 percent. The average rate on low-duty raw materials was cut from 3.2 percent to 2.2 percent. In general, the more technologically complex the product, the higher was the tariff cut. For additional detail, see *World Economic Survey*, 1969–1971, United Nations, New York, 1971, pp. 150–158.

trial product, therefore, is it likely to benefit from the most-favored nation clause.

In order to create a forum for their own point of view and, perhaps, a focal institution for concerted action, the underdeveloped countries have established the United Nations Conference on Trade and Development (UNCTAD). Through UNCTAD the underdeveloped nations are attempting to gain acceptance for their above-summarized trade policies, such as access to the domestic markets of advanced countries, industrialization, import substitution, commodity agreements, etc.

The differences between advanced and underdeveloped nations in their attitudes toward international trade represent one of the most complex issues of our time. We have tried to use some of our analytical tools to understand the basis of the disagreement. This is all we can do. Any attempt to offer a simple resolution in this area would be not only futile but arrogant. Complex questions rarely have simple answers.

SUMMARY

The orthodox trade theory of comparative advantage is, essentially, static in nature.

Changes in demand may cause changes in trade patterns; demand, in turn, is affected by international trade.

Changes in the availability of production factors and technology will affect trade from the supply side. If factor growth favors the production potential of exports, an increase in exports is likely. If factor growth favors the production potential of imports, a reduction of imports or a reversal of the trading pattern will occur, depending on the extent of factor growth.

A two-way relationship exists between growth and trade. While growth affects trade volume and trading patterns, export-led growth has been observed in a number of industrial countries.

The fact that most countries who export mostly primary products are poor suggests to some that such countries are poor *because* they export primary products. This belief leads to rejection of the theory which determines the trading pattern, i.e., comparative advantage.

Underdeveloped countries claim that their terms of trade have gradually declined, thus denying them the welfare gains normally associated with productivity gains.

A declining proportion of rising world income spent on primary products, and differences in competitiveness between industrial and primary producers, are among the most often cited reasons for this decline in the terms of trade.

No conclusive empirical evidence for these claims has yet been presented.

The underdeveloped countries are seeking easier access to the primary product markets of the advanced countries. Commodity agreements are designed to reduce the instability of primary product prices on the world market. They have in general failed to serve this purpose.

On the import side, underdeveloped countries reserve the right of strict control. Imports which are necessary to national development plans have priority over consumer goods. Import restrictions are further designed to protect infant industries.

Underdeveloped countries generally do not subscribe to GATT's basic philosophy of multilateral and reciprocal trade liberalization. UNCTAD was established to provide underdeveloped countries with a forum for their own point of view and an institution for concerted action.

SUGGESTED FURTHER READINGS

A good general discussion on trade and development may be found in James C. Ingram, *International Economic Problems* (John Wiley & Sons, Inc., New York, 1966), chap. 5. See also Charles P. Kindleberger, *International Economics*, 5th ed. (Richard D. Irwin, Inc., Homewood, Ill., 1973), chaps. 4, 5, and 10. For a detailed study and an extensive bibliography, see G. M. Meier, *International Trade and Economic Development* (Harper & Row Publishers, Incorporated, New York, 1967). On the underdeveloped countries' point of view, see Raul Prebish, "Commercial Policy in the Underdeveloped Countries," *American Economic Review*, May, 1959. Also by Prebish, United Nations Conference on Trade and Development, *Towards a New Trade Policy for Development*, a report by the Secretary-General of the Conference (United Nations, New York, 1964). For up-to-date information in this area, see the latest issue of *World Economic Survey* (United Nations, New York).

Chapter 7

The Multinational Corporation

Before we conclude this section of our study, which deals with resource allocation and comparative advantage, let us turn to a relatively new topic in this area, the multinational corporation.

There are various definitions of what constitutes a multinational corporation. Rather than using any one particular definition, let us work here with a very general notion, according to which a multinational corporation is a very large firm which operates in several countries. This means firms with annual sales in the hundreds of millions of dollars and networks of affiliates which may cover fifty foreign countries. Most lists of the important multinationals include about 300 firms, two-thirds of which are based in the United States.[1]

---

[1]The number of firms with one or more foreign affiliates is, of course, much higher. We are concerned here only with the giants.

RELEVANCE FOR INTERNATIONAL TRADE

It may be useful to consider the ways in which the existence of multinational firms is relevant to a study of international economics. Considerable flows of goods and services, for example, may be counted as international trade because they cross national borders, but they remain internal to one firm if they are shipments between parent company and foreign affiliate. Such flows are set in motion by the requirements of corporate strategy, which does not always lead to the same result as basic comparative advantage.

Other trade in goods and services which does not fall into this intrafirm category is also likely to be affected. The establishment of an affiliate in a foreign country may displace exports of the parent company to that country and perhaps even to third countries. Foreign affiliates will become exporters and importers in their own right. Again, the resulting trade flows are perhaps better explained by corporate strategy than by our model of comparative advantage.

Finally, there are the immense international flows of investment capital generated by the multinationals. We recall from our comparative advantage model that trade was explained by international differences in factor endowments. The factors of production were assumed to be mobile only within national borders. International factor movements, of course, may reduce the need to move goods. Although capital flows have always been an important part of international economic relations, they have come to be more strongly identified with multinational corporate strategy, and as such they have acquired a new perspective.

HISTORICAL DEVELOPMENT

Large firms with networks of foreign affiliates are by no means new-comers to the international scene. We need only think of the British East India Company, chartered in 1600 by Queen Elizabeth I. This company held a position of dominance as the world's largest and most powerful corporation for nearly 200 years. Other early examples of multinational enterprise include German banks such as the House of Rothschild and East India companies chartered by Holland, Denmark, Spain, Austria, and Sweden. On the North American continent the Hudson's Bay Company had a vast area of almost exclusive trading. Most of these colonial companies were trading concerns, engaged predominantly with such commodities as spices, tea, rum, and furs.

The next phase in the development of multinational enterprise began with the industrial revolution in the nineteenth century. It reflected the industrializing countries' rising need for raw materials. The result was the multinational resource-oriented company in mining, smelting, petroleum, and plantation agriculture.

Manufacturing abroad did not gain importance until well into the twentieth century; most of it began after World War II. The explosive growth of the multinational manufacturing corporation began in the mid-fifties, much of it (but by no means all) by U.S. firms in Western Europe.

SIZE AND DISTRIBUTION

Before we enter into some of the issues associated with the multinational sector of the world economy, let us try to gain a brief impression of its dimensions. The combined sales of all multinational corporations in 1971 have been estimated at about $500 billion.[2] This would amount to about 20 percent of the world's gross national product, excluding the communist countries. The sales of the ten largest multinationals were more than $3 billion, which is greater than the gross national product of some 80 countries. Sales abroad of affiliates of multinational companies to nonaffiliates were estimated at $250 billion in 1971. This figure is of interest if we view producing and selling abroad as an alternative to conventional exports. It turns out that these $250 billion are roughly equal to the total exports of the developed noncommunist countries ($242 billion in 1971) and not much smaller than total world exports ($300 billion).

Since the foreign sales of multinational corporations have grown more rapidly than world exports, these comparisons may lead one to the expectation that production abroad will eventually replace exporting as the predominant vehicle of international trade. In any event, the few figures cited here, even though they are only rough approximations, indicate the importance of the multinational corporate sector.

Some more detailed data are available for U.S.-based companies.

---

[2]The data for this section are from a United Nations study, *The Multinational Corporation in World Development*, a paper prepared by the United Nations Secretary-General for the use of the Group of Eminent Persons on Multinational Corporations (United Nations, New York, 1973).

Table 7-1   U.S.-based MNCs in World Trade (in billions of dollars)

	Value in 1970	Percent increase 1966–1970
World exports of all merchandise	309.2	53
U.S. MNC-related exports	72.8	69
World exports of manufactured goods	201.4	65
U.S. MNC-related manufactured exports	38.8	73
Breakdown of U.S. MNC-related exports of manufactured goods:		
Exports from U.S.:	21.7	59
to MOFAs*	8.8	62
To others	12.9	53
Exports of MOFAs:	17.0	93
To parent companies in U.S.	4.8	120
To affiliates in third countries	6.0	81
To unaffiliated buyers in third countries and U.S.	6.2	86

*Majority-owned foreign affiliates.
Source: Implications of Multinational Firms for World Trade and Investment and for U.S. Trade and Labor,
Report to the Committee on Finance of the U.S. Senate and its Subcommittee on International Trade, 93d Cong.,
1st Sess., Government Printing Office, 1973, p. 279.

Table 7-1 shows that 23 percent of total world exports were accounted for by U.S. multinational corporations through direct exports of the parent companies and through the exports of their affiliates. In manufacturing this share was 19 percent.

It is interesting to note that about two-thirds of the affiliates' exports were either to other affiliates abroad or to their parent companies in the United States. If we add to this the exports by the parent companies to their affiliates, we find that about $20 billion or 10 percent of world exports in manufactured goods were intracompany shipments by U.S. firms.

In terms of growth rates, Table 7-1 shows that the exports of the U.S. multinationals have exceeded the world average. Finally, we may apply to this export figure in Table 7-1 an estimate that about 80 percent of the U.S. affiliates' output is sold in their local markets abroad.[3] This gives us a

[3]*Implications of Multinational Firms for World Trade and Investment and for U.S. Trade and Labor*, Report to the Committee on Finance of the United States Senate and its Subcommittee on International Trade, 93d Cong., 1st Sess., Government Printing Office, 1973, p. 278.

figure of $85 billion as the output of U.S. affiliates abroad in manufacturing for 1970.[4]

CORPORATE STRATEGY AND COMPARATIVE ADVANTAGE

If the figures given above are even approximately correct, the key to explaining a large and growing portion of all international trade must be found in the corporate strategies of multinational companies. The most immediate question arising in this context is to what extent this will qualify or even invalidate our basic model of comparative advantage. This is a very complex question, and it can be approached in various ways.

First, and most simply, we may view the significance of multinational operations in terms of factor mobility. The company in this view simply produces a particular product or component of a product wherever this involves the lowest cost. Its large size and global vision enable such a firm to regard the world as its field of operations. Its large resources permit extensive planning and testing of projected sites, products, and markets. It may produce some component for which labor is an important input in a country with abundant labor resources, taking advantage of local skills and crafts. Raw materials may be extracted in another country, while the finished product may be sold in yet another country.

The end result of this type of operation is entirely in agreement with the basic thrust of comparative advantage, which is, after all, that each good should be produced in the lowest-cost country. This, we recall, is the meaning of efficient resource allocation on a global scale. The only difference between our conventional model and the multinational type of operation is that the former places all emphasis on the international movement of products, while the latter rests more heavily on the movement of factors of production.

One of the factors moved in great quantities across national borders is, of course, capital. The general direction of such capital flows is presumably from capital-rich countries, where yields are low, to capital-poor countries, where yields are high. A given unit of capital, in other

---

[4]Manufacturing accounts for 45 percent of the net assets of U.S. affiliates abroad. Petroleum accounts for another 33 percent, followed by public utilities (9 percent), mining and smelting (5 percent), and others (8 percent). See *Implications of Multinational Firms*, op. cit., p. 404.

words, will be more productive in a capital-poor country, where many promising investment projects go unexploited, than in a capital-rich country. According to this approach, then, the movement of capital will improve resource allocation from a global viewpoint.

Important as capital movements may be, it is possible that their significance has been overemphasized until recently, when the U.S. government imposed restrictions on capital exports by its multinational corporations. It subsequently turned out that these firms were quite able to raise the capital required by their affiliates in capital markets abroad, especially in Western Europe. Since the growth of U.S. affiliates was not noticeably slowed down by the U.S. restrictions, it appears that abundant capital resources were not the only factor enabling U.S. firms to expand abroad. Perhaps more important were factors such as managerial skills and advanced technologies. These are very important factors of production, the movement of which across national borders may be among the most crucial aspects of trade today.

In short, as far as the ultimate result of our comparative advantage model, i.e., efficient resource allocation on a global scale, is concerned, multinational corporate operations could be viewed as leading to the same result. In fact, it might be expected to go further in the direction of global efficiency than trade in products only would be able to go. The key to this view is integration of the world economy by virtue of the multinationals' global vision of their operations. Technology is spread quickly and evenly, capital moves into underdeveloped areas, economies of scale are more readily exploited. Supporters of this view use the U.S. economy, and more recently the European Common Market, as examples of the benefits derived from such integration, in which large corporations have played an important role.

OLIGOPOLIST STRATEGY

But there are other views. Some students of multinational corporations emphasize industry structure as a key element in the analysis of their conduct. They attach much importance to the fact that most multinational companies operate in an oligopolistic environment. Oligopoly means "few sellers," i.e., an industry in which a handful of giant firms dominate. An oligopolistic industry structure differs in many ways from a purely competitive structure, which consists of large numbers of relatively small firms. Some of these differences have a bearing on our discussion.

The competitive firm will typically exhibit independent behavior in the sense that it is primarily geared to objective considerations of cost and price, rather than to the activities of its competitors. Pure competition has been a formal, if mostly implicit assumption required for the argument of comparative advantage. This point can be intuitively seen by once more recalling efficiency of global resource allocation as the cornerstone of this argument. It means production at lowest possible cost, and competitive industries with their emphasis on cost considerations are best suited to bring about this result.[5] Competition in its pure form is a very impersonal concept. The one objective guideline to which all competitors are subject is least-cost production. All those who fail to meet this objective will be unable to sell their product and will drop out of the industry. A firm which does not survive under pure competition is unlikely to feel that it has been "put" out of business by its competitors. First, there are so many competitors that it makes no sense to single out any one of them. Secondly, the market share vacated by the leaving firm is so small that the resulting increase for each of the remaining firms is insignificant. The remaining firms, therefore, have little to gain from the departure of just one firm.

All this is very different where oligopoly is concerned. Here we have a few firms who are constantly aware of each other's activities. Each firm watches jealously over its market share, and one firm's loss will show up as the other firms' gain. The peace among oligopolist rivals is often an uneasy one, usually maintained by certain tacit ground rules which tend to limit the degree of direct price competition. Such peace, however, is unlikely to prevail in situations where new markets are still to be secured. This tends to be the case in new industries where the shares of the domestic market are yet to be settled and in established industries after the domestic market is spoken for and the industry begins to look abroad for further expansion.

A company's decision to move into a particular foreign market, then, may be explained by its desire to beat its rivals to an as yet unclaimed

[5]It is not possible here to fully develop this topic. The reader may wish to consult any textbook on microeconomic principles for a comparison between pure competition and oligopoly; for example, see L. W. Weiss, *Case Studies in American Industry*, 2d ed., John Wiley & Sons, Inc. (New York, 1971), chaps. 2, 4, and 7.

market or by the wish to wrest at least part of the new market from earlier arrivals. In either case, considerations of cost and resource allocation tend to be secondary, and comparative advantage will not explain such movements.

Take, for example, the market for automobiles in Argentina. This market aroused the interest of the U.S. and European automobile corporations in 1959, when Argentina's government announced a compulsory domestic production program, meaning that cars would have to be locally produced rather than imported. A few years later virtually all major car makers as well as some minor ones had plants in Argentina. A market amounting to less than 2 percent of the U.S. domestic market was divided among 13 companies producing 70 different models of cars and trucks. In bad years as little as 20 percent of plant capacity was used. Even in good years no plant used 100 percent of its capacity; the industry was too overcrowded. Costs were high. Fiat cars, for example, cost more than twice as much to produce in Argentina as in Italy. Consequently, profits were lower than those made by the parent companies in their home countries. This situation was certainly not indicative of efficient international resource allocation. By 1969, some of the minor firms had been bought out by the majors. Fiat of Italy was moving toward leadership in terms of its market share.[6]

PRODUCT CYCLES

What is suggested in the preceding section is not that oligopolist strategy completely ignores profits for the sake of market shares, but that this strategy tends to work with a much longer time horizon than does static economic analysis. Before there can be profits, there must be markets. For those with sufficient stamina to survive in the long run, there will eventually be profits. This view is supported by the observation that on the whole foreign affiliates seem to have been about equally profitable as their parent companies at home.[7]

The need for a long time horizon in the analysis of multinational corporate strategy is emphasized by the concept of *product cycles*, which

---

[6]For this and other examples of automotive investment abroad, see J. Wilner Sundelson, "U.S. Automotive Investments Abroad," in *The International Corporation, A Symposium*, Charles P. Kindleberger, ed., The M.I.T. Press, Cambridge, Mass., 1971.

[7]*Implications of Multinational Firms*, op. cit., p. 434.

points out certain patterns in the life of a product.[8] The sequence usually begins with some technological advance leading to the introduction of a new product. In the first phase of its life cycle the product conquers the domestic market. During the next phase, the product is exported. A successful export good, however, will sooner or later confront its producers with the need to move production closer to the foreign markets, and thus begins the third phase of the product cycle. There are a number of reasons for this. Foreign markets, which first were opened up by exports, may have become large enough to allow large-scale production abroad, with its inherent cost savings. Transportation costs and tariffs are also often important considerations. In addition, the innovative technology in question may have become fairly commonplace by now. This will invite foreign producers to begin imitation. The decision to establish affiliates abroad therefore is often a defensive one, designed to protect what were export markets heretofore.

The last phase of the product cycle begins as the product becomes so standardized that it can now be produced anywhere by anyone. Its technology is no longer the special province of a few firms. The cycle will have run its full course when the product is actually imported by the country which had originally introduced it. Textiles are often described as a product which has run its full course through the product cycle. Automobiles appear to be close to the last stage of standardization, with production now occurring in most parts of the world, some of it resulting in imports by the original export countries. Computers seem to be in the second phase, where exports still predominate.

THE UNITED STATES VERSUS WESTERN EUROPE

Having discussed the general background for our topic, let us now turn to some of the issues which have given this topic much exposure lately. These issues may be divided into two areas with fairly clear differences. One is the multinational corporation in the developed world, especially the "invasion" of Western Europe by U.S. companies. The other concerns the relationship between the multinationals and their host countries in the developing world.

---

[8]For a detailed exposition see R. Vernon, "International Investment and International Trade in the Product Cycle," *Quarterly Journal of Economics*, vol. 80, May 1966.

In 1967 a French journalist published a best-selling book in which he argued that Europe was well on its way to being colonized by American industrial giants.[9] Using phrases such as "assault," "penetration," and "conquest," he speculated that American industry in Europe may soon become the third leading world industrial power after the United States proper and Russia. *The American Challenge* popularized an issue which had been developing for some time. Western Europe had indeed become the major area of U.S. corporate expansion abroad. This was particularly the case in the EEC countries where U.S. firms, experienced in large and integrated market operations, were quicker to see their opportunities than European firms. Table 7-2 shows the very rapid growth of U.S. direct investment in Europe during the last decade.

European concern is not so much with the mere fact that large amounts of U.S. capital have been invested as with the forms which this investment has taken. It is true, for example, although seldom pointed out, that European investment in the United States is about equal to U.S. investment in Europe. The important difference lies in the fact that European investment is mostly in portfolio form, i.e., stocks and bonds in U.S. companies, while U.S. investment is mostly of the direct type, i.e., wholly owned subsidiaries or affiliates in which majority interests are

[9]J. J. Servan-Schreiber, *The American Challenge* (English translation), Atheneum Publishers, New York, 1968.

Table 7-2   U.S. Direct Investment Abroad (in billions of dollars)

Area	Book value at year-end			
	1929	1950	1960	1970
Canada	2.0	3.6	11.2	22.8
Europe	1.4	1.7	6.7	24.5
Japan	0.3		0.4	1.5
Other developed areas		0.4	1.3	4.4
Latin America	3.5	4.4	8.4	14.7
Middle East			1.1	2.0
Other less-developed areas			1.4	4.6
Unallocated	0.3	1.7	1.5	3.6
Total	7.5	11.8	32.0	78.1

Source: Implications of Multinational Firms for World Trade and Investment and for U.S. Trade and Labor, report to the Committee on Finance of the United States Senate and its Subcommittee on International Trade, 93d Cong., 1st Sess., Government Printing Office, 1973, p. 97.

held. This means that U.S. management goes along with U.S. capital, while European capital in the United States is managed by U.S. firms.[10]

At issue then is not U.S. investment in Europe as such, but the penetration of European industrial life by U.S. management it signifies. The impact on the European economies is significant. In Belgium and Luxembourg, for example, 13 percent of manufacturing labor is employed by U.S. affiliates. The corresponding figures for the United Kingdom, West Germany, and France are 8, 5, and 4 percent respectively.[11] More than 10 percent of total EEC merchandise exports are accounted for by U.S. affiliates.[12]

HIGH-TECHNOLOGY INDUSTRIES

Perhaps more significant than the figures listed above is the pattern of U.S. investment in terms of the industries in which it is concentrated. These industries are commonly described as science-based, research-intensive, high-technology, or, simply, knowledge industries.[13] Such industries tend to play a crucial role in the process of economic growth for several reasons: They increase productivity in their own sector; the technological knowledge they generate tends to spill over into other sectors of the economy; they provide better and cheaper inputs for other industries.

A second type of industry with which U.S. investment tends to be associated is characterized by large economies of scale in combination with high-income elasticity of demand for its products. Such industries experience large increases in demand as consumers' incomes rise, and, due to the economies of scale, they are in a good position to satisfy this demand, expand, and make profits.[14] Automobiles are perhaps the best example in this area.

[10]To the extent that U.S. affiliates have raised their own capital in Europe, it may even be said that U.S. management is independent of U.S. capital.

[11]*Implications of Multinational Firms*, op. cit., p. 621.

[12]Ibid., p. 354.

[13]One way of measuring technological intensity is to take research and development spending as percent of industry sales. Some examples of high-technology industries are electrical machinery, drugs, industrial chemicals, instruments, transportation equipment, radio, TV, electronic components, farm machinery, computers, and office machines. *Implications of Multinational Firms*, op. cit., p. 561.

[14]On the interaction between U.S. investment and growth in Europe see John H. Dunning, "Technology, United States Investment, and European Economic Growth," in *The International Corporation*, op. cit., p. 14.

We conclude that U.S. investment in Europe is not only large in absolute terms, but also strategically placed in the growth sectors. What inferences shall we draw from these observations? Some argue that European concerns are unfounded. The American advantage seems to lie mainly in the factor of technological and managerial knowledge. Why should such knowledge, they ask, be generated at equal rates throughout the world? In terms of maximization of goods and services available for consumption, it may well be more efficient to import technology developed elsewhere than to duplicate it by costly research efforts. The import of technology, furthermore, must not necessarily go hand in hand with foreign management. It can be obtained by licensing arrangements or joint ventures with foreign firms. This approach, of course, views knowledge simply as a factor of production, a view which may leave many dissatisfied.

Be this as it may, one need not accept the view that the present trend of American-European industrial relations will continue indefinitely. Already there are indications that European companies, on the average, have had higher growth rates than American firms, even though American affiliates in Europe seem to have grown faster yet than European firms.[15] Europe has its multinational giants too. Some of these firms are quite comparable in size with their American rivals.[16] In addition, European governments are currently favoring mergers between European firms for the purpose of creating companies sufficiently large to operate in the expanded EEC market and to stand up to their American rivals. This merger movement appears to be gaining momentum, and, with it, European management is adopting the global vision long held by U.S. companies.

Perhaps one can apply something resembling the product cycle concept to the spread of modern management techniques. These techniques were first developed by American firms in the process of integrating their vast domestic market. The exporting phase arrived when U.S. firms moved overseas. But there is no reason to believe that the cycle will stop here. Modern management techniques, particularly as applied to multinational operations, are being rapidly adopted by foreign firms. Indeed, they are beginning to be exported by European and Japanese firms into other parts of the world. As the standardization of multinational management progresses, the cycle will have run its course when foreign

---

[15]See Stephen Hymer and Robert Rowthorn, "Multinational Corporations and International Oligopoly: The Non-American Challenge," in *The International Corporation*, op. cit., p. 57.

[16]Some of the largest are Unilever (Anglo-Dutch), Nestlé (Swiss), Royal Dutch-Shell (Anglo-Dutch), and British Petroleum (British).

multinationals have gained enough experience and resources to begin operations in the U.S. domestic market on a broad scale.

There are certain aspects of oligopoly theory which would support such a view. In a world of equally large corporations with similar global strategies there is little reason to expect that the U.S. market should remain forever the exclusive domain of U.S. firms.[17]

THE MULTINATIONALS IN DEVELOPING COUNTRIES

When it comes to concern over domination by foreign companies, the less developed countries have a much better case than the Europeans. For one thing, the days of colonialism and gunboat diplomacy are not too far in the past to dissipate all memories. The presence of a giant foreign corporation in a less developed country, furthermore, is likely to be much more visible than it would be elsewhere. As a percentage of total capital formation foreign investment tends to be much higher in developing countries than in developed countries. Finally, a large proportion of the multinationals' operations in the developing world consists of extracting petroleum, copper, bauxite, and other natural resources.[18]

If all these factors are taken into account, it is not surprising that claims of exploitation and neoimperialism are frequently heard. This is countered with assertions that without the multinationals' know-how and capital, the host countries would be unable to operate these industries and would thus forego tax revenue, profit shares, employment, and the generally associated spill-over benefits.

In order to approach this controversy in a reasonably objective manner, it is best to put aside the colonial past and face modern realities. Even so, the developing country is often at a disadvantage when new contracts with foreign firms are negotiated. The developing country has the resource, but the company it is dealing with has the technology and capital to extract it, the management to coordinate its flow to its destination, and the market to sell it. While the host country may have alternate bids, the company may have alternate hosts.

Only after the company has been established for years will the host

---

[17]Along these lines see Hymer and Rowthorn, op. cit., pp. 74–81.

[18]In the Middle East about 90 percent of foreign investment is in petroleum. In South America 28 percent is in petroleum and 39 percent in manufacturing. In Africa 59 percent of foreign investment is in petroleum and mining and 19 percent in manufacturing. In Asia the share in extractive industries is 40 percent (petroleum and agriculture), while 30 percent is in manufacturing. *The Multinational Corporation in World Development*, op. cit., p. 33.

country, depending on its strategy, begin to acquire some of the necessary technology, learn about the size of its mineral deposits, and gain a degree of power over the company's fixed assets. Gradually the terms may move in favor of the host country, as profit shares, taxes, and various other aspects of the company's operation are renegotiated.[19] Occasionally, the company's profitability is squeezed to the limit, and it will suspend operations and leave the country. In other instances the host country may choose to nationalize the company's assets under its jurisdiction.[20] More often, the host government and the firm will share the profits in a ratio depending on each side's bargaining strength.

From the viewpoint of the multinational corporations the anticipation of this process leads to heavy discounting of future profits, especially when political instability is added as a further risk factor. This must be weighed against considerations of market share rivalry, which is an important part of oligopolist strategy as we have seen above.

THE MULTINATIONAL CORPORATION AND THE HOME COUNTRY

So far we have been concerned mainly with the impact of multinational companies on host countries. In recent years some issues have also arisen with regard to their effect on home countries. In the United States, for example, phrases such as "runaway" capital and "job exports" point to concern over the effect of the U.S.-based multinationals on domestic U.S. investment and employment. Definitive answers to these questions are not available because they involve comparisons between what is (i.e., the present state of affairs) and what would have been in the absence of multinational business. Most answers, as we will see, depend on the assumptions made concerning such possible alternatives.

Take, for example, the investment issue. The phrase "runaway" capital implies that investments are being made abroad instead of at home. Investment abroad in this sense reduces investment at home and therefore involves a loss for the domestic economy in terms of income and employment. Critics of multinational corporations assert, conse-

---

[19]For a description of this process in the petroleum industry see M. A. Adelman, "The Multinational Corporation in World Petroleum," in *The International Corporation*, op. cit., p. 227.

[20]A statement made by the Kennecott Copper Corporation, which had its mines in Chile expropriated in 1971, may be found in *Multinational Corporations*, A Compendium of Papers Submitted to the Subcommittee on International Trade of the Committee of Finance of the U.S. Senate, 93d Cong., 1st Sess., Government Printing Office, 1973, p. 251.

quently, that domestic investment would be higher if these firms did not invest abroad.

It has been argued, on the other hand, that investment abroad occurs in addition to, rather than instead of, domestic investment. There is evidence that firms with extensive foreign investment also tend to lead in domestic investment, while firms who do not invest abroad are also low on the domestic scale.[21] This observation, however, does not settle the issue. In the absence of investment opportunities abroad the high-investment companies might have increased their domestic investment even further.

This dependence of the outcome on the assumptions made is equally evident as we turn to the employment question. On the surface it might appear that the home country could gain much in terms of employment if the multinationals were to bring their affiliates home and produce for the export market. But this assumes that U.S. exports would be perfect substitutes for the sales of the affiliates to foreigners. The crucial assumption therefore concerns the percentage of sales abroad which could be maintained by exporting rather than producing abroad. The higher this percentage, the more jobs could be repatriated and the higher is the domestic job loss due to operating affiliates abroad.

But this percentage cannot be measured. The companies tend to assert that it is very low. They claim that much of the foreign investment occurred in order to protect markets developed originally by exports. The loss of the investments would therefore be quickly followed by the loss of the markets. Local producers would be able to take over, and competition from third countries would move in. This is consistent with our earlier disucssion of oligopolist strategy.

Others argue that the key variable here is the dispersion abroad of advanced technology by U.S. affiliates. Without the affiliates, they claim, this dispersion would be slowed, and U.S. exports would retain greater advantages over longer periods. In this view the percentage of foreign sales maintainable through exporting is higher, and the domestic job loss due to the multinationals is accordingly larger.[22]

---

[21]*Implications of Multinational Firms*, op. cit., p. 328.

[22]A recent estimate shows greatly different results depending on the assumptions made. A net domestic U.S. loss of 1.3 million jobs resulted from the assumption that exporting would be a perfect substitute for producing abroad. This loss declined to 418,000 jobs when it was assumed that 50 percent of affiliate production would be replaced by local foreign production. Finally an attempt was made to estimate market shares maintainable through exports on the basis of past U.S. export performance. This assumption led to a net gain of 490,000 jobs. *Implications of Multinational Firms*, op. cit., pp. 645–671.

NATIONAL INDEPENDENCE AND THE MULTINATIONAL COMPANY

The rapid growth of multinational firms in recent years has touched off a very broad debate over their impact on national independence. Many see an inherent conflict between the global vision of the multinational firm and the national outlook of the nation-state. "Geocentric" technology meets "ethnocentric" nationalism.[23] Some predict that the nation-state as we know it today will have to yield in order to accommodate tomorrow's technology.[24] To others, the conflict signals the need to establish control mechanisms by which the multinational corporation can be brought back into the conventional international order.

Rather then adding our own speculation to this debate, let us consider some of the ways in which the multinational corporation infringes upon national sovereignty. Most generally speaking, the relationship between government and private business in a market economy is based on certain parameters, set by the government, within which business is allowed to operate. The government, which is responsible for the overall functioning of the economy, collects taxes, stimulates employment, fights inflation, redistributes income, enforces antitrust laws, etc. In developing countries, furthermore, governments usually establish broad economic objectives which often tie firms to certain locations, prescribe particular products to be made, restrict the use of foreign exchange, etc.

The ability of multinational firms to avoid or circumvent government regulations is much greater than that of the domestic firm. Consider, for example, monetary policy, which is perhaps the most important single tool a government has to fight inflation, maintain desirable employment levels, control its balance of payments, and even affect the rate of economic growth to some extent.[25] A vital aspect of monetary policy is the government's ability to tighten credit. This can be done by restricting the volume of loans made by the banks. Multinational corporations, however, have credit sources abroad. They are largely independent of the monetary policy pursued by any single government, which consequently sees its ability to use this very important tool frustrated.

To make matters worse for the host government, multinational corporations today are served by a banking system which itself consists of large multinational banks, able to move credit quickly and in great

---

[23]S. Rolfe, "Updating Adam Smith," *Interplay*, vol. 2, November 1968.
[24]G. W. Ball, "The Promise of the Multinational Corporation," *Fortune*, vol. 75, no. 6, June 1967.
[25]This topic will be treated in greater detail in Chapters 12 and 13 below.

volume across national borders with little regard for national monetary policies. In fact, as a result of this multinational banking system, countries may experience results that are just the opposite of those normally associated with a tight money policy. When the government moves to tighten credit, interest rates will rise. High interest rates, however, will attract credit from abroad, especially when a well-organized multinational banking system with vast sources of credit stands ready to take advantage of precisely this situation.[26]

This ability of the multinationals to frustrate government policy reaches into many other areas. A company can evade taxes and foreign exchange restrictions by adopting accounting techniques which understate or exaggerate the value of intracompany shipments. A company's wage policy may run counter to local income redistribution programs. While the national plan may call for the development of the hinterland, a company may wish to locate in urban areas. The host government may be interested in higher employment, but a firm may wish to introduce labor-saving technology. Finally, the marketing techniques of foreign corporations may create consumer preferences which greatly differ from locally accepted standards.

There is little doubt that the multinational corporation plays an important role in international trade. Whether or not its impact is beneficial for the world economy is emerging as one of the great modern issues. As we have seen in this chapter, it is unwise to make sweeping generalizations on this subject. Those who see the world drifting into the grasp of a greedy clique of supermanagers are surely presenting a biased view. It is difficult, on the other hand, to accept as universally valid the claim that the multinational corporation is the great modern conveyor of the gains from trade, exposing locally protected markets to the fresh winds of international competition. The truth, as usual, lies somewhere in between.

SUMMARY

The multinational corporation is relevant to international trade for these reasons: Some international trade is intracompany trade; the establish-

---

[26]This banking system came to be known as the Euro-currency system, of which the Euro-dollar system composed the major part. The West German government repeatedly and the U.S. government in 1969 have seen their tight money policies largely rendered ineffective by the ample availability of funds through the Euro-dollar system.

ment of affiliates abroad may replace exports; extensive factor movements occur.

From colonial trading companies over resource orientation in the nineteenth century, multinational business has spread into manufacturing after World War II.

Multinational corporations account for one-fifth of the noncommunist world's production. United States companies alone account for almost one-fourth of world exports. If production abroad by affiliates is viewed as a form of trade, multinational business accounts for about one-half of world trade.

To the extent that multinational operations are purely competitive, their effect on the world economy is in agreement with comparative advantage. To the extent that oligopoly prevails, the effect may be different.

Exporting will be followed by producing abroad if the life of a product is viewed in terms of the product cycle.

United States investment in Europe is not only extensive, but also concentrated in high-technology growth industries. Concerns about Europe's colonialization by U.S. industry seem exaggerated in view of recent countermoves by European industry.

The relationship between the multinationals and their less developed host countries may be viewed as a bargaining situation which initially favors the company. Over time, the host country's terms tend to improve.

Home countries may be concerned with runaway capital and loss of potential jobs due to the multinationals' operations. Evidence in this area is inconclusive.

Multinational business with its global outlook has on occasion frustrated the policy objectives of nation-states and reduced the independence of national policy making.

SUGGESTED FURTHER READINGS

Two official reports repeatedly cited in this chapter contain a great deal more material than was used here. The first is *The Multinational Corporation in World Development*, a paper prepared by the United Nations Secretary-General for the use of the Group of Eminent Persons on Multinational Corporations (United Nations, New York, 1973). The second is *Implications of Multinational Firms for World Trade and Investment and for U.S. Trade and Labor*, report to the

Committee on Finance of the United States Senate and its Subcommittee on International Trade, 93d Cong., 1st Sess. (Government Printing Office, 1973). This report is accompanied by a collection of business and labor views, entitled *Multinational Corporations*, A Compendium of Papers submitted to the Subcommittee on International Trade of the Committee on Finance of the U.S. Senate, 93d Cong., 1st Sess. (Government Printing Office, 1973). For collections of articles see *The International Corporation, A Symposium*, Charles P Kindleberger, ed. (The M.I.T. Press, Cambridge, Mass., 1971), and *Multinational Enterprise*, John H. Dunning, ed. (Praeger, Inc., New York, 1972).

Chapter 8

The Balance of International Payments

Having studied in the preceding chapters the conditions under which trade takes place, we now turn to the statement which records all such trading transactions. This statement is the *balance of international payments.* It records all economic transactions between residents of the recording country and residents of all other countries for a specified period of time.

With the possible exception of census statistics, the balance of international payments is the oldest form of economic data. Long before governments had developed sophisticated income and sales tax networks, they derived tax revenue from international trade. In the great early trading nations such as England, Holland, Spain, and Portugal, it was relatively easy for the government to record and tax merchandise shipments at their ports of entry. We therefore owe the long-standing tradition of balance of payments accounting more to the royal need for tax funds than to purely scholarly interest.

Before we go into the accounting procedures, let us emphasize that we are not interested in the balance of payments because it represents an application of accounting techniques. Rather, our interest lies in practical issues involving the balance of payments. Much of the current international monetary debate, for example, centers on the problem of chronic U.S. deficits and the international value of the dollar.

An understanding of this problem, however, must be based on the link between the foreign exchange market, where the value of the dollar is determined, and the balance of payments. In order to understand this link we must become acquainted with the basic technical mechanisms involved both in the balance of payments and the foreign exchange market. For this reason the present brief chapter covers balance of payments accounting. The next chapter will then take up the foreign exchange market.

DEFICITS AND SURPLUSES

According to the accounting principle of double-entry bookkeeping, each transaction between a resident and a nonresident leads to two entries in the balance of payments. Usually one of these entries is a credit and one is a debit. In the balance of payments of country A, for example, a $100 merchandise export by A would be entered as follows:

Table 8-1   A's Balance of Payments

Debits		Credits	
Payments received	$100	$100	Merchandise exports

A $150 merchandise import by A would lead to the following entries:

Table 8-2   A's Balance of Payments

Debits		Credits	
Merchandise imports	$150	$150	Payments made

Already we have proceeded far enough to ask the obvious question: How is it possible for the balance of payments to show a deficit or a surplus? If each transaction leads to one debit and one credit entry, the balance of payments should always balance.

This is correct. The *accounting balance of payments,* i.e., the sum of all credits minus the sum of all debits can never be anything but zero.

When we refer to deficits and surpluses, we have in mind a concept which differs from that of the accounting balance. In order to develop this concept, let us take a closer look at the entries following each of the transactions in Tables 8-1 and 8-2.

ACTIVE VERSUS PASSIVE ENTRIES

Consider, for example, the $100 merchandise export of country A. Can we make a conceptual distinction between the two entries associated with this transaction? Foreigners wish to buy $100 worth of country A's products. Their motive for this purchase is autonomously based on their active preference for A's product. The "export" entry is therefore independent of any other entry in A's balance of payments. The same cannot be said about the other entry, "payments received," which passively follows from the active "export" entry. In order to make this distinction clear, an analogy may be used. Consider your purchase of a magazine from a newsstand. You buy the magazine because you wish to have it and not because you wish to make payment for it. Making payment is the passive consequence of your active decision to obtain the magazine.

We conclude that one of the two entries belonging to each transaction is *active,* while the other one is *passive.* If the active entry is a credit, the passive entry must be a debit, and vice versa.

Considering now the $150 imports of country A, it is evident that the debit entry "merchandise imports" is active and that the credit entry "payments made" is its passive corollary. We conclude that if the active entry is a debit, the passive entry must be a credit.

The distinction between active and passive entries leads us directly to a concept of imbalance in the balance of payments. In Table 8-3 both the export and the import transactions are reflected in four entries. The active entries are placed into the "active account," and the passive entries are placed into the "passive settlements account."

Note that the accounting balance of payments, i.e., the sum of all credits ($250) minus the sum of all debits ($250), balances. Country A, however, has imported more than it has exported and has consequently made more payments than it has received. Intuition tells us that country A should have a deficit in its balance of payments.

Table 8-3   A's Balance of Payments

Debits		Credits	
Active account			
Merchandise imports	$150	$100	Merchandise exports
Net active (deficit)	*50*		
Passive settlements account			
Payments received	$100	$150	Payments made
Net passive		*50*	*(Deficit)*
Accounting balance	$250	$250	

If we look at the two accounts in Table 8-3 separately, we find a net debit in the active account ($150 − $100 = $50) and a net credit in the passive account ($150 − $100 = $50). This leads us to a very useful definition of balance of payments deficit and surplus. A country has a balance of payments deficit if *active debits exceed active credits,* or, what amounts to the same thing, if *passive credits exceed passive debits.* A country has a balance of payments surplus if *active credits exceed active debits,* or, what is the same thing, if *passive debits exceed passive credits.*

We will adhere to these simple definitions throughout our discussion of the balance of payments in this and the following chapter. Our next task is to outline how the distinction between active and passive entries affects the myriad of different international transactions conducted each day by a country such as the United States.

ACTIVE ENTRIES

To determine when an active entry is a credit and when it is a debit, we need only look back at Table 8-3. An active entry is a credit *when payment is received for it.* An active entry is a debit *when payment must be made for it.* This simple criterion serves well not only for merchandise imports and exports, but also for most other transactions. It may be useful to consider a small sample of possible transactions.[1]

Services

Country A may sell services to foreigners in the form of transportation, tourism, and insurance, for example. Such service exports are active

---

[1] A more detailed list will be given in Chapter 10, which deals with the actual United States balance of payments.

credits because payment is received for them. The balancing passive debits record the payment received. Service imports, by the same token, are active debits balanced by passive credits.

Unilateral Transfers

Country A may decide to give foreign aid to another country.[2] Although this is a unilateral transfer, one active and one passive entry will be made. We know that the active decision to give foreign aid results in payments made to foreigners just as, for example, the active decision to buy imports results in payments made to foreigners. Foreign aid given, therefore, carries an active debit entry along with the passive credit entry "payments made."

Lending and Borrowing

Suppose residents of country·A have decided to lend money to foreigners. The transaction clearly requires the payment of this money to foreigners. The active entry "lending" is therefore a debit, balancing the passive credit "payments made." Borrowing from foreigners, on the other hand, will result in payments received from foreigners. The active entry "borrowing" is a credit, while the corresponding passive entry "payments received" is a debit.

Example

To provide an example, let us assume that country A has engaged in the following international transactions during 1970: Country A has:

(a) Exported merchandise $100
(b) Imported merchandise   150
(c) Sold services to foreigners   70
(d) Bought services from foreigners   50
(e) Paid foreign aid   80
(f) Lent to foreigners   95
(g) Borrowed from foreigners   30

It should be easy to determine A's balance of payments deficit by simply going down this list and adding all active credits and subtracting all active debits. A's balance of payments is shown in Table 8-4.

[2]We are speaking here of outright gifts of grants. Certain types of preferential loans are also commonly listed under foreign aid. In terms of balance of payments accounting, such loans should be placed under "lending and borrowing" below.

Table 8.4   A's Balance of Payments for 1970

Debits			Credits
Active account			
[b]Merchandise imports	$150	$100	Merchandise exports[a]
[d]Service imports	50	70	Service imports[c]
[e]Foreign aid	80	30	Borrowing[g]
[f]Lending	95		
	$375	$200	
Net active (deficit)	175		
Passive settlements account			
[a, c, g]Payments rec.	$200	$375	Payments made[b, d, e, f]
Net passive		$175	(Deficit)
Accounting balance	$575	$575	

Country A's balance of payments deficit follows from our definitions above. Active credits exceed active debits by $175. Passive credits exceed passive debits by $175. Note again that total credits equal total debits. The accounting balance, therefore, balances.

THE PASSIVE SETTLEMENTS ENTRIES

The passive settlements account in Table 8-4 contains only two summary entries because it was possible to add all payments received and to add all payments made. In the real world these payments can take many different forms. We therefore turn now to some different ways in which international payments may be made.

International payments are typically made by check drawn on a bank in the exporting country, in the importing country, or in any third country. Since bank accounts or balances are usually denominated in the local currency, this means that an international transaction may be settled in the currency of the exporting country, the importing country, or any third country. Let us assume that the United States exports $100 worth of merchandise to the United Kingdom. What are some of the alternate forms of payment for these exports?

1   The U.K. importers deposit $100 worth of pounds sterling in the U.S. exporter's account in a London bank. In this case the passive settlement entry in the U.S. balance of payments may be called "increase in foreign balances $100."

2   The U.K. importers may deposit $100 worth of Swiss francs in the U.S. exporter's account in a Swiss bank. The passive entry would again be "increase in foreign balances $100."

3   The U.K. importer may draw on his dollar account with his New York bank in order to pay the U.S. exporter. In this case dollar balances in the United States owned by foreigners would decline. Let us name the resulting passive settlement entry in the U.S. balance of payments "decrease in domestic balances due foreigners."

Alternatives (1) through (3) show two basic types of passive payment entries, "increase in foreign balances" and "decrease in domestic balances due foreigners." Both are passive debit entries, since they reflect alternate ways to balance the active credit "merchandise exports." Note that the difference between these two types of passive payment entries lies essentially in the difference between the currencies used for payment; if the domestic currency (in our example, U.S. dollars) is used, the entry takes the form of "domestic balances due foreigners." These balances are checking accounts in U.S. banks owned by foreign residents. If a foreign currency is used, the entry becomes "foreign balances," or checking accounts owned by U.S. residents in banks abroad.

Without repeating the whole argument in terms of U.S. imports, it can be seen that the active debit "merchandise imports" could be balanced by a passive credit entry named either "decrease in foreign balances" or "increase in domestic balances due foreigners."

We conclude that our passive entries can be placed in the category of either "foreign balances" or "domestic balances due foreigners." Increases in foreign balances and decreases in domestic balances due foreigners are passive debits. Decreases in foreign balances and increases in domestic balances due foreigners are passive credits.

In Table 8-5 we enter once more the list of country A's transactions which formed the basis for Table 8-4. But now we assume that the passive settlements entries can take different forms. Payment for merchandise and service exports (*a* and *c*), for example, is assumed to be received in terms of foreign currencies. These two active credit entries are therefore balanced by the passive debit entry "increase in foreign balances" (*a* and *c*).

Payment for merchandise imports (*b*), likewise, is made in terms of foreign currencies, resulting in a decline in A's holdings of such foreign

Table 8-5   A's Balance of Payments for 1970

Debits		Credits	
Active account			
[b]Merchandise imports	$150	$100	Merchandise exports[a]
[d]Service imports	50	70	Service exports[c]
[e]Foreign aid	80	30	Borrowing[g]
[f]Lending	95		
	$375	$200	
Net active (deficit)	175		
Passive settlements account			
[a, c]Increase in foreign		$150	Decrease in foreign
balances	$170		balances[b]
[g]Decrease in domestic bal-		225	Increase in domestic bal-
ances due foreigners	30		ances due foreigners[d, e, f]
[a, c, b]Net increase in for-		$195	Net increase in domestic bal-
eign balances	20		ances due foreigners[d, e, f, g]
Net passive		175	(Deficit)
Accounting balance	$575	$575	

currencies. The corresponding passive credit entry is therefore a "decrease in foreign balances" *(b)*.

The payments to foreigners required by service imports *(d)*, foreign aid *(e)*, and lending *(f)* are all made in terms of A's own currency. This may be done by crediting foreigners' bank accounts in A. The balancing passive credit entry is accordingly an "increase on domestic balances due foreigners" *(d, e, f)*.

This leaves item *g*, i.e., borrowing. We assume that the foreign lenders advance these funds to A's residents in terms of A's currency. To this purpose foreigners must draw on their balances in A's currency. From A's point of view this means a "decrease in domestic balances due foreigners" *(g)*, a passive debit which balances the active credit entry "borrowing."

A's balance of payments deficit remains, of course, the same as in Table 8-4. But we now have more information about the nature of this deficit. If we take the net figures of the settlements entries in each of the two categories, we can make the following statement: As a consequence of the international transactions conducted by country A during 1970, its foreign balances have increased by $20, but its domestic balances owed to foreigners have increased by $195. This leaves country A with a net deterioration in its payments position of $175.[3]

ERRORS AND OMISSIONS

At this point we might give some thought to the practical task of compiling a nation's balance of international payments. If we recall that each and every transaction between domestic and foreign residents is presumably reflected in the balance of payments, the considerable magnitude of this task becomes apparent.

Furthermore, it is one thing to postulate a balanced accounting balance on conceptual grounds, but quite another thing to achieve such a balance by showing that the net figure in the passive account actually equals the net figure of the active account. This equality would mean that foreign balances and domestic balances due foreigners had in fact changed by the exact amount of active entries.

In order to apply the double-entry method in practice, both entries of each transaction must be known to the recorder. While this is the case with most transactions, there are others where only one entry, usually the passive one, becomes known. Such borderline transactions may be due to gaps in the recording network or to illegal transactions.

Consider, for example, illegal imports of marijuana. Conceptually, the active entry should be a debit under "merchandise imports." This part of the transaction goes unrecorded for obvious reasons. But the induced entry will eventually be recorded if the dollars paid the foreign marijuana growers, after possibly changing hands abroad several times, show up in a New York bank account as an increase in domestic balances due foreigners. Foreigners' bank balances in U.S. banks are routinely surveyed by the U.S. Department of Commerce, which in this case has a passive credit entry on its hands without the corresponding active entry. In order to keep the accounting balance intact, some balancing active debit must be entered. In the U.S. balance of payments this entry is called "errors and omissions."

Or, consider an American tourist who buys $1,000 worth of foreign

---

[3]This laborious distinction between foreign and domestic balances is not simply a matter of accounting finesse. We will see in Chapter 10 that much of the U.S. deficit has been financed in terms of domestic balances due foreigners.

exchange in New York and spends these travel funds in Europe. Again, the active entry should be a debit under "travel," while the passive entry takes the form of a decrease in foreign balances. While the passive entry will be recorded, the active entry may not be recorded. Once more, "errors and omissions" will be debited to keep the accounting balance intact.

In short, if the active and passive accounts do not balance, the passive settlements account is accepted as correct and the active account is adjusted by means of the residual active errors and omissions entry. There is good reason for this procedure: The passive settlements account consists basically of data gathered from official agencies and large private banks with international business. Data for the active account, on the other hand, come from a great variety of sources. Compared with the active account, therefore, the passive settlements account is more reliable.

A COMPLICATION

The conceptual framework we have developed so far is designed to help us understand the actual balance of payments with particular reference to the United States. In view of this particular emphasis, a special conceptual point requires our attention. This point concerns the domestic balances due foreigners, which we have identified as passive payment entries. In the United States balance of payments, this entry takes the form of increases in liquid liabilities to foreigners. According to our discussion above, these liabilities may reflect dollars accepted by foreigners in payment for sales to the United States. But how do we actually measure these liabilities?

Suppose foreign commercial banks report an annual increase of $5 billion in short-term dollar claims on the United States. If we view the whole $5 billion as passive payment for active United States imports, we may be overlooking another possible explanation of these funds. United States residents may have made the active decision to borrow short-term money from foreign commercial banks. This transaction leads to the familiar two entries according to our guidelines developed above: The active credit (borrowing) will be an increase in short-term liabilities to foreign commercial banks, while the balancing passive debit may take the form of increases in foreign balances, or—what is more likely—decreases in domestic balances due foreigners. In short, we have the practical problem of deciding to what extent the $5 billion increase in foreign short-term dollar claims on the United States reflects a passive settlement credit or an active borrowing credit. The outcome of this decision will obviously affect the U.S. balance of payments. It may in fact make the difference between surplus and deficit.[4]

SUMMARY

Balance of payments accounting uses the double-entry bookkeeping method.

Each transaction leads to two entries, one of which is active and the other one passive.

If the active entry is a credit (debit), the balancing passive entry is a debit (credit).

The accounting balance of payments always balances.

A balance of payments surplus is defined as the excess of active credits over active debits or as the excess of passive debits over passive credits.

A balance of payments deficit is defined as the excess of active debits over active credits or as the excess of passive credits over passive debits.

All passive entries can be placed in one of two categories, foreign balances and domestic balances due foreigners.

Increases in foreign balances and decreases in domestic balances due foreigners are passive debit entries. Decreases in foreign balances and increases in domestic balances due foreigners are passive credit entries.

If actual data do not result in a zero accounting balance, the passive settlements figure is taken to be correct and the active account is adjusted by means of an "errors and omissions" entry.

When working with actual data, it is sometimes difficult to determine whether increases in short-term liabilities to foreigners represent passive domestic balances due foreigners or active borrowing from foreigners.

[4]See Chapter 10 below for an example.

SUGGESTED FURTHER READINGS

Balance of payments accounting receives more or less standard treatment by most texts. For comparisons among some of them, see: P. T. Ellsworth, *The International Economy,* 3rd ed. (The Macmillan Company, New York, 1965), chap. 16; Ingo Walker, *International Economics, Theory and Policy* (The Ronald Press Company, New York, 1966), chap. 11; Charles P. Kindleberger, *International Economics,* 5th ed. (Richard D. Irwin, Inc., Homewood, Ill., 1973), chap. 18. For balance of payments data and different concepts, see Chapter 10 of this book.

The Foreign
Exchange Market

In the preceding chapter it was pointed out that our primary interest does not rest with accounting procedures but with the balance of payments as an analytical tool. As we enter now into a discussion of the foreign exchange market, we will more clearly understand the meaning of this statement. The balance of payments, as we shall see, is closely related to the foreign exchange market. In fact, the balance of payments and the foreign exchange market are alternate ways of looking at the same thing, i.e., a country's international payments position.

In order to demonstrate the close link between the two concepts, let us first discuss the basic components of the foreign exchange market. One way in which international trade differs from domestic trade is the fact that different currencies are used in international trade. For example, an American resident who wishes to buy a British sports car may have to make payment to the British producer in terms of pounds sterling. The American resident will therefore have to buy pounds sterling. Pounds

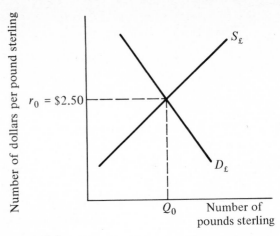

Figure 9-1

sterling may be bought in the foreign exchange market. Their price in terms of dollars is called the *the rate of exchange* between dollars and pounds sterling.

The foreign exchange market has no particular single location; it exists wherever funds are exchanged from one currency into another. As in any other market, the price in the foreign exchange market is determined by the interaction between supply and demand.

Assume that the world consists of two countries, the United States and the United Kingdom. Figure 9-1, in this case, shows the foreign exchange market from the U.S. point of view. The volume of foreign currency (i.e., sterling) is measured along the horizontal quantity axis, and the price per unit of foreign currency (i.e., dollars per pound sterling) is measured along the vertical price axis. The point of intersection between the supply curve and the demand curve shows the equilibrium level (r_0) of the exchange rate and the equilibrium level (Q_0) of the sterling volume traded.

Figure 9-2 is intended to demonstrate the similarity between the foreign exchange market and any other market, such as the market for apples. In both cases the quantity units of whatever is being traded must be defined on the horizontal axis.

The price on the vertical axis always refers to the amount of money per quantity unit as defined on the horizontal axis. An exchange rate of $2.50, for example, refers to the price in terms of dollars of one pound

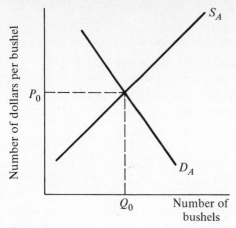

Figure 9-2

sterling. The same exchange rate can be expressed as £0.40 (1/2.5). It refers to the price of one dollar in terms of sterling. If the exchange rate is expressed in this way, the quantity on the horizontal axis must be stated in terms of dollars. Figure 9-3, therefore, shows the same foreign exchange market as Figure 9-1, but from the viewpoint of the United

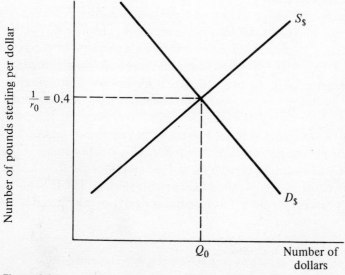

Figure 9-3

Kingdom. The demand for sterling in Figure 9-1 is equivalent to the supply of dollars in Figure 9-3, and the supply of sterling in Figure 9-1 is equivalent to the demand for dollars in Figure 9-3. These identities are rather obvious in our two-country world, since buying sterling means selling dollars and selling sterling means buying dollars. It will be convenient for us to use the presentation of Figure 9-1 rather than that of Figure 9-3 for the remainder of this chapter.

THE BALANCE OF PAYMENTS AND THE FOREIGN EXCHANGE MARKET

In our diagrams so far, we have drawn an upward-sloping supply curve and a downward-sloping demand curve for foreign exchange. It is important to study these curves in some detail. Let us go back, for example, to the U.S. resident who buys a British sports car and makes payment in terms of pounds sterling. We have already seen that these sterling funds must be bought by the U.S. importer in the foreign exchange market. We can therefore say that the import (an active debit in the U.S. balance of payments) can also be viewed as demand for foreign exchange. Upon further reflection, it appears that not only merchandise imports but all active debits on the U.S. balance of payments represent demand for foreign exchange if we assume that all payments are made in terms of foreign exchange.[1]

This identity of active debits and demand for foreign exchange follows directly from our definitions in the preceding chapter: Any active debit represents a purchase from a foreigner, be it a purchase of goods, of services, or of securities.[2] If payment for all these purchases is made in terms of foreign exchange, then the necessary amount of foreign exchange must be bought in the foreign exchange market with domestic currency.

The sum of active debits in the balance of payments is thus identical to the quantity of foreign exchange demanded. This identity continues to hold even if we allow for the possibility that payments for purchases from foreigners are made in dollars rather than pounds sterling. The U.S. buyer of a British sports car would in this case pay the price of the car in dollars

---

[1]This assumption will be relaxed shortly.
[2]Buying a foreign corporate bond, for example, amounts to lending to foreigners.

to the British producer. The British producer, however, has no use for dollars as such; he must pay his wage bill, his capital cost, etc., in terms of pounds sterling rather than dollars. He will therefore sell the dollar funds for pounds sterling in the foreign exchange market. As we have already seen, however, sales of sterling are equivalent to purchases of dollars. It follows that the U.S. import of a British sports car has once more led to demand for sterling. The only difference lies in the person of the buyer of sterling; while previously the buyer of sterling was the U.S. importer, it is now the U.K. exporter.

Without repeating the whole argument for U.S. exports, we may state that the sum of active credits in the U.S. balance of payments is identical to the quantity of sterling supplied. The argument is analogous to our discussion above. United States exporters are sellers of pounds sterling if they receive payment for their exports in sterling. If payment for U.S. exports is made in dollars, U.K. importers must buy dollars, i.e., sell sterling in the foreign exchange market.

Having established these very important identities, we must now consider their meaning. It is intuitively plausible that the demand for a country's currency by foreigners should reflect the demand for its exports by foreigners. If we also recall that the demand for dollars and the supply of pounds sterling are the same thing, we have established our important identities between balance of payments concepts and foreign exchange market concepts.

THE SLOPES OF SUPPLY AND DEMAND

Consider the supply and demand curve of Figure 9-1 in the light of our latest findings. The meaning of the upward-sloping supply curve is as follows: As the number of dollars obtained by U.S. exporters for each pound sterling rises, they will be willing to increase their sales of exports to the United Kingdom. In other words, as sterling becomes more expensive in terms of dollars, U.S. exporters will wish to increase their sales to the sterling country. The positive slope of the sterling supply curve is therefore plausible.

The demand curve in Figure 9-1 can be explained in similar terms. As the number of dollars needed by U.S. importers to obtain one pound sterling increases, they will wish to reduce their purchases of imports from the United Kingdom. As sterling becomes more expensive in terms of dollars, U.S. importers will reduce their purchases from the sterling country.[3]

EQUILIBRIUM IN THE FOREIGN EXCHANGE MARKET

If foreign exchange supply and demand are a function of the exchange rate, and if autonomous credits and debits are identical to supply and demand, then active credits and debits must also be a function of the exchange rate. For each given rate of exchange, in other words, there will be one quantity value of active credits and one quantity value of active debits.

Consider, for example, the quantity values associated with r_1 and r_2 in Figure 9-4, where r is defined as the dollar price of sterling. At r_1, the quantity of foreign exchange demanded (£500) exceeds the quantity supplied (£200) by £300. We have excess demand for £300 sterling at r_1. Active debits in the U.S. balance of payments exceed active credits by £300.

[3]This rationale for normally sloped curves in the foreign exchange market does not imply that the supply curve must necessarily have a positive and the demand curve a negative slope. Rather, it is shown above that such normal slopes can reasonably be assumed to exist.

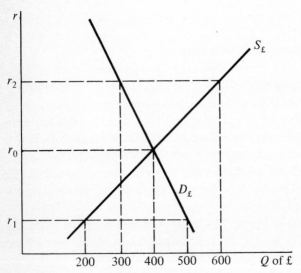

Figure 9-4

We conclude that excess demand for pounds sterling is equivalent to a deficit in the U.S. balance of payments. Similarly, at r_2 we notice excess supply of sterling and hence a balance of payments surplus of £300.

We know that neither r_1 nor r_2 can be the equilibrium price in the market described by Figure 9-4. An equilibrium price or exchange rate is defined as that rate at which neither excess demand nor excess supply exists. We are of course referring to r_0. At r_0 the quantity of sterling demanded (£400) is equal to the quantity of sterling supplied (£400). The foreign exchange market is in equilibrium. This also implies that active credits in the U.S. balance of payments are equal to active debits and that the balance of payments is therefore in equilibrium.

We have arrived at the crucial conclusion that equilibrium in the foreign exchange market is equivalent to equilibrium in the balance of payments.

An obvious question arises immediately: How can the foreign exchange market and, therefore, the balance of payments *not* be in equilibrium? Every student of economic principles knows that r_0 is the only price which will be able to exist for any appreciable time in Figure 9-4.

The answer rests on the ability of the exchange rate to clear the foreign exchange market, i.e., to attain its equilibrium value. Suppose, for example, that the governments of our two countries have agreed to fix the exchange rate at a predetermined level, let us say at r_1, in Figure 9-4. In this case of a fixed exchange rate we can see that a U.S. deficit would occur, since active debits would exceed active credits in the U.S. balance of payments.

This leads us to the general conclusion that imbalance in the balance of payments may occur if the exchange rate is fixed, but it will not occur if the rate is flexible enough to attain its equilibrium level.

Obviously, this result is of considerable relevance to the discussion of fixed versus flexible exchange rates. We must not be misled, however, by the ease with which we have arrived at our result into an overly simplistic attitude toward this discussion. An informed judgment in this area should be withheld until more has been said about the technical as well as the institutional aspects of the foreign exchange market. For the time being, let us continue our discussion of the conceptual links between the balance of payments and the foreign exchange market before we address ourselves empirically to the U.S. balance of payments in the next chapter.

SHIFTS IN THE FOREIGN EXCHANGE MARKET

Let us consider, for example, a sudden increase of U.S. demand for British products and its effect under a system of flexible as well as fixed exchange rates. In Figure 9-5, the foreign exchange market and the balance of payments are originally in equilibrium at r_0. The balance of payments at point A in Figure 9-5 is given in Table 9-1.[4]

Now U.S. residents wish to buy more British goods. This increase in demand is assumed to be independent of the exchange rate, i.e., more is demanded at r_0 than at any other exchange rate. We are therefore faced with a shift to the right of the demand curve for sterling to the position indicated by $D_\pounds'$. The new demand curve now intersects the supply curve $S_\pounds$ at point B. If the exchange rate ($r = \$/\pounds$) is allowed to move to its new equilibrium level, it will rise to r_1. In other words, the dollar depreciates relative to the pound sterling because the dollar price per pound sterling rises. The U.S. balance of payments reaches equilibrium as soon as the rate of exchange has moved from r_0 to r_1. At r_0, originally, a deficit equal to the distance between points A and C opens up in response to the sudden increase in demand for sterling. But just as any other market eliminates excess demand by an increase in price, the foreign exchange market equates active credits and active debits at point B. Table 9-2 shows the U.S. balance of payments at point B in Figure 9-5. Note that both exports and imports in Table 9-2 increased over their level in Table 9-1.

[4]Note that Table 9-1 and the following tables state the U.S. balance of payments in terms of sterling rather than dollars. This is necessary because the balance of payments tables relate directly to the foreign exchange market diagram, in which all quantities are sterling quantities. In order to obtain the U.S. balance of payments figures in terms of dollars, we need only multiply the sterling figures by the appropriate rate of exchange (r). This would be r_0 in Tables 9-1 and 9-3 and r_1 in Table 9-2.

Table 9-1   U.S. Balance of Payments at Point A ($r = r_0$)

Debits			Credits
Active account			
Imports	200	200	Exports
Passive settlements account			
(+) Foreign balances	200	200	(−) Foreign balances
Accounting balance	400	400	

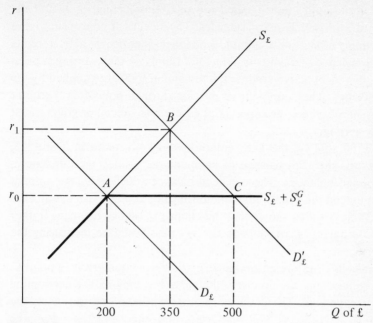

Figure 9-5

Assume now that the rate of exchange is fixed at r_0, and consider the same shift in the demand curve for sterling. Excess demand for sterling at r_0 tends to drive the exchange rate above r_0. The U.S. authorities, in order to keep the rate at r_0, will have to sell sterling at the rate r_0.[5] These additional sales of sterling will bend the supply curve horizontally to

[5]In fixing the rate of exchange, the authorities therefore rely on market forces. The fixed rate is not "frozen" by official decree, which would make it illegal to buy or sell foreign exchange at any other rate. Rather, the rate is "pegged" at a given level by means of official purchases or sales of foreign exchange.

Table 9-2   U.S. Balance of Payments at Point B $(r = r_1)$

Debits			Credits
	Active account		
Imports	350	350	Exports
	Passive settlements account		
(+) Foreign balances	350	350	(−) Foreign balances
Accounting balance	700	700	

the right until supply and demand are once more equal at r_0 and the tendency of r to rise beyond r_0 subsides. This occurs at point C in Figure 9-5. The supply of sterling at point C is no longer identical to active credits in the U.S. balance of payments. Of a total supply of £500 sterling at point C, only £200 reflect active credits; the remaining £300 are supplied by the U.S. authorities. The supply curve passing through point C is therefore labeled $S_£ + S_£^G$, where the superscript G refers to official or government supply of sterling.

The £300 sold by the U.S. authorities can be found in Table 9-3, which records the U.S. balance of payments at point C as a decline in official foreign balances. These official balances decline by the amount needed to extend the supply curve of sterling horizontally from point A to point C. Table 9-3 also shows that the change in official balances (rather than private balances) remains as the net passive figure measuring the U.S. deficit.

Technically, the foreign exchange market is in equilibrium at point C. But this equilibrium has precisely the same meaning as the accounting balance of payments. The price r_0, in other words, no more reflects the autonomous activities of U.S. importers and exporters than does the accounting balance of Table 9-3. Accordingly, we may distinguish between autonomous equilibrium and technical equilibrium. Autonomous equilibrium in the foreign exchange market occurs when supply and demand reflect active credits and debits and are equal to each other.

Table 9-3   U.S. Balance of Payments at Point C ($r = r_0$)

Debits			Credits
Active account			
Imports	500	200	Exports
Net active (deficit)	300		
Passive settlements account			
Increase in private foreign balances	200	200	Decrease in private foreign balances
		300	Decrease in official foreign balances
Net passive		300	Decrease (deficit) in official foreign balances
Accounting balance	700	700	

Technical equilibrium, on the other hand, involves official intervention in the sense that the authorities shift the supply or demand curve in order to keep the exchange rate at a given level. Autonomous equilibrium in the foreign exchange market means balance of payments equilibrium; technical equilibrium does not.

After the shift in demand from $D_£$ to $D_£'$, the dollar may be considered overvalued at r_0 in the sense that it would decline in value if it were not supported by official sales of sterling. The rationale of considering the dollar overvalued even though the foreign exchange market is technically in equilibrium at point C is precisely the rationale of considering the U.S. balance of payments (Table 9-3) in deficit even though the accounting balance technically balances.

Thus, in order to maintain r_0 in the face of an autonomous increase in demand for sterling, the U.S. government must part with an amount of its sterling reserves equal to the excess of autonomous demand ($D_£'$) over autonomous supply ($S_£$) at r_0. Since this excess is by definition equal to the U.S. balance of payments deficit, the deficit at r_0 is paid for, or financed by, official sales of sterling.

It should be easy now to construct a case in which the autonomous supply rather than the demand for sterling suddenly shifts to the right. All conclusions are exactly reversed: If flexible, the rate of exchange would decline, i.e., the dollar would appreciate relative to the pound sterling. If the rate were fixed at r_0, a U.S. surplus would result which would be financed by official purchases of sterling in the foreign exchange market. The dollar, in this case, would be considered undervalued at r_0.

A careful derivation of these conclusions with the help of the proper diagram and balance of payments tables could provide a useful exercise at this point.

Let us summarize our findings with regard to the fixed rate of exchange: Unless the rate is fixed precisely at the level where the foreign exchange market is in autonomous equilibrium, the authorities will have to intervene (in order to establish technical equilibrium at the fixed rate). If excess demand for foreign exchange occurs at the fixed rate, the balance of payments will be in deficit, and the authorities must sell foreign exchange. In case of excess supply and a balance of payments surplus at the fixed rate, the authorities will buy foreign exchange. In accounting terms, the deficit will be reflected by a net passive credit entry showing a decline in official foreign balances. The surplus takes the form of a net passive debit entry indicating an increase in official foreign balances.

THE FOREIGN EXCHANGE MARKET AND
THE INTERNATIONAL MONETARY SYSTEM

In our discussion so far we have established the basis for understanding a good deal about actual international monetary arrangements. But this discussion has been theoretical in the sense that we have dealt with two pure forms of foreign exchange market organization, i.e., that of flexible exchange rates and that of fixed exchange rates. These two pure forms are extremes, neither of which has ever been very important as an actual working proposition.

Rather, the foreign exchange markets of the real world have typically reflected some compromise between rigidly fixed and freely flexible exchange rates, as we shall see in the following discussion.

THE CLASSIC GOLD STANDARD

The classic gold standard, in effect from approximately 1870 to 1914, was a form of exchange market organization which provided for almost completely fixed rates of exchange. Let us see how this system worked.

The gold standard may be described as a commitment on the part of a national government to buy and sell a specified amount of gold for a specified amount of its own currency. If such a commitment exists in two countries, the rate of exchange between the two currencies will be fixed and determined by the ratio of the gold parities.

Let us assume, for example, that the United States stands committed to buy and sell one fine ounce of gold for $35. Similarly, the United Kingdom is assumed to buy and sell one fine ounce of gold for £14. In this situation, anyone who wishes to buy dollars for sterling can buy 1/14 ounce of gold for one pound sterling from the U.K. treasury and sell 1/14 ounce of gold for 2.5 dollars to the U.S. treasury. One pound sterling thus always exchanges for 2.5 dollars; the rate of exchange ($r = \$/£$) is fixed at $2.50.

Similarly, sterling can be obtained for dollars by buying 1/35 ounce of gold from the U.S. treasury for one dollar and by selling the gold for £0.4 to the U.K. treasury. In this case, the rate of exchange ($r = £/\$$) is equal to £0.4. Obviously, $2.5 for one pound or £0.4 for one dollar amounts to the same rate of exchange.

Under the gold standard, then, a country can change the rate of exchange by changing the price of gold in terms of its own currency. If, for example, the United States were to increase the price of gold to $42 per ounce of gold, the rate of exchange ($r = \$/\pounds$) would rise to $3.00 per one pound sterling ($42/14 = 3$). Defined as the sterling price per dollar, the exchange rate ($r = \pounds/\$$) would decline from £0.4 to £0.33.

GOLD AND THE FOREIGN EXCHANGE MARKET

Let us now integrate the gold standard, as described above, into our framework of the foreign exchange market and the balance of payments. It appears that the buyer of sterling now has two ways of obtaining sterling: He may buy it in the foreign exchange market, or he may go through the gold parity links as explained above. In Figure 9-6, $r = 2.500$ is the exchange rate reflecting the gold parities (35/14). This rate is defined as the *mint parity* rate. If our buyer can obtain sterling for this price directly in the foreign exchange market, he will not bother to sell dollars for gold and buy sterling for gold, because he would not be able to improve on this price.

In fact, he might do worse, considering that he would have to ship

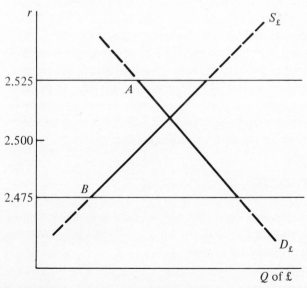

Figure 9-6

gold from the United States to the United Kingdom, which would involve costs of transportation, insurance, etc. The existence of these costs means that the buyer of sterling would probably accept a price of sterling in the foreign exchange market slightly higher than mint parity at $2.50. If the cost involved in using the gold link is equal to 1 percent of $2.50 for each dollar converted, he will buy sterling in the foreign exchange market rather than use the gold standard up to a price of $2.525 per pound sterling. Any higher price will induce him to ship gold for sale to the U.K. treasury. The price of $2.525, then, is the maximum which can be charged for sterling in the foreign exchange market. This is shown in Figure 9-6 by the horizontal line drawn through $r = 2.525$. Point A in Figure 9-6 may accordingly be called the U.S. gold export point.

If we put ourselves into the position of the seller of pounds sterling, we can see that the gold standard also imposes a minimum price of sterling on the foreign exchange market. Sellers cease to deal in the market and begin to ship gold from the United Kingdom to the United States as the price of sterling falls below $2.475, or more than 1 percent below mint parity. Point B in Figure 9-6 is the U.S. gold import point.

The interaction between the gold standard and the foreign exchange market in this way produces an intermediate solution between a freely flexible and a rigidly fixed rate of exchange.[6] As we can see in Figure 9-6, the equilibrium rate of exchange may fall anywhere between the upper and the lower gold point (i.e., anywhere between 2.525 and 2.475). Between these points, it is determined by supply and demand for sterling. Between the gold points, in other words, the rate of exchange is allowed to clear the market and to provide for balance of payments equilibrium.

Note that the equilibrium rate of exchange does not have to be equal to mint parity ($2.500). The mint parity level simply serves as a point of reference, in the sense that mint parity plus and minus 1 percent in Figure 9-6 establishes the range of exchange rate flexibility.

THE SETTLEMENT PROCESS

Shifts of the type discussed in Figure 9-5 may be used to demonstrate the operation of a gold standard system. In Figure 9-7 we consider three different shifts in the demand for sterling.

---

[6]This compromise solution, of course, comes quite close to a fixed rate system because the range of flexibility under the classic gold standard was very narrow.

The shift from $D_£^0$ to $D_£^1$ results in a higher r, i.e., a small depreciation of the dollar. The effect is similar to that under a flexible rate system. The same holds for $D_£^2$, but we realize that this is the largest shift which can be accommodated by a change in the exchange rate, because r_2 is the ceiling rate. The balance of payments, as we know, returns to equilibrium after each of these first two shifts.

The third shift, from $D_£^2$ to $D_£^3$, is a different matter. Buyers of sterling are unwilling to pay the rate r_3. Instead, they will obtain an amount of sterling measured by the distance between points A and B in Figure 9-7 at the rate r_2 by exporting gold to the United Kingdom.[7] The U.K. treasury in this way supplies that amount of sterling which is needed to fill the excess demand gap AB at the rate r_2. We may show this in Figure 9-7 by extending the sterling supply curve from point A to the right in horizontal fashion.

---

[7]The rate at which sterling is obtained from the U.K. treasury is mint parity. To this we must add the cost of shipping and insurance, so that the actual cost of sterling in terms of dollars adds up to r_2.

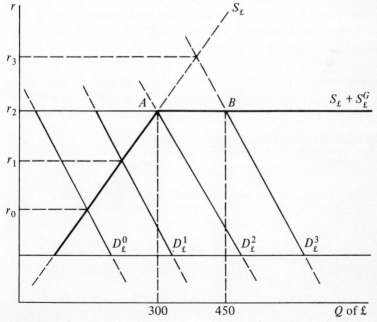

Figure 9-7

The U.S. balance of payments after the third shift is outlined in Table 9-4. Active debits exceed active credits by £150. The passive credit "gold exports" reflects the U.S. deficit and the distance between points A and B in Figure 9-7.

Note that this form of settlement, in which gold transfers provide the net settling entry, is completely automatic in the sense that governments need not enter the foreign exchange market. All the government has to do is to adhere to its commitment under the gold standard to buy and sell its own currency for gold at the specified rate.

THE GOLD-EXCHANGE STANDARD

World War I marked the end of the classic gold standard era. During the war itself, the recovery period afterward, and finally the Great Depression, the organization of foreign exchange markets was undergoing many changes.[8] Various types of arrangements alternated as efforts to reestablish the classic gold standard eventually had to be given up.

What emerged after World War II was a system which still provided for substantially fixed rates of exchange, although it was a good deal less automatic, and in which the importance of gold was greatly reduced. This system is known as the *gold-exchange standard.* National currencies were still defined in terms of gold, but this definition was essentially a

[8]The period between the two World Wars will be discussed in greater detail in Chapter 14.

Table 9-4   U.S. Balance of Payments at Point B $(r = r_2)$

Debits			Credits
Active account			
Imports	450	300	Export
Net active (deficit)	150		
Passive settlements account			
Increase in foreign balances		300	Decrease in foreign balances
	300		
		150	Gold exports
Net induced		150	Gold exports (deficit)
Accounting balance	750	750	

formality, since—with the exception of the United States—nations no longer stood ready to redeem their currencies in gold. We recall that the commitment by all participating nations to do just that had been the basis of the classic gold standard.

The maintenance of fixed exchange rates became a matter of government policy rather than—as had been the case under the classic gold standard—the automatic result of given gold parities. The gold-exchange standard, in other words, amounts to an agreement between national governments to peg their currencies at agreed-upon levels. The basic mechanism by which fixed rates were maintained has already been explained in Figure 9-5 above and the related discussion: Whenever there is excess demand for foreign exchange at the fixed rate and the rate therefore threatens to rise, the authorities will close the gap by selling foreign exchange. Whenever there is excess supply, the authorities will buy foreign exchange.

All that remains to be added is the fact that under the gold-exchange standard the rate of exchange is allowed to fluctuate within a narrow range around its official parity. This, of course, was also true under the classic gold standard, but for a different reason. Under the classic gold standard, the range of flexibility was determined by the cost of shipping gold. Under the gold-exchange standard, this range is simply a matter of agreement among national governments.

KEY CURRENCIES

So far, the difference between the two systems has been described in terms of automatic settlement by private gold shipments versus an officially managed pegging mechanism. But the difference goes considerably further than that. If, under the gold-exchange standard, governments were prepared to buy and sell foreign exchange in order to peg their currencies, they required stocks of foreign exchange reserves for this purpose. It would have been extremely cumbersome, however, to keep on hand reserves in all those foreign currencies against which the domestic currency might have to be supported. Instead, the bulk of all international reserves consisted of a few key currencies, among which the U.S. dollar was by far the most important.[9] Not only was the dollar acceptable

---

[9]The other major key currency was the pound sterling, which was used heavily in those parts of the world which either had been or still were associated with Britain. This use of sterling declined after 1967.

throughout the world, constituting therefore a good reserve asset against liabilities in any other currency, but it was also convertible into gold. In addition, many foreign countries used the dollar to settle transactions among themselves which did not involve the United States.

What evolved was something close to a dollar standard in the sense that the dollar was the common denominator in terms of which all exchange rates were defined. The dollar, in turn, remained convertible into gold, which led to the terms gold-exchange or gold-dollar standard.

THE KEY CURRENCY COUNTRY AND
THE GOLD-EXCHANGE STANDARD

One of the interesting conclusions so far is the fact that a national currency may also function as an international key currency. This dual role of its money has important implications for a country whose currency serves as international reserve asset. While we are not yet prepared for a full discussion of this subject, it will be useful at this point to analyze its effect on the link between the foreign exchange market and the balance of payments.

Let us assume that the United States, as key currency country, has a balance of payments deficit. This deficit, as we have seen above, could be reflected in a decline of foreign balances or in the U.S. gold stock. In both cases, the deficit shows up as excess demand for foreign exchange at the fixed rate of exchange. The decline in foreign exchange reserves or gold is the result of the official pegging operations at that rate.

Now let us consider the fact that the dollar is a key currency. This means that foreign countries are willing to hold dollars as international reserves in large quantities. Let us also recall the passive settlement entry "domestic balances due foreigners" which was explained in the previous chapter. A U.S. deficit, then, may be settled by an increase in domestic balances due foreigners, which simply means that foreigners have accepted U.S. dollars in payment for their net exports to the United States *and* that these foreigners are willing to hold these dollars rather than to sell them in the foreign exchange market. The foreign exchange market, consequently, remains unaffected by the U.S. deficit. There is no pressure on the U.S. dollar to fall below its given rate in response to this deficit. This conclusion is a very important aspect of the international position of the United States at the present time. We will therefore elaborate somewhat further.

We might assume, for example, that the passive settlement account in the U.S. balance of payments contains entries in terms of domestic balances due foreigners only. This would mean that all payments resulting from the active entries have been made in dollars. The deficit then takes the form of a net passive credit entry showing a net increase in domestic balances due foreigners. In this case, the identities derived earlier between active credits and the supply of foreign exchange, and active debits and the demand for foreign exchange, are no longer valid for the simple reason that no foreign exchange is used in this situation. If all international transactions are settled in dollars, there is no need for a foreign exchange market at all.

We need not make such unrealistic assumptions to arrive at our conclusion that the rate of exchange may not be affected by the U.S. deficit. All we need to assume is that the net passive credit entry measuring the U.S. deficit takes the form of an increase in domestic balances due foreigners.

This is demonstrated in Figure 9–8 and Table 9–5. If the original equilibrium is at point A in Figure 9–8, we know that payments are made in sterling or in dollars which are immediately converted into sterling.[10] Now let the U.S. demand for British goods suddenly increase. If no change occurs in the payments arrangements, we would have a shift in demand for sterling from $D_\pounds$ to $D_\pounds{}^1$.

If we assume, however, that (1) the additional U.S. imports are financed in dollars and (2) the U.K. exporters who receive these dollars do not convert them into sterling, no shift in the demand for sterling will take place. Instead, the distance between points A and B in Figure 9–8 reflects a U.S. deficit financed by increases in domestic balances due foreigners. Note that in this case the rate of exchange remains at r_o, in autonomous equilibrium.[11]

We have autonomous equilibrium (at point A) in the foreign exchange market, but a balance of payments deficit (at point B).

In Table 9–5, which shows the U.S. balance of payments corresponding at point B in Figure 9–8, we have financed £500 of U.S. imports by

---

[10]This follows directly from our derivation of the supply and demand curves for sterling.

[11]Actually, the U.K. exporters who receive payment in dollars are likely to sell them for sterling without delay. However, this does not affect our argument so long as the dollars are bought by someone else abroad at the given exchange rate. The actual process is likely to be as follows: The U.K. exporter sells the dollars to his commercial bank in Britain for sterling. If this bank has international business, it may hold the dollars as transactions balances or reserves. Otherwise, the commercial bank will sell the dollars to the Bank of England, which will add them to its official reserves. As long as each of these transactions takes place at r_0, our conclusions are not affected. Someone abroad adds dollars to his reserves and thereby withholds them from the foreign exchange market.

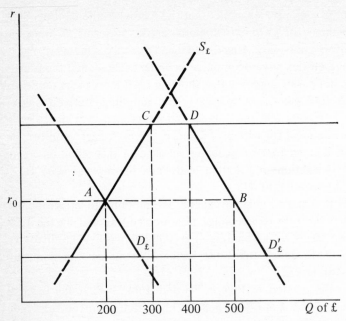

Figure 9-8

Table 9-5 U.S. Balance of Payments at Point *B* *(r = r_0)*

Debits			Credits
	Active account		
Imports	500	200	Exports
Net active (deficit)	300		
	Passive settlements account		
Increase in foreign		200	Decrease in foreign balances
balances	200		
		300	Increase in domestic balances due foreigners
Net passive		*300*	*Increase in domestic balances due foreigners (deficit)*
Accounting balance	700	700	

£200 of decreases in foreign balances, and the remaining £300 by increases in domestic balances due foreigners. These £300 reflect the sudden shift in U.S. demand for U.K. goods, i.e., the distance between *A* and *B* in Figure 9-8.

Thus, changes in the balance of payments do not lead to changes in the exchange rate or the official stock of gold or foreign balances to the extent that domestic balances due foreigners are involved. In fact, the U.S. authorities need not intervene in any way.

A key currency country is in a sense exempt from the pressures which the balance of payments may exert on the foreign exchange market. Such a country can presumably continue to show deficits without being forced to reduce its gold stock or its stock of foreign currency reserves as long as its foreign trading partners remain willing to accumulate balances in the key currency.

Of course, this position is not without its drawbacks. Dollar balances in foreign hands may be viewed as a *potential* if not an actual supply of dollars on the foreign exchange market. Should anything happen to the general confidence in the dollar, potential supply can quickly become actual supply, as foreigners wish to divest themselves of their dollar holdings. In such an eventuality, the U.S. authorities would be confronted with excess supply of dollars (i.e., excess demand for foreign exchange) which could far surpass the dimensions of the U.S. deficit at that particular time. The resulting pressure on the dollar would not merely reflect the most recent deficit. Rather, it would be primarily related to the total stock of foreign-held dollar balances, i.e., the cumulative deficit of many years. This "overhang" of previously accumulated dollar balances was an important factor, for example, in the dollar crisis of 1971, and it remains a concern in the ongoing debate over the reform of the system.

DEVALUATION AND REVALUATION

Although the gold-exchange standard was designed, as we have seen, as a system of fixed exchange rates, its actual record in maintaining fixed rates in the long run compares unfavorably with that of the classic gold standard. Currency devaluation and revaluation occurred repeatedly and quite frequently during the late 1960s and early 1970s. Currency devaluation is official action by which the heretofore fixed price of the domestic currency in terms of foreign currency is reduced. By revaluation we understand the officially announced increase in the price of the domestic currency in terms of foreign currency.

Suppose Figure 9-9 portrays the foreign exchange market from the French point of view and the French balance of payments. We assume that r_1 represents the agreed-upon parity rate of the franc in terms of the

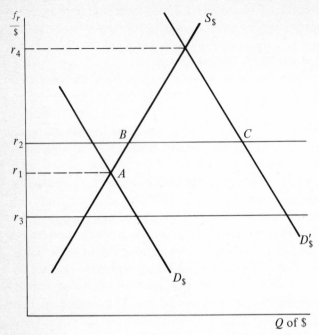

Figure 9-9

U.S. dollar. The rates r_2 and r_3 reflect the support limits within which the French government has agreed to maintain the franc. We start at point A, where the foreign exchange market and the balance of payments are in equilibrium at the rate r_1. Now we assume an outward shift of demand for dollars to $D_\$'$. This shift may have been caused, for example, by an increase in French demand for imports. The exchange rate now moves toward r_4, a weakening of the franc in response to the deterioration in the French balance of payments as reflected by the shift in demand for foreign exchange.

In order to maintain the rate at r_2, the support limit, the French authorities would have to sell an amount of dollars which is measured by the distance between points B and C in Figure 9-9. This action would extend the dollar supply curve horizontally to the right and establish technical equilibrium at point C.

The French authorities, however, may not have enough dollar reserves for this purpose. Previous deficits may have exhausted the French stock of international reserves, including gold. Forecasts may predict further deficits at the rate r_2. Under these circumstances, the French may decide to devalue the franc. This devaluation would consist of an announcement by the French government that henceforth the parity rate is to be, for example, r_4. The new parity, in this case, was chosen to achieve autonomous equilibrium in the foreign exchange market and, consequently, equilibrium in the balance of payments.

INTERNATIONAL NEGOTIATIONS ⌄

Such policy devaluations are normally preceded by intense international negotiations. The reason for such negotiations is easy to see in that an exchange rate, by definition, involves at least two currencies. Devaluation of the franc against the dollar implies revaluation of the dollar against the franc. If the dollar's rate against all other currencies, furthermore, remains unchanged, the devaluation of the franc against the dollar also means devaluation of the franc against all other currencies.

Keeping this in mind, let us take another look at Figure 9-9, but this time from the point of view of France's trading partners. The French deficit *B–C* in Figure 9-9 represents the sum of all other countries' surpluses with France. This does not mean however that each of these countries has a surplus in its overall balance of payments. Britain, for example, while running a surplus in her trade with France may have deficits with Germany, Japan, etc. The British balance of payments, therefore, may also be in deficit. The French devaluation, by reducing or eliminating the French deficit with Britain, will put an additional burden on Britain's overall deficit. This burden, in fact, may be heavy enough to force Britain into devaluation of sterling as a consequence of the original French devaluation.

We can see that the British devaluation, in addition to the French one, now puts even more pressure on other deficit countries. Some may follow suit, and with each additional devaluation the pressure on the remaining currencies mounts.[12] It is also evident that each subsequent devaluation of another currency cancels more and more of the intended effect of the original devaluation of the franc. It is for this reason that a country which plans to devalue its currency normally consults with its major trading partners.

---

[12]Such chain reactions occurred during the 1930s, with disastrous effects on the volume of international trade. See Chapter 14 below.

CONTROLLED FLOATING ⁺

Under a properly functioning gold-exchange standard, fixed exchange rates (within small margins of flexibility) are the rule, and rate alterations are exceptions. Such a system, as we shall see later, requires a certain basic alignment between different economies which is maintained by mechanisms of internal adjustment within each country. If these internal adjustment mechanisms do not function adequately, the gold-exchange standard will be subjected to severe stresses. We will leave the discussion of these adjustment mechanisms for subsequent chapters and maintain our present focus on the foreign exchange market. Here the problem of basic misalignment between different economies will be reflected in frequent and heavy pressures for exchange rate alterations.

When such pressures continue to occur in several major countries at the same time, it becomes extremely difficult for any given country to negotiate effectively for a planned devaluation or revaluation. Other countries are likely to be unsure about the future of their own currencies. If a country, on the other hand, resorts to unilateral action without prior consultation, the chances for retaliation are greatly increased.

In situations of this type, a country may allow its currency to float. As we can see in our foreign exchange market diagrams, the floating currency could automatically find its equilibrium level and hence bring the balance of payments back into equilibrium. But in order to obtain this result, the country in question must be willing to allow its currency to rise or fall to whatever level is required to clear the foreign exchange market. Few countries have displayed this indifference to the international value of their currencies. Instead, the authorities have tended to intervene in accordance with some notion about the level to which their currencies should float.[13] To the extent, then, that the authorities' notion of the desirable rate differs from the equilibrium rate, a floating rate remains consistent with balance of payments deficit or surplus.

This is demonstrated in Figure 9-10. Let us assume that Britain allows sterling to float in response to the pressures of a large deficit (A–B) at the sterling support limit r_2. But the rate r_5 may represent too large a depreciation of sterling. The authorities may let sterling float to r_4 and then sell dollars (C–D) in order to maintain that rate. This, of course, means a British deficit (C–D) at the rate r_4.

---

[13]Such floating with intermittent official intervention has recently come to be termed "dirty" floating.

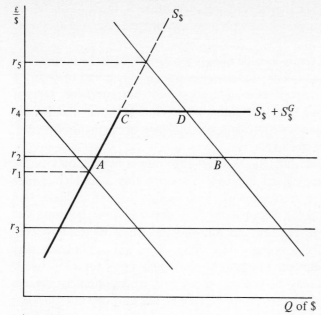

Figure 9-10

Controlled floating was used by Germany and the Netherlands in a somewhat different manner in 1971. The German mark and and the Dutch guilder had been under strong upward pressure for some time. Revaluation became necessary, but the negotiations over the degree of the revaluations became hopelessly deadlocked at a time of widespread uncertainty. The German and Dutch authorities, consequently, let their currencies float for a period of about six months. In this way market forces (rather than negotiations and estimates) determined the extent to which the exchange rate would have to be changed in order to bring about autonomous equilibrium in the foreign exchange market. After these new rates had been in operation for some time, the mark and the guilder were officially revalued and fixed at, or close to, the new equilibrium rate.

THE SYSTEM IN TRANSITION

Controlled floating occurred with increasing frequency as the gold-exchange standard showed signs of serious disintegration during the early

1970s. It is important, however, not to confuse a situation in which controlled floating is prevalent with a system of freely flexible exchange rates.

In a system of freely flexible rates, each country must be prepared to let the exchange rate fall or rise to whatever level is required to clear the foreign exchange market. The authorities must not intervene. Only if these conditions are met will autonomous equilibrium in the foreign exchange market and its equivalent (i.e., balance of payments equilibrium) be consistently achieved.

Under controlled floating, the exchange rate is flexible only to the extent which meets official approval. This presents a problem which becomes immediately clear when we recall the fact that any exchange rate involves two currencies. Suppose the U.S. dollar and the Japanese yen are floating. Each government has some notion as to what the dollar/yen rate should be. These notions may differ. The U.S. authorities may envisage a high dollar/yen rate, the Japanese may press for a low one.[14] Each government may be willing to back its own notion by the appropriate foreign exchange sales or purchases. But only one rate can exist at any one time. If confusion and disruption of the trade flow between the two countries are to be avoided, they must come to some agreement on the terms under which each currency's floating will be controlled.

This, however, will ultimately amount to an agreement on the levels at which each government will intervene in the foreign exchange market. Controlled floating, whenever it has occurred, has generally been viewed as an emergency measure to be employed only as a last resort. Widespread floating, accordingly, has been taken as a transitory stage in a system awaiting more basic reform.[15]

EXCHANGE CONTROL

All the foreign exchange schemes we have discussed in this chapter have one important element in common. They are all based on the market mechanism. Government interference may alter the outcome of the market mechanism, but it does so by using supply and demand. This has the very important result that once an exchange rate is determined,

---

[14]A high dollar/yen rate means that U.S. exports are cheap in Japan. A low rate means that Japanese exports are cheap in the United States.

[15]We will address ourselves to this question in greater detail in Chapter 15.

everyone has unrestricted access to it. Anyone can buy or sell unlimited quantities of foreign exchange.

All this is very different under a system of *exchange control,* where foreign exchange transactions are officially regulated. In the extreme case, for example, all foreign exchange transactions between private individuals may be prohibited. Importers may have to obtain their foreign exchange funds from the government and exporters may have to surrender their foreign exchange receipts to the government at rates set by the government. There is no market for foreign exchange in this case.

The purpose of such controls is, of course, the correspondingly complete control over the balance of payments. For example, a government may establish a system of *multiple exchange rates.* For imports deemed essential, foreign exchange will be made available cheaply. For less essential imports the price will be set higher, and for undesirable imports no licenses and foreign exchange will be made available. It is easy to see that every entry in the balance of payments could conceivably be controlled in this way. Common side effects of exchange control are black markets and various forms of smuggling.

Take, for example, the case of East Germany during the 1950s and early 1960s. The East-mark could be bought in Western Europe at a small fraction of its officially controlled rate in terms of Western currencies.[16] If one could enter East Germany with East-marks bought at such bargain prices, one could, for example, buy famous Zeiss Ikon cameras for a pittance in terms of Western currencies. In order to enforce its exchange control, the East German authorities had to control their border as well. Severe penalties awaited anyone, foreigner or resident, who was caught with unaccounted-for sums of East-marks on his way into East Germany. In addition, our camera buyer would face the same penalties on his way back out, if he could not prove that the funds for that camera had been obtained at the officially controlled exchange rate.

Exchange control can of course be practiced to various degrees. Many Western countries have established such controls on a limited basis over certain foreign currencies and certain trade and investment categories. Such practices were particularly prevalent in Western Europe after World War II. Many underdeveloped countries use exchange control in order to ensure that their scarce foreign exchange reserves are used for

---

[16]This means ultimately that some East Germans did not agree with their government's priorities. They were willing to pay much more for some Western goods than the authorities would allocate for imports of these goods.

imports of essential capital goods rather than luxuries. Finally, by the very nature of their domestic economic systems, communist countries practice exchange control as a regular aspect of their foreign trade.

SUMMARY

Active credits in the balance of payments are identical to autonomous supply of foreign exchange.

Active debits are identical to autonomous demand for foreign exchange.

These identities hold whether or not the domestic or a foreign currency is used for international payments. They provide the basic link between the balance of payments and the foreign exchange market.

Autonomous equilibrium in the foreign exchange market is the logical equivalent of equilibrium in the balance of payments.

In order to achieve autonomous equilibrium, the rate of exchange must be free to adjust to autonomous market forces.

An exchange rate pegged below its autonomous equilibrium level leads to balance of payments surplus, while an overvalued currency results in a deficit.

A pegged exchange rate is an equilibrium rate only in the sense that total supply of foreign exchange equals total demand. This concept of technical equilibrium is a mirror image of the accounting balance of payments where total credits equal total debits.

The gold standard provides for exchange rates which are fixed within a narrow range around mint parity. If supply or demand shifts fall within this range, they will be absorbed by changes in the exchange rate. Larger shifts lead to deficits or surpluses, which are settled automatically by gold exports or imports.

The gold-exchange standard provides for fixed exchange rates, which are maintained by official sales and purchases of foreign exchange.

Currencies such as the U.S. dollar which are held by many countries as international reserves are called key, or reserve, currencies. Under the gold-exchange standard, most official interventions in the foreign exchange market for the purpose of maintaining the fixed exchange rate consist of sales or purchases of key currencies.

A key currency country is exempt from the immediate pressure which a balance of payments deficit normally exerts on the foreign exchange market. But key currency balances held by foreigners may be viewed as a potential supply of that key currency.

Devaluation or revaluation is an alteration of the fixed exchange rate by official policy. Such alterations normally require prior consultations with major trading partners.

Controlled floating occurs when a currency is allowed to float in response to autonomous market forces, but when the government reserves the right to intervene whenever this is deemed necessary. Controlled floating should not be confused with a system of freely flexible exchange rates.

Exchange control differs from the other foreign exchange arrangements in that it disregards market forces altogether. Various degrees of exchange controls can be found throughout the world.

SUGGESTED FURTHER READINGS

A thorough treatment of foreign exchange operations may be found in Alan Holmes and Frances H. Schott, *The New York Foreign Exchange Market,* 2d ed. (New York, 1959). See also R. Z. Aliber (ed.), *The International Market for Foreign Exchange* (Praeger, Inc., New York, 1969). For an advanced discussion of the link between the foreign exchange market and the balance of payments, see Gottfried Haberler, "The Market for Foreign Exchange and the Stability of the Balance of Payments," *Kyklos,* vol. 3, 1949.

The United States Balance of Payments

In the two previous chapters we have studied the basic concepts of the balance of payments and the foreign exchange market. These concepts will now be put to the test as we turn to actual balance of payments data for the United States.

THE DOUBLE-ENTRY SYSTEM

Table 10-1 reproduces the official presentation of the U.S. balance of payments for the years 1960, 1965, and 1968–1972. The present chapter will be devoted almost entirely to studying this table. In order to see how the data are entered in this table, let us first consider the concept of double-entry bookkeeping. We recall from Chapter 8 that each transaction leads to one credit and one debit entry and that the accounting balance must, therefore, always balance. This principle was also used in Table 10-1. The sum of all (positive) credit entries is equal to the sum of all (negative) debit entries.[1]

---

[1]It may be a useful, if somewhat tedious, exercise to put this proposition to the test, using Table 10-1. Take any given year and add all those positive entries which are not subtotals. (Line 1, for example, is a subtotal and must therefore be omitted.) Then add all those negative entries which are not subtotals. You will find that the two sums are equal to each other. A small discrepancy may occur due to the fact that the entries in Table 10-1 are rounded off to millions of dollars.

Table 10-1 U.S. Balance of International Payments (in millions of U.S. dollars)

Line	(Credits +; Debits —)	1960	1965	1968	1969	1970	1971	1972
1	Merchandise Trade balance	4,906	4,942	612	621	2,164	-2,689	-6,816
2	Exports	19,650	26,438	33,576	36,417	41,963	42,770	48,840
3	Imports	-14,744	-21,496	-32,964	-35,796	-39,799	-45,459	-55,656
4	Military transactions, net	-2,752	-2,122	-3,143	-3,344	-3,374	-2,894	-3,541
5	Travel and transportation, net	-964	-1,318	-1,565	-1,784	-2,061	-2,432	-2,583
6	Investment income, net	2,841	5,294	6,220	5,975	6,259	7,995	7,901
7	U.S. direct investment abroad	2,945	5,162	6,519	7,340	7,920	9,455	10,293
8	Other U.S. investment abroad	994	1,930	2,714	3,199	3,506	3,443	3,499
9	Foreign investments in the United States	-1,098	-1,798	-3,013	-4,564	-5,167	-4,903	-5,891
10	Other services, net	77	301	302	442	574	748	819
11	Balance on goods and services	4,107	7,098	2,425	1,911	3,563	727	-4,219
12	Remittances, pensions, and other transfers	-628	-1,028	-1,202	-1,301	-1,474	-1,529	-1,557
13	Balance on goods, services, and remittances	3,479	6,070	1,223	610	2,089	-802	-5,776
14	U.S. government grants (excluding military)	-1,664	-1,808	-1,707	-1,644	-1,734	-2,045	-2,208
15	Balance on current account	1,815	4,263	-484	-1,035	356	-2,847	-7,983
16	U.S. government capital flows excluding non-scheduled repayments, net	-1,158	-1,819	-2,538	-2,106	-1,829	-2,117	-1,708
17	Nonscheduled repayments of U.S. government assets	54	221	269	-87	244	225	127

18	U.S. government nonliquid liabilities to other than foreign official reserve agencies	215	66	110	267	−433	−486	214
19	Long-term private capital flows, net	−2,100	−4,577	1,198	−50	−1,398	−4,149	107
20	U.S. direct investment abroad	−1,674	−3,468	−3,209	−3,254	−4,400	−4,765	−3,339
21	Foreign direct investment in the United States	141	57	319	832	1,030	−67	322
22	Foreign securities	−663	−759	−1,226	−1,494	−942	−909	−619
23	U.S. securities other than Treasury issues	282	−357	4,389	3,112	2,190	2,282	4,502
24	Other, reported by U.S. banks	−147	9	430	477	198	−814	−1,102
25	Other, reported by U.S. nonbanking concerns	−39	−59	495	277	526	124	343
26	*Balance on current account and long-term capital*	−1,174	−1,846	−1,444	−3,011	−3,059	−9,374	−9,243
27	Nonliquid short-term private capital flows, net	1,405	−154	230	−640	−482	−2,420	−1,634
28	Claims reported by U.S. banks	−951	−200	−44	−658	−1,023	−1,807	−1,530
29	Claims reported by U.S. nonbanking concerns	−363	−103	−485	−73	−361	−555	−243
30	Liabilities reported by U.S. nonbanking concerns	−91	149	759	91	902	−58	139
31	Allocations of special drawing rights (SDR)					867	717	710
32	Errors and omissions, net	−1,098	−476	−399	−2,470	−1,174	−10,927	−3,806
33	*Net liquidity balance*	−3,676	−2,477	−1,610	−6,122	−3,851	−22,002	−13,974
34	Liquid private capital flows, net	273	1,188	3,251	8,824	−5,988	−7,763	3,677
35	Liquid claims	−35	1,057	−558	162	252	−1,072	−1,139
36	Reported by U.S. banks	−44	525	−61	−209	−99	−566	−733
37	Reported by U.S. nonbanking concerns	9	532	−497	371	351	−506	−406

Table 10-1 (Continued)

Line	(Credits +; Debits −)	1960	1965	1968	1969	1970	1971	1972
38	Liquid liabilities	308	131	3,809	8,662	−6,240	−6,691	4,816
39	To foreign commercial banks	140	116	3,387	9,166	−6,508	'6,908	3,905
40	To international and regional organizations	335	−291	48	−63	181	682	102
41	To other foreigners	−167	306	375	−441	87	−465	809
42	Official reserve transactions balance	−3,403	−1,289	1,641	2,702	−9,839	−29,765	−10,297
	Financed by changes in:							
43	Nonliquid liabilities to foreign official reserve agencies reported by U.S. gov.		123	1,806	−162	535	341	189
44	Nonliquid liabilities to foreign official agencies reported by U.S. banks		−38	534	−836	−810	−539	400
45	Liquid liabilities to foreign official agencies	1,258	−18	−3,101	−517	7,637	27,615	9,676
46	U.S. official reserve assets, net	2,145	1,222	−880	−1,187	2,477	2,348	32
47	Gold	1,703	1,665	1,173	−967	787	866	547
48	SDR					−851	−249	−703
49	Convertible currencies		−349	−1,183	814	2,152	381	35
50	Gold tranche position in IMF	442	−94	−870	−1,034	389	1,350	153

Source: Survey of Current Business, U.S. Department of Commerce, June 1972, March 1973.

Let us briefly review the meaning of the double-entry system and how it applies to Table 10-1. In Chapter 8 we discussed the general rule that each transaction has one active and one passive entry. If the active entry is a credit, the balancing passive entry must be a debit, and *vice versa*. Consider, for example, line 5 in Table 10-1. Transactions involving travel and transportation resulted in an active debit entry of $2.06 billion in 1970. This reflects net U.S. imports of travel and transportation services. How were these net imports paid for? The balancing passive credit entry could, for example, be part of line 49, which indicates that the U.S. stock of convertible foreign currencies has declined by $2.15 billion in 1970. It is more likely, of course, that payment for the net imports of travel and transportation services took several different forms. The balancing passive credit entry may therefore be found as part of several items such as line 45, which reflects an increase in dollars held by foreign central banks in 1970, or even line 47, which reports the loss of U.S. gold in 1970.

THE CURRENT ACCOUNT

Now that we have put Table 10-1 into a more familiar perspective, let us go down the columns of this table, simply describing the nature of various entries. The current account, which is added up in line 15, consists basically of entries pertaining to transactions in goods and services and transfers. Military transactions, for example, include not only the provisions bought abroad for U.S. armed forces stationed abroad, but also U.S. military aid. Investment income is equivalent to a service export in the sense that U.S. corporations, by investing abroad, are making the services of their capital available to foreigners. These services, an active credit (lines 7 and 8), are not to be confused with the actual lending of capital, which is an active debit in the capital account (lines 20 and 22).

Private transfers contain items such as aid to foreigners provided by private U.S. charitable organizations or money sent by U.S. residents to relatives abroad.[2] Official transfers or government grants reflect U.S. foreign aid to the extent that it consists of outright unilateral gifts rather than loans, which are found under government lending in the capital account (line 16, for example).

---

[2]It will be recalled from Chapter 8 that unilateral transfers of the type described here lead to one active and one passive entry like all other transactions.

THE LONG-TERM CAPITAL ACCOUNT

This account contains the active entries of all long-term lending and borrowing transactions. The negative debit entries in this account reflect, primarily, increases in U.S. long-term lending to foreigners. They may, however, also reflect decreases in U.S. borrowing from foreigners. In line 18, for example, we find a credit entry for 1969 and a debit entry for 1970. This means that nonliquid government liabilities to private foreigners have increased in 1969 but decreased in 1970. During 1969, in other words, the United States has increased its borrowing in this category while in 1970 this borrowing has declined.

Private long-term capital flows are detailed by the types of such flows. Direct investment, for example, concerns the direct purchase of foreign plant and equipment as opposed to the purchase of foreign stocks and bonds. The establishment of a subsidiary abroad by a U.S. corporation would be included under U.S. direct investment abroad in line 20. A certain pattern emerges when we compare U.S. investment abroad (lines 20 and 23) with foreign investment in the United States (lines 21 and 23). While U.S. residents prefer direct investment abroad, foreigners invest more heavily in U.S. stocks and bonds than directly in U.S. plant and equipment.

THE SHORT-TERM CAPITAL ACCOUNT

The active entries of all short-term lending and borrowing transactions make up the short-term capital account. Since it is difficult, however, to determine without ambiguity what is and what is not an active short-term capital entry, we are confronted with several alternative ways of stating this active short-term capital account. In Table 10-1 we find short-term capital entries in three different places. Private short-term capital entries are reported in lines 27 and 34. Official short-term capital entries are shown in lines 43 to 45. This distribution reflects the judgment that official short-term capital entries are definitely passive entries. In fact, the passive official capital category also contains U.S. long-term liabilities to foreign official agencies. We can therefore safely exclude all official short-term capital flows from the active short-term capital account.

This leaves us with private short-term capital entries (lines 27 and 34). It is with regard to these two lines that we have alternatives. We may consider only the so-called "nonliquid" short-term private capital flows of line 27 as active entries and as such eligible for the active short-term capital account. Or, we may accept all private capital entries as active components of the short-term capital account. Let us, for the time being, adopt this second alternative but keep the first alternative in mind for later discussion.

The short-term capital account, then, consists of all private short-term lending and borrowing (lines 27 and 34).[3] Increases in U.S. liabilities reflect borrowing and are entered as active credits. Once more it should be noted that debit entries can be associated with U.S. borrowing if a *decline* in borrowing has taken place. United States liabilities to foreign commercial banks, for example, showed a large increase in 1969 and a decline in 1970 (line 39). This reflects the fact that in 1969 U.S. residents borrowed heavily from foreign banks, while in 1970 they paid back a substantial part of the borrowed funds.

ERRORS AND OMISSIONS

This item (line 30) is an active balancing entry estimating those active entries which for some reason have not been reported as such but for which the corresponding passive entries show up in the official settlements account. The conceptual discussion of this item may be recalled from Chapter 8.

ALLOCATION OF SPECIAL DRAWING RIGHTS (SDRs)

Special drawing rights are a newly created form of international reserves. Beginning in 1970 countries have received their allocations of these reserve assets. Line 31 simply represents an active counter-entry to line 48, which shows the increase in the U.S. stock of SDRs. This procedure is analogous to the way in which the unilateral transfers in the current account are handled.[4]

---

[3]Note that both lines are subtotals. Line 27 is the sum of lines 28 through 30, and line 34 is the sum of lines 36, 37, and 39 through 41.

[4]Lines 31 and 48 do not have to show equal amounts of SDRs. Line 31 reports original allocations, whereas line 48 shows by how much the stock of SDRs has increased during the current year. If some of the originally allocated SDRs are spent during the current year, line 31 will show a larger figure than line 48. The difference could be balanced by an active merchandise import, for example. SDRs will be discussed in greater detail in Chapter 15.

THE OFFICIAL SETTLEMENTS ACCOUNT

Here we finally come to the collection of all passive entries. The sum of the official settlements account, therefore, must be equal to the sum of all previously discussed active entries.[5] The official settlements account consists essentially of entries pertaining to U.S. liabilities to foreign official agencies and official U.S. reserve assets.

In terms of our conceptual framework developed in Chapter 8, we recognize "domestic balances due official foreigners" in lines 43 to 45 and "foreign balances" in line 46.[6] Using now our definitions for balance of payments deficit or surplus, we may state with regard to Table 10-1: In 1972 active credits exceeded active debits by $10.3 billion. This measures the U.S. balance of payments deficit for that year. Alternatively, we may find this deficit in the excess of passive credits over passive debits.

Let us hasten to say that the discussion so far was primarily designed to reconcile the actual data of Table 10-1 with our conceptual framework developed in the two previous chapters. The resulting measurement of the actual U.S. balance of payments deficit is only one of several possible measures, as we shall see below.

INTERDEPENDENT ENTRIES

Before we take up the question of deficit or surplus in detail, let us briefly consider the U.S. balance of payments in its entirety as opposed to the above item-by-item discussion. Although each item reflects a separate category of entries, certain relationships exist between categories, of which most are very subtle but some are quite obvious. Such interrelationships are occasionally overlooked when a country attempts to correct a balance of payments deficit by directly changing one particular item.

For example, it has been argued that foreign aid (line 14) should be reduced in order to help reduce the U.S. deficit. At first sight a reduction of the active debit in line 14, along with the reduction in whatever

---

[5]Lines 43 through 46 are the sum of the official settlements account. Compare this with line 42, which is the sum of all active entries. Except for their signs, these sums must be equal if the accounting balance is to be zero.

[6]Line 46 is, of course, a subtotal. Its components are gold, SDRs, and convertible currencies, all reserve assets as we have already seen. The gold tranche position with the IMF is an automatic drawing right on the International Monetary Fund, which amounts to a reserve asset. (More about this gold tranche and the IMF in Chapter 15.)

constitutes the corresponding passive credit, would indeed reduce the U.S. deficit. But most U.S. foreign aid is tied aid, in the sense that aid funds are given with the provision that they be spent on U.S. goods and services. A reduction in aid would therefore also reduce U.S. exports (line 2). A cut in foreign aid may, therefore, have no net effect on the U.S. balance of payments. Even if foreign aid were not tied, a reduction in aid would probably lead to some decline in exports. On the other hand, if no foreign aid would have been available, foreigners might have imported some of those U.S. goods which were made available to them through U.S. aid. In this case, a reduction of aid might have improved the U.S. balance of payments.

Another example of similar nature concerns U.S. lending to foreigners. Beginning in the mid-1960s, first by voluntary and then by mandatory guidelines, the U.S. government sought to reduce lending to foreigners (lines 20 and 22) in order to improve the U.S. balance of payments position. Again, lines 20 and 22 are large debits, and their reduction would indeed lead to a smaller deficit. But we cannot overlook investment income (lines 7 and 8) in this connection. If the guidelines were to reduce U.S. investment abroad, a decline in the earnings from these investments seems a likely consequence sooner or later. Arguing along these lines, critics have called the guidelines a case of killing the goose which lays the golden egg. Still another point to be raised in this connection involves U.S. imports (line 3). Some of the products manufactured by U.S. subsidiaries abroad are sold in the U.S. domestic market. Investing abroad (a debit) generates not only investment income (a credit) but also imports (a debit). The exact net effect on the U.S. balance of payments is therefore difficult to determine.

Yet another case of selective control involves restrictions on the amount of money tourists are allowed to take out of the country. Such restrictions exist in many countries. The U.S. government has contemplated restrictions of this nature at one time a number of years ago. The aim is to reduce the debit entry on travel (line 5). Tourists would be asked to declare their traveling funds when leaving the country, with the understanding that more than a certain limit is not allowed. Let us assume that the total amount of *declared* travel funds leaving the country is actually reduced in this way. The active debit in line 5 will therefore decline. But let us now also assume that the limit is very low and that many tourists actually take more money than they declare to the officials. As the tourists now spend both declared and undeclared funds abroad, these funds may be assumed to find their way into the holdings of foreign central banks.[7] The active debit for travel will now be smaller than the passive credit "liquid liabilities to foreign official agencies" by the amount of undeclared funds. As we know, the Department of Commerce will correct this imbalance by adding the difference to errors and omissions, as an active debit entry. Thus a reduction of debits in line 5 has led to an addition to debits in line 32.

MEASUREMENTS OF SURPLUSES OR DEFICITS

Having discussed most of the items listed in the U.S. balance of payments and some of their interrelationships, we are now ready for the question of deficits and surpluses. If we recall the concept of the zero accounting balance and the way in which it applies to Table 10-1, we can arrive at a deficit or surplus by simply drawing a horizontal line through Table 10-1. The particular location of this line determines what kind of balance of payments measurement we have chosen. All entries above the line are then defined as active entries, which are settled or financed by all (passive) entries below the line. It is, of course, possible to place this line in some random fashion and arrive at a measurement which is meaningless. On the other hand, there is no single location of this line which is agreed upon as the single most useful measurement. This is the reason why we have different measurements of balance of payments surpluses or deficits. In the following we will discuss three such measurements, their derivation and their meaning.

THE OFFICIAL RESERVE TRANSACTIONS BALANCE

To arrive at our first measurement, let us draw a line between lines 42 and 43 in Table 10-1. The result is the *official reserve transactions balance*. This balance fits well into our conceptual framework of Chapters 8 and 9, since all entries below this line are clearly passive settlements entries. Table 10-2, using the figures of Table 10-1, summarize the official reserve transactions balance for the year 1972. The line under errors and

---

[7]This occurs, for example, if U.S. tourists buy local foreign currencies with their dollars. Foreign central banks may buy these dollars in order to support the price of the dollar in the foreign exchange market.

Table 10-2   U.S. Official Reserve Transactions Balance, 1972 (in millions of dollars)

Current account (lines 1, 4–6, 10, 12, 14)	−7,983
Long-term capital account (lines 16–19)	−1,260
Short-term capital account (lines 27, 34)	2,043
Allocations of SDRs (line 31)	710
Errors and omissions (line 32)	−3,806
Official reserve transactions balance (line 42)	−10,297
Financed by:	
Official settlements account (lines 43–46)	10,297
Accounting balance	0

Source: Table 10-1.

omissions in Table 10-2 divides all entries into active (above the line) and passive (below the line).

The official reserve transactions balance is designed to reflect *actual* foreign exchange market pressure on the dollar as a result of transactions during the year in question between the United States and other countries. As such, this balance provides a good illustration of our conceptual link between the foreign exchange market and the balance of payments. All entries below the line are directly relevant to official buying or selling of dollars. In 1971, for example, foreign official agencies increased their holdings of U.S. dollars by $27.4 billion (lines 43 to 45, Table 10-1). Most of these dollars were bought by foreign central banks in the foreign exchange market in order to support the price of the dollar in terms of their own currencies. Another $2.3 billion in official reserves (line 46) was used by the U.S. authorities themselves to buy dollars in the foreign exchange market.[8]

THE NET LIQUIDITY BALANCE

If we draw the line across Table 10-1 between lines 33 and 34, we arrive at an alternate measure, the so-called *net liquidity balance*. This balance is intended to serve as a broad indicator of *potential* pressure on the U.S.

---

[8]One could argue that the dollar purchases by foreign central banks do not represent direct pressure on the United States. They do, however, represent pressure on the dollar since without these purchases the dollar would have declined in the foreign exchange market.

dollar in the foreign exchange market. Let us consider the reasoning behind this concept.

The net liquidity balance dates back to about 1955, when U.S. officials began to wonder how accurately the official reserve transactions balance reflected the true international position of the United States.[9] Their main concern was with the rising volume of liquid liabilities to *private* foreigners, especially to foreign commercial banks (line 39). The practice among foreigners of accepting dollars in payment for their sales to the United States was becoming more and more widespread. Many foreign recipients of such dollar payments, furthermore, did not sell these dollars in the foreign exchange market, but kept them on deposit in their commercial banks. They had good reasons for doing this, since the U.S. dollar as a key currency can be used in practically all international transactions.

How did this development affect the U.S. balance of payments? Normally, as a foreigner receives dollars for an export sale to the United States, he sells the dollars in the foreign exchange market for his domestic currency. These dollars then are likely to end up in his domestic central bank.[10] In this case, the export sale to the United States will result in the following two entries in the U.S. balance of payments: The active debit entry is an import (line 3), and the passive credit entry is an increase in liquid liabilities to foreign official agencies (line 45). As expected, this transaction contributes to a U.S. deficit under both the official reserve transactions balance and the net liquidity balance definitions.

But now consider an alternate way of settling this transaction. Suppose now the foreign exporter deposits his dollar receipts in his commercial bank rather than selling them in the foreign exchange market. The active debit entry will remain the same, i.e., U.S. imports (line 3). But the balancing credit entry must now be made in line 39 as an increase in liquid liabilities to (private) foreign commercial banks. From the point of view of the official reserve transactions balance, both of these entries are above the line. They have, therefore, no effect on the U.S. balance of

[9]The liquidity balance concept was revised to its present (1973) form in 1971. Before that time, the liquidity balance had somewhat different meaning, since most U.S. short-term claims were kept above the line, while short-term liabilities were entered below the line. This asymmetric treatment was corrected in 1971.

[10]The sale of dollars in the foreign exchange market will tend to depress the price of dollars in terms of the foreign currency in question. The foreign central bank, under a system of pegged exchange rates, will buy these dollars in order to prevent a decline in the price of the dollar. Such dollar purchases may also occur under controlled floating. (See Chapter 9.)

payments under this definition. In other words, a complete import transaction has been duly recorded, but the official reserve transactions balance show no deficit.

It was therefore suggested that liquid liabilities to foreign commercial banks (line 39), along with those other parts of the short-term capital account which are essentially passive settlement entries, should be moved below this line. The result was the net liquidity balance. Which parts of the short-term capital account are active and which are passive is, obviously, a somewhat arbitrary decision.[11] Conceptually, it is easy to understand that short-term capital entries which are settlement or financing entries should be placed below the line. In practice, however, such distinctions are not easily drawn.

That part of the short-term capital account which was left above the line was labeled "nonliquid" in Table 10-1 (line 27), while the part placed below the line was named "liquid." If a phrase such as "nonliquid short-term private capital flows" (line 27) appears as a contradiction in terms, we can substitute "active" for "nonliquid" and "passive" for "liquid." In this way we can reconcile the intent of the net liquidity balance with our conceptual framework which requires that all passive entries be made below the line.

In the light of the discussion above, it may be useful to state once

[11]For the conceptual background of this problem, see Chapter 8.

Table 10-3   U.S. Net Liquidity Balance, 1972 (in millions of dollars)

Current account (lines 1, 4–6, 10, 12, 14)	−7,983
Long-term capital account (lines 16–19)	−1,260
Nonliquid private short-term capital (line 27)	−1,634
Allocations of SDRs (line 31)	710
Errors and omissions (line 32)	−3,807
Net liquidity balance (line 33)	−13,974
Financed by:	
Liquid private short-term capital (line 34)	3,677
Official settlements account (lines 43–46)	10,297
	13,974
Accounting balance	0

Source: Table 10-1.

more the difference between the official reserve transactions balance and the net liquidity balance: The official reserve transactions balance is in deficit if *actual* pressure on the dollar has been absorbed through dollar purchases by foreign central banks or U.S. authorities, or both. The net liquidity balance considers *potential* pressure in addition to *actual* pressure. It is possible, for example, that no actual pressure exists—that neither foreign nor U.S. authorities have bought (or sold) dollars, and the official reserve transactions balance is in equilibrium. But if there have been net increases in private foreign holdings of liquid dollars, the net liquidity balance will be in deficit. These private dollars held abroad are considered a potential supply of dollars in the foreign exchange market by the net liquidity concept.

THE BALANCE ON CURRENT ACCOUNT AND LONG-TERM CAPITAL

Table 10-4, again using the data from Table 10-1, develops the third and final major balance of payments measure, the *balance on current account and long-term capital,* also called the *basic balance.* This measure is based on the belief that the short-term capital account contains so many temporary and volatile items that it should be placed altogether below the line. Since these short-term items, it is argued, do not really affect a country's basic or long-term economic position, they are better disregarded when calculating the balance of payments. The basic balance,

Table 10-4   U.S. Basic Balance, 1972 (in millions of dollars

Current account (lines 1, 4–6, 10, 12, 14)	−7,983
Long-term capital account (lines 16–19)	−1,260
Basic balance (line 26)	−9,243
Financed by:	
Short-term capital account (lines 27, 34)	2,043
Allocations of SDRs (line 31)	710
Errors and omissions (line 32)	−3,807
Official settlements account (lines 43–46)	10,297
	9,243
Accounting balance	0

Source: Table 10-1.

therefore, considers only current account and long-term capital account entries as active.

Admittedly, the basic balance does not attempt to link the balance of payments to the foreign exchange market. Rather, it is intended as an indicator of long-term trends in a nation's international position. As such, it is not as relevant to questions of immediate concern as the two other measures, and its use is less frequent.

PROPER USE OF DIFFERENT BALANCES

By drawing the line across Table 10-1 in three different places, we have derived three different balance of payments definitions. By now it is obvious that it makes little sense to talk about the U.S. balance of payments in terms of a single figure without at least specifying which one of the measures is being used.

In 1969, for example, the United States had a deficit of $6.1 billion in the net liquidity balance and a surplus of $2.7 billion in the official reserve transactions balance. A look at Table 10-1 explains that the difference was largely due to a very substantial increase in U.S. liquid liabilities to foreign commercial banks (line 39). These liabilities reflected potential downward pressure on the U.S. dollar. Actual pressure, on the other hand, was in the opposite direction, as we can see from the official settlements account, which shows a decrease in U.S. liabilities to official foreigners and an increase in U.S. reserve assets. An adequate description, therefore, of the state of the U.S. balance of payments should include not only both measures but also an explanation of the relationship between the two concepts.

THE U.S. BALANCE OF PAYMENTS PROBLEM

Regardless of what definition is used, the U.S. balance of payments has been generally in deficit for about twenty years now. This trend has been described as the U.S. balance of payments problem or the dollar problem. In order to discuss it, let us turn to a set of data which is different from but related to the balance of payments data used so far. Table 10-5 describes the international monetary position of the United States over the last decade. While the balance of payments uses flow data, which measure

changes during each year, Table 10-5 consists of stock data, which show
the total U.S. stock of certain assets and liabilities at the end of each
year.[12] Table 10-5 in a sense keeps the cumulative score of annual changes
reported by the balance of payments in Table 10-1. For reasons of clarity,
only three items were chosen to represent the U.S. international monetary position. This is possible because these three items correspond
to the major items measuring the U.S. balance of payments deficit
under both the net liquidity and the official reserve transactions balance.[13]

Table 10-5 shows that as a result of the deficit (according to the net
liquidity definition) the stock of U.S. reserve assets has declined by $7.2
billion during the twelve years in question. Since the stock of reserve
assets consists largely of gold, this corresponds approximately to the loss
of U.S. gold. The remaining part of the deficit was financed by an increase
in liabilities to foreigners of $57.8 billion.[14]

LIABILITIES TO OFFICIAL VERSUS PRIVATE FOREIGNERS

Let us take a closer look at the liabilities to foreigners in the last two lines
of Table 10-5. We recall from our previous discussion, particularly in

[12]Take official reserve assets, for example: Table 10-1 shows a decrease in these assets for 1970 of
$2.5 billion. This figure can also be obtained from Table 10-5 by subtracting the stock figure of official
reserve assets at the end of 1970 ($14.5 billion) from the stock at the end of 1969 ($17.0 billion). The other
two items in Table 10-5 are related to Table 10-1 in similar fashion. Liquid liabilities to private foreigners
are thus related to line 38 in Table 10-1, and liabilities to foreign official agencies are related to lines 43–45
in Table 10-1.
[13]A look at Table 10-1 shows that liquid claims (line 35) are disregarded in Table 10-5. These claims
are relatively small and do not affect our discussion significantly.
[14]$(21.4 + 57.9) - (9.1 + 12.4) = 57.8$.

Table 10-5   U.S. International Monetary Position 1960–1972 (in billions of U.S. dollars)

	1960	1965	1966	1967	1968	1969	1970	1971	1972
Official reserve assets	19.4	15.4	14.9	14.8	15.7	17.0	14.5	12.2	12.2
Liquid liabilities to private foreigners	9.1	12.9	15.1	16.4	20.1	28.9	22.6	16.6	21.4
Liabilities to foreign official agencies	12.4	16.2	14.7	16.7	13.5	17.0	24.4	47.6	57.9

Source: *Survey of Current Business*, U.S. Department of Commerce, October 1968–1972, March 1973.

Chapter 9, that liquid liabilities to foreign official agencies represent dollars which have been bought by foreign central banks in the foreign exchange market in order to prevent the price of the dollar in terms of their own currencies from falling. Before 1971, under the gold-exchange standard, such dollar purchases were made under the then existing arrangements to peg exchange rates. Thereafter, as many currencies were subject to controlled floating, these dollar purchases reflected mainly European and Japanese reservations against letting their currencies float too far upwards against the dollar.

To the extent that rather than holding liquid dollars, foreign central banks, acquired, say, U.S. government bonds, they also held nonliquid claims on the United States. But the nature of all such officially held claims on the United States, liquid and nonliquid, is similar in the sense that they are readily marketable.[15]

Now let us compare lines 1 and 3 of Table 10-5. Using foreign exchange market terminology, we may view line 3 as a measure of foreign governments' ability to drive the price of the dollar down by selling their dollar holdings. Line 1, on the other hand, may be viewed as the U.S. government's ability to absorb this downward pressure by buying dollars in exchange for its official reserves, i.e., gold, foreign exchange, etc.[16] Table 10-5 shows that until 1969 U.S. reserve assets were roughly sufficient to cover U.S. liabilities to foreign official agencies. From this point of view, the U.S. balance of payments has presented a problem only since 1970.

So far, of course, we have disregarded liquid liabilities to *private* foreigners. The fact that private foreigners have freely chosen to hold (rather than to sell) these dollars does not altogether justify this disregard. Private foreigners may at any time sell their dollars in the foreign exchange market, where they could be acquired by foreign official agencies. On the other hand, private foreigners may have good reasons for maintaining dollar balances. Such balances are convenient for anyone with international business because the dollar, as a key currency, is widely accepted throughout the world. In short, whether or not these balances affect the U.S. international financial position depends on how

---

[15]Under the gold-exchange standard before August 1971, all such claims could be presented to the U.S. Treasury in exchange for U.S. gold.

[16]Before 1971 this comparison had a somewhat different meaning. Under the gold-exchange standard, line 3 in Table 10-5 represented potential foreign claims on the U.S. gold stock, while line 1 essentially measured the U.S. gold stock.

likely they are judged to be sold in the foreign exchange market. To the extent that this likelihood is judged high, a problem has existed since 1960 and before, because the stock of U.S. reserve assets has been quite inadequate to cover liabilities to both private and official foreigners. This judgment, of course, is crucial to the distinction between the net liquidity and the official reserve transactions balance.

Until the end of 1969, private foreigners continued to accumulate ever larger dollar balances, thus giving credence to balance of payments optimists who supported the official reserve transactions definition. The liquidity definition appeared pessimistic because the evidence pointed toward a seemingly unlimited capacity of private foreigners to absorb dollar balances. The U.S. balance of payments for 1968 and 1969, showing surpluses on the official reserve transactions balance and deficits on the net liquidity balance, highlights these opposing views.

The turning point came in 1970. Table 10-5 shows how liabilities to foreign official agencies increased sharply during this year, while liquid liabilities to private foreigners declined by a comparable magnitude. What had happened was precisely what advocates of the liquidity balance had feared. Private foreigners sold part of their dollar balances in the foreign exchange market, and foreign official agencies were obliged to buy them in support of the dollar. In 1971 this trend continued; in addition to previously accumulated private dollars foreign official agencies acquired large sums of dollars which were reaching the market from current sources. The increase in liabilities to foreign official agencies, therefore, far exceeded the decline in liabilities to private foreigners. By 1971 it was quite clear that the U.S. position was problematic. It therefore came as no surprise to many observers when in August 1971 President Nixon took the historic step of abolishing the official link between gold and the U.S. dollar, thereby effectively eliminating the gold-exchange standard.

THE DOLLAR AND THE U.S. DEFICIT

In our discussion of the foreign exchange market in the previous chapter, we have concluded that a key currency country is in a sense exempted from the pressures the balance of payments may exert on its currency. The U.S. dollar is a good example of this. According to Table 10-5, the cumulative U.S. deficit (liquidity definition) for 1960–1971 was $49.9 billion.[17] Of these $49.9 billion, $7.5 billion did not exert pressure on the dollar because they were held in private balances abroad. The remaining $42.4 billion became excess demand for foreign exchange at the dollar rate which was essentially fixed during the period in question. But $35.2 billion of this $42.4 billion excess demand was absorbed by foreign central banks. This leaves the United States with a reserve loss due to supporting its own currency of only $7.2 billion, or one-seventh of its cumulative deficit. The dollar, consequently, has resisted devaluation far longer (i.e., until December 1971) than one would have expected by simply looking at the large deficits of the past decade.

INTERNATIONAL INDEBTEDNESS

The foregoing discussion has led us to the conclusion that there certainly has been a problem with the U.S. balance of payments during 1970–1972 and possibly also during earlier years. Let us conclude this chapter by placing the problem in its proper perspective lest we come away from the discussion of the balance of payments thinking of the United States as a debt-ridden or even poor country.

Table 10-6 presents the U.S. balance of international indebtedness. Like Table 10-5, it contains year-end stock figures. But unlike Table 10-5, which shows *selected* assets and liabilities, it includes *all* U.S. assets and liabilities. In short, it shows the overall international indebtedness position of the United States.

Table 10-6 shows the United States as a net international creditor of $57.8 billion in 1971. A closer examination reveals that this net creditor position is due to the fact that U.S. net long-term claims on foreigners far exceed U.S. net liquid liabilities to foreigners.

Exactly what perspective does this put on the U.S. balance of payments? We must recall the distinction between wealth and solvency. The balance of payments measures not wealth but solvency. It is possible for a firm with substantial net long-term assets to run into financial problems for lack of cash on hand.

---

[17]Calculated as follows: Decline in official reserve assets ($7.2 billion) plus increase in liabilities to foreign official agencies (35.2 billion) plus increase in liquid liabilities to private foreigners ($7.5 billion) equals $49.9 billion.

Table 10-6   U.S. Balance of International Indebtedness (in billions of U.S. dollars)

	1960	1965	1970	1971
U.S. claims on foreigners				
Direct investments	31.9	49.5	78.1	86.0
Foreign stocks and bonds	9.6	15.2	19.6	21.7
Long-term loans	3.1	6.4	7.0	7.9
Private short-term claims	4.8	10.1	15.2	18.6
Long-term government credits	14.0	20.2	29.7	31.8
Government foreign currencies and other short-term assets	2.9	3.2	2.5	2.4
Official reserve assets	19.4	15.4	14.5	12.2
Total	85.7	120.3	166.6	180.6
Foreign claims on the United States				
U.S. stocks and bonds	9.9	15.5	25.6	29.9
Direct investments	6.9	8.8	13.2	13.7
Other long-term claims	2.3	3.9	7.9	7.6
Short-term commercial credits	0.6	1.0	3.7	3.8
Liquid claims of private foreigners	9.1	12.9	22.6	16.6
Claims of foreign official agencies	11.9	16.7	24.4	51.2
Total	40.7	58.8	97.4	122.8
U.S. net creditor position	45.0	61.5	69.2	57.8

Source: *Survey of Current Business*, U.S. Department of Commerce, October 1971 and 1972.

SUMMARY

The actual presentation of the U.S. balance of payments reflects the use of the double-entry method.

The current account consists of all active entries pertaining to transactions in goods, services, and unilateral transfers.

The long-term capital account contains all active entries resulting from long-term borrowing and lending transactions. Exceptions are long-term liabilities to foreign official agencies, which are entered in the official settlements account.

The short-term capital account contains all active entries pertaining to private short-term borrowing and lending transactions. Two different views of what constitutes an active or "nonliquid" short-term capital entry lead to two different balance of payments definitions.

The official settlements account consists of passive entries. It is divided into liabilities to foreign official agencies and U.S. official reserve assets.

The official reserve transactions balance is the sum of the current account, the long-term capital account, both the "nonliquid" and the "liquid" part of the short-term capital account, errors and omissions, and allocations of SDRs. If this sum is a net credit (debit), the official reserve transactions balance is in surplus (deficit).

The net liquidity balance is the sum of the current account, the long-term capital account, the "nonliquid" part of the short-term capital account, errors and omissions, and allocations of SDRs. If this sum is a net credit (debit), the net liquidity balance is in surplus (deficit).

The basic balance, or the balance on current account and long-term capital, is the sum of the current and the long-term capital accounts. If this sum is a net credit (debit), the basic balance is in surplus (deficit). The basic balance is an instrument of long-term analysis and is not used as frequently as the other two measures.

The official reserve transactions balance is designed to reflect actual pressure on the dollar, while the net liquidity balance measures actual as well as potential pressure.

Many balance of payments items are interrelated in such a way that a change in one active entry may bring about a compensatory change in another active entry.

The United States has had a balance of payments problem in 1970–1972 in the sense that U.S. offical reserve assets did not cover U.S. liabilities to foreign official agencies. If U.S. liquid liabilities to private foreigners are added to those U.S. liabilities which should be covered by official reserve assets, a problem has existed much longer.

Whether or not net liquid liabilities to private foreigners should be covered by official reserve assets is a question of judgment. No definitive answer can be given. This is the basic reason for the coexistence between the net liquidity and the official reserve transactions balances.

The fact that the dollar is a key currency has largely exempted U.S. authorities from the market pressures on the dollar which we would normally associate with extensive balance of payments deficits. This exemption, however, has not been without limits, nor has it been permanent, as developments in the early 1970s have shown.

The balance of international indebtedness weighs the total stock of a country's international assets against the total stock of its international liabilities. This balance shows the United States in a large net creditor position.

SUGGESTED FURTHER READINGS

A useful item-by-item description of the U.S. balance of payments, as well as definitions, may be found in David T. Devlin, "The U. S. Balance of Payments: Revised Presentation," *Survey of Current Business*, U.S. Department of Commerce, vol. 51, no. 6, June 1971, p. 24.

The *Survey of Current Business* also presents commentaries on quarterly U.S. balance of payments developments at regular intervals. More detailed data, especially on long- and short-term capital flows, are carried in the monthly *Federal Reserve Bulletin* issued by the Board of Governors of the Federal Reserve System. For more advanced discussions of alternative balance of payments measurements, see Charles P. Kindleberger, "Measuring Equilibrium in the Balance of Payments," *Journal of Political Economy,* December 1969; Fritz Machlup, "Three Concepts of the Balance of Payments and the So-Called Dollar Shortage," *Economic Journal,* March 1950; and Walter Lederer, "The Balance on Foreign Transactions: Problems of Definition and Measurement," *Special Papers in International Economics,* Princeton, N.J., September, 1963.

Forward Exchange, Speculation, and Arbitrage

From our discussion of the balance of payments in the preceding chapters, the short-term capital account emerges as particularly interesting. We have seen that different views on the short-term capital account lead to different views on the balance of payments and our international position in general. It will therefore be helpful to study some of the principal factors which set short-term capital flows in motion. In the present chapter, we first develop certain necessary concepts and then apply them to a number of real-world situations.

THE FORWARD EXCHANGE MARKET

Let us begin with the example of a U.S. exporter who has shipped merchandise to a U.K. resident and expects to be paid for this merchandise shipment in three months from now. The payment is to be made in pounds sterling. The U.S. exporter is in a speculative position with regard to these sterling funds receivable: If the pound sterling should depreciate in terms of dollars during these three months, he will receive fewer dollars for his merchandise than if payment had been made immediately. If the pound sterling should appreciate, on the other hand, he will receive more dollars.

Merchandise exporters do not typically wish to be in speculative positions, which add an element of uncertainty to their business. The forward exchange market gives our exporter an opportunity to hedge against this uncertainty. He can sell his receivable sterling funds in the forward exchange market. This involves the following contract between our exporter (i.e., the seller of forward sterling) and the buyer of forward sterling: The seller agrees to deliver to the buyer a given amount of sterling in three months from now, and the buyer agrees in exchange to deliver to the seller a given amount of dollars in three months from now.[1] The terms of the exchange, i.e., how many dollars will exchange for how many pounds sterling, are expressed by the *forward rate of exchange.* Note that this rate is agreed upon *at present.* Our U.S. exporter, by entering into this forward contract, has eliminated that element of uncertainty from his exporting business which is caused by unforeseeable changes in the rate of exchange. He now knows exactly how many dollars he will receive in three months from now.[2]

Whom might we picture as the buyer of these forward sterling funds? Consider, for example, a U.S. importer who has been given three months to make payment in sterling for a merchandise shipment received from the United Kingdom. This importer is in just the opposite position of the exporter discussed above. He will need pounds sterling in three months from now. Should sterling appreciate (depreciate) in the meantime, he will have to pay more (less) dollars for his imports than at the present or "spot" rate of exchange. The importer, who is not interested in taking such a speculative position, will consequently wish to buy forward sterling.

We may conclude, in general, that anyone with foreign exchange receivable at some future date will sell forward exchange, while anyone with foreign exchange payable will buy forward exchange. Both buyers'

[1] The time period is, of course, subject to agreement between buyer and seller. Frequently used periods are 1 month, 3 months, and 6 months.
[2] Consider the following example. A U.S. exporter ships $1,000 worth of semiconductors to Britain. At the current spot rate of, say, $2.50 per pound sterling, this means £400. Payment in sterling is expected in three months. Assume now that the spot rate falls to $2.40 per pound sterling during these three months. In this case, the £400 will be worth only $960. Our exporter will have lost $40 due to depreciation of sterling. But suppose now that he has sold the £400 forward for dollars at the time of the merchandise shipment, when the forward rate was, say, $2.48 per pound. As the forward contract comes due, he receives $992 for his £400. His loss of $8 may be viewed as an insurance fee. He knows he will not lose more than $8 regardless of what happens to the spot rate during the three months in question.

and sellers' actions are motivated by their desire to avoid the exchange risk.

The forward rate $(\$/£)_f$ is determined by supply and demand in the forward exchange market. In Figure 11-1 a normal upward-sloping supply curve and a downward-sloping demand curve were drawn. This, of course, implies certain assumptions about the behavior of sellers and buyers. The quantity of forward sterling which sellers are willing to sell is thus shown as an increasing function of the forward rate. In other words, we are assuming that sellers' willingness to sell forward sterling increases as they receive more dollars per pound of forward sterling. The negative slope of the demand curve, on the other hand, means that buyers become less willing to buy forward sterling as its price in dollars rises.

SPOT VERSUS FORWARD RATES

A clear distinction must be made between the spot rate of exchange, which expresses the price of foreign exchange at present, and the forward

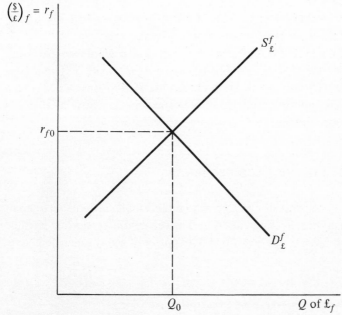

Figure 11-1

rate, which is defined as the price (agreed upon at present) at which foreign exchange will sell at a certain future date. Both rates are known at present, but the forward rate applies to a transaction which will take place in the future.

At this point, a question arises regarding the relationship between the spot and the forward rate. Why should the forward rate differ from the spot rate? Let us go back to our example used above. If we assume that the U.S. exporter wishes to sell exactly as much forward sterling as the U.S. importer wishes to buy, there is no reason for the forward rate to differ from the spot rate. To show this, we need only to think of the exporter and the importer as members of the same export-import firm. This firm would have equal amounts of sterling receivable and payable in three months. Its net position would not be risky, and there would be no need for hedging. In fact, there would be no need for a forward market. Consider, however, the possibility of sterling payable exceeding sterling receivable. The firm would have to buy forward sterling to cover its net position.

Let us go one step further and consider the situation from an aggregate point of view. Suppose all exporters and importers combined have a position reflecting net demand for forward sterling. This net or excess demand will tend to drive the price of forward sterling above the price of spot sterling. Excess supply of forward sterling, by similar reasoning, would drive the forward rate below the spot rate.

Although we may conclude that the spot and forward rate are likely to differ, the nature of this difference is not as easily explained as suggested here. This is due to the fact that the forward market, besides hedgers, contains another group of buyers and sellers, whose behavior is a great deal more difficult to assess—i.e., speculators.

SPECULATION AND FORWARD EXCHANGE

Let us define as a speculator anyone who intentionally accepts an open or uncovered position reflecting either sterling receivable or sterling payable at a future date.[3] We recall that the U.S. exporter of our discussion above,

---

[3]Note that we are concerned here with speculation in forward exchange only. It is, of course, also possible to speculate in the spot market. A speculator, for example, may buy spot exchange in the expectation that the spot rate will rise. However, this type of speculation does not concern us here.

for example, found himself at one point in such an uncovered position with sterling receivable. His position involved a risk (from sterling depreciation) as well as the chance of a gain (from sterling appreciation). His desire to cover this uncovered position led him to the forward market, where he sold forward sterling.

The speculator specializes in taking uncovered positions in the expectation of a gain. For example, a speculator who expects the future spot rate $(\$/\pounds)_s$ to be higher than the current forward rate $(\$/\pounds)_f$ will buy forward sterling. When this forward contract comes due, he expects to be able to sell these sterling funds at a higher price in the spot market.[4] It is necessary here to distinguish between the forward rate and the future spot rate. The forward rate, as we know, is the dollar price at which the speculator agrees *now* to buy sterling at a certain future date. The future spot rate is the spot rate which will exist at that future date. The forward rate is known now, the future spot rate is not.

We conclude that speculators will buy or sell forward exchange depending on their expectation regarding the future spot rate. If the future spot rate is expected to exceed the forward rate, speculators will buy forward exchange. If the reverse is expected, they will sell forward exchange.

Except for special circumstances, all speculators will not share the same expectations. It is therefore typical to find speculators on both sides of the forward market at the same time.

Consequently, the forward rate, as determined by supply and demand, is related not only to the hedgers' desire to avoid risks but also to the speculators' desire to take risks.

ARBITRAGE

So far we have discussed the forward market as reflecting the activities of hedgers and speculators. No particular reference to short-term capital flows has yet emerged. Let us now turn to this reference by considering a special type of hedger, the interest arbitrageur.

---

[4]Suppose the three-month forward rate $(\$/\pounds)_f$ is $2.40 per pound sterling. Suppose also that the speculator expects the spot rate $(\$/\pounds)_s$ to be $2.42 in three months from now. Let him now buy £1,000,000 forward at the price of $2,400,000. According to his expectation he will be able to get $2,420,000 for these £1,000,000 in the spot market three months from now. He expects a profit of $20,000.

An arbitrageur, in general, is one who buys at a lower price and sells at a higher price in a situation where both prices are known to him. In the spot market for foreign exchange, for example, sterling may be slightly cheaper in Beirut than it is in Hong Kong. Foreign exchange arbitrageurs will take advantage of this rate differential by buying sterling in Beirut and selling it in Hong Kong. This arbitrage activity will tend to raise the price of sterling in Beirut and lower it in Hong Kong until the two rates are equal. Note that arbitrage does not involve risk taking, because both his buying price and his selling price are known to the arbitrageur.

Interest arbitrage is based on the same priciple but involves interest rate differentials as well as spot and forward exchange rates. Assume, for example, that the interest rate in the United States (i_{US}) is lower than the interest rate in Great Britain (i_{UK}). If arbitrageurs would now borrow money in the United States at the low rate and lend it in the United Kingdom at the higher rate, they should make a profit. But this leaves out the following considerations: The dollars borrowed in the United States must be converted into sterling before they can be lent in the United Kingdom. Furthermore, the dollars borrowed in the United States will eventually have to be repaid with the sterling proceeds from the loan made in the United Kingdom. This means that sterling will have to be converted back into dollars at the time when both loans come due. Evidently, then, the arbitrageur's profit depends not only on the interest rate differential but also on the exchange rates.

Let us put this proposition into two simple formulas, assuming that arbitrageurs borrow in the United States in order to lend in the United Kingdom.

$$\$100 \ (1 + i_{US}) = R \tag{1}$$

Relation (1) states R as the amount of dollars which will have to be paid back in, say, three months in the United States. The amount borrowed is $100. If the rate of interest for three months is 2 percent, R will be equal to $102.

$$\$100 \ \frac{1}{r_s} \ (1 + i_{UK}) \ r_f = S \tag{2}$$

S in relation (2) expresses the amount of dollars which will be received back from the United Kingdom. Its components are as follows: The $100 borrowed in the United States are converted into sterling. If the spot rate is defined as $r_s = (\$/\pounds)_s$, this means dividing \$100 by r_s. Now we have \$100 worth of sterling which is to be lent in the United Kingdom. The amount of sterling receivable after three months will be the amount of sterling lent out, i.e., \$100 $1/r_s$, multiplied by $1 + i_{UK}$.

At this point the arbitrageur is in a speculative position with sterling receivable in three months. He is risking depreciation of sterling, and he will cover his position by selling forward sterling. This explains the presence of the forward rate r_f in relation (2).

From relations (1) and (2) we conclude that interest arbitrage depends not only on the interest rates but also on the spot and forward exchange rates. Rather than simply comparing i_{US} with i_{UK}, we must compare R with S in order to decide where to borrow and where to lend.

Let us assume, for the moment, that S is larger than R. This means that a profit can be made by borrowing dollars in the United States, converting them into sterling, lending the sterling in the United Kingdom, and selling it forward for dollars. The amount of dollars we end up with after this operation exceeds the amount of dollars we will have to pay back in the United States. Note that this profit is made without taking an exchange risk, i.e., without speculating. All four relevant rates are known at the outset of the operation.

$$R < S \tag{3}$$

$$(1 + i_{US}) < \frac{r_f}{r_s}(1 + i_{UK}) \tag{4}$$

Relations (3) and (4) simply describe the operation. Relation (4) results from substituting (1) and (2) into relation (3).

ARBITRAGE EQUILIBRIUM

Let us go one step further now and recall that arbitrage in general tends to eliminate those price differences which have originally brought the arbitrageurs into action. Will this also happen with interest arbitrage? Consider the activities resulting from our example above, where S is assumed to be larger than R.

1   Arbitrageurs borrow dollars in the United States. This will tend to put upward pressure on the rate of interest (i_{US}).

2 They buy spot sterling. This will tend to raise the price of spot sterling (r_s).

3 They lend sterling in the United Kingdom. This will tend to put downward pressure on the rate of interest (i_{UK}).

4 They sell forward sterling. This will tend to lower the price of forward sterling (r_f).

The effect of these changes on relation (4) is easy to see. The left-hand side (1 + i_{US}) increases because i_{US} rises. The right-hand side, r_f/r_s (1 + i_{UK}), decreases because r_f and i_{UK} fall while r_s rises. How long will these tendencies remain in effect? As long as arbitrageurs continue to borrow in the United States and lend in the United Kingdom. Not until R has become equal to S, or until the sides of relation (4) are equal, will this arbitrage activity cease.

$$\frac{r_f}{r_s} = \frac{1 + i_{US}}{1 + i_{UK}} \tag{5}$$

We conclude that interest arbitrage shows the same equalizing tendencies as arbitrage in general in the sense that it will equate R and S. Relation (5) expresses this equality or equilibrium in a form slightly altered from relation (4).

THE NET ARBITRAGE MARGIN

Relation (5) is a very important practical formula regarding the international flow of short-term capital. It may be referred to as the *net arbitrage margin*. It determines the relative attractiveness of a particular international financial center for investors of short-term capital. If, for example,

$$\frac{r_f}{r_s} > \frac{1 + i_{US}}{1 + i_{UK}} \tag{6}$$

London is the relatively attractive center for short-term investments. If, on the other hand,

$$\frac{r_f}{r_s} < \frac{1 + i_{US}}{1 + i_{UK}} \tag{7}$$

the net arbitrage margin is in favor of New York, and investors would place their funds in New York rather than in London.

Only if equality, i.e., relation (5), prevails, will the net arbitrage margin be neutral or zero. In this case, investors are indifferent between the two centers, and capital does not flow or flows in a random pattern.

SHORT-TERM CAPITAL FLOWS TODAY

It is not necessary to assume, as we have done so far, that money invested in one center must be borrowed in the other. Let us simply observe that there is a vast amount of short-term capital ready at any time to flow toward attractive financial centers. These funds are owned by investors in all parts of the world, such as U.S. corporations with temporarily uncommitted cash balances, British banking and investment houses, or oil shieks of the Middle East. What all these investors have in common is the continual search for the most attractive center to place their funds.[5] The effects on a balance of payments can under certain conditions be quite unsettling because of the short-term nature and the magnitudes of such flows.

In order to see the relationship between the net arbitrage margin and capital flows more clearly, let us use a simple diagram. In Figure 11-2 the interest differential is measured on the vertical axis, and the ratio of the exchange rates is measured along the horizontal axis. A 45-degree line drawn through this diagram describes all possible combinations of the four rates which result in a zero net arbitrage margin or which will, in other words, satisfy the equilibrium relation (5). Any point above the 45-degree line will then reflect a margin in favor of New York, as does relation (7). Any point below the line will favor London, as indicated in relation (6).

Figure 11-2 suggests a zero net arbitrage margin as the state of equilibrium, in the sense that any nonzero margin will cause capital to flow in such a way as to reestablish equilibrium. We have discussed this tendency when we derived the net arbitrage margin by moving from

[5]According to a recent U.S. Tariff Commision study, some $268 billion (!) in such funds were held at the end of 1971 by private institutions on the international scene. The "lion's share" of these funds was controlled by U.S.-based multinational companies and banks. *The Wall Street Journal,* Feb. 13, 1973.

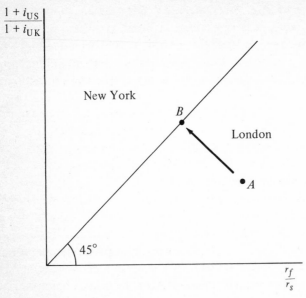

Figure 11-2

relation (4) to relation (5). The movement can be traced in Figure 11-2 by the arrow pointing from point A to point B.[6]

FLEXIBILITY OF INTEREST AND EXCHANGE RATES

Note that the equilibrating movement from point A to B in Figure 11-2 was based on the assumption that all four rates change. From a practical point of view, this is not likely to happen.

National interest rates, for example, are controlled by institutions which are in charge of monetary policy, such as the Federal Reserve System. In general, these institutions use the rate of interest as a tool to achieve objectives of domestic economic policy such as price stability and full employment. It is unlikely, therefore, that the rate of interest

[6]Recall that a margin in favor of London (at point A) induces the following changes: i_{US} goes up and i_{UK} goes down. This would be a movement to the north from point A. But in addition, r_s goes up and r_f goes down. This would be a move to the west from point A. The combined effect is therefore the arrow pointing northwest from A.

would be allowed to change in response to international capital flows if such a change were inconsistent with these policy objectives. It is possible, on the other hand, for the attraction (or repulsion) of international capital flows to become in itself a policy target. In this case, the rate of interest would be adjusted by policy in such a way as to achieve that net arbitrage margin which would generate the desired capital flow.

From a practical point of view, then, we may conclude that changes in interest rates are more likely to reflect economic policy than autonomous market forces. Whether or not they are equilibrating in the sense of Figure 11-2 depends on whether or not they are consistent with national objectives of monetary policy.

The spot exchange rate is subject to similar constraints. We know that under a system of fixed exchange rates the spot rate is pegged within narrow limits. In a situation of controlled floating it usually will be allowed to adjust to a nonzero net arbitrage margin only if the resulting change is consistent with broader policy objectives or as a matter of last resort. There are many instances in which the monetary authorities of a country have adjusted the rate of interest in order to relieve the spot exchange rate from pressure generated by short-term capital flows. This has occurred both under a system of fixed exchange rates and under controlled floating. In fact, as we shall see below, much of the contemporary relevance of this net arbitrage margin lies in the area of policies designed to maintain a given exchange rate.

This leaves the forward rate as the most flexible component of the net arbitrage margin. There are no international agreements with regard to pegging the forward rate. In general, therefore, we may expect the forward rate to carry out most of the adjustment called for by nonzero arbitrage margins. Yet even here the possibility of official intervention exists. Monetary authorities have, on occasion, bought or sold forward exchange for the specific purpose of affecting the forward rate and thereby the net arbitrage margin.

SOME APPLICATIONS

We are now ready to apply the framework developed above to a number of real-world situations. Let us begin with a relatively simple case involving the spot rate and the rate of interest.

In November 1967 the pound sterling was officially devalued by 15 percent. A few days later the Federal Reserve raised the U.S. interest rate from 4.0 to 4.5 percent. We can explain the link between these two policy measures with the help of Figure 11-3. Prior to the sterling devaluation the net arbitrage margin favored New York at point A.[7] The resulting large capital flows out of London were part of the reason for the sterling devaluation. The devaluation from \$2.80 to \$2.40 per pound was a decrease of the spot rate r_s as defined previously (i.e. \$/£). The effect of this decrease on the net arbitrage margin is shown in Figure 11-3 as the horizontal move from point A to point B. At point B the margin was now in favor of London. The U.S. authorities were, of course, aware of this shift and became concerned about its possible effect on the U.S. balance of payments. They therefore raised the U.S. interest rate as a precautionary measure in an attempt to move the net arbitrage margin closer to equilibrium. This is shown in Figure 11-3 by the vertical move from B toward C.

[7]This will be explained in the following example.

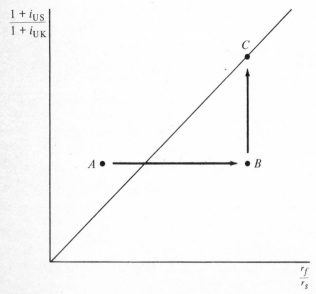

Figure 11-3

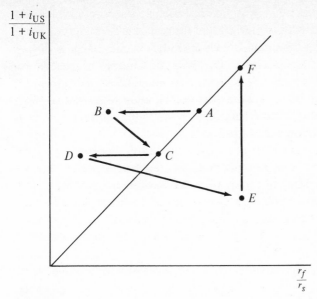

Figure 11-4

STERLING DEVALUATION

As our next application, let us use the net arbitrage margin to study some of the circumstances surrounding the 1967 devaluation of sterling. We start at some point before the devaluation with a net arbitrage margin at, or close to, equilibrium, that is, point A in Figure 11-4.[8] The U.K. overall balance of payments had shown persistently large deficits for several years. It was general knowledge that the Bank of England was running out of the reserves necessary to finance this deficit at the fixed exchange rate.

Speculators in increasing numbers began to expect that it would soon become necessary to devalue the pound sterling. They consequently expected the future spot rate to be lower than the forward rate and began to sell large amounts of forward sterling. These heavy forward sales put downward pressure on the forward rate and shifted the net arbitrage margin from point A in Figure 11-4 to point B.

---

[8]Our reason for placing point A on the equilibrium line is to point out that the persistent U.K. balance of payments deficit was due to causes other than short-term capital flows.

The Bank of England now found itself in an awkward situation where speculative forward sales of sterling and the resulting deterioration of the net arbitrage margin compounded the already existing balance of payments pressure on the spot rate. The Bank of England reacted in two ways. It raised the U.K. interest rate, and it bought forward sterling. In Figure 11-4 this policy is shown as the combination of a vertical move downward from point B and a horizontal move to the right from point B. The result is the move from B to C.

Note that as far as short-term capital flows are concerned, points C and A are equivalent since both represent equilibrium points. But the Bank of England had to pay a price for reestablishing this equilibrium. At point C the U.K. rate of interest was higher than it had been at A. It is not clear to what extent this increase was consistent with the domestic goals of U.K. economic policy at that time. Apart from this important consideration, it must be observed realistically that interest rates cannot rise indefinitely. For example, given a bank rate of 5.0 percent at point A, the Bank of England had a margin of only two or possibly three percentage points left for controlling the net arbitrage margin via the interest rate.[9] If the bank rate was 6.5 percent at point C, the possibilities for this type of policy were very nearly exhausted.

The second difference between points A and C concerns the purchases of forward sterling (i.e., sales of forward dollars) by the Bank of England. Although these purchases tended to move the arbitrage margin back toward equilibrium, they involved future obligations of the Bank of England to deliver dollars in quantities possibly exceeding its present stock of dollar reserves. This observation was not lost on the speculators.

At point C in Figure 11-4 speculative behavior became crucial once more.[10] In order to visualize the speculators' disposition at point C, let us recall what was said about their disposition at point A: Their expectation that sterling would have to be devalued was based on the large U.K. balance of payments deficit. This deficit still existed at point B. By moving the arbitrage margin from point B to C, the Bank of England had corrected only that additional component of the overall deficit, which was due to short-term capital flows caused by the move from A to B. The

---

[9] The particular interest rate used by the Bank of England for policy purposes is called the bank rate.

[10] On several previous occasions the sequence of events ended at point C. Such occasions were sterling crises in which the Bank of England was able to relieve speculative pressure by bank rate policy and forward purchases of sterling.

policy move from *B* to *C* was a temporarily successful defense of sterling against speculative attack, but it had done little to correct the deficit which had already existed at point *A*.[11] From the speculators' point of view, therefore, the situation at point *C* was not really different from the original situation at point *A*. On the contrary, the Bank of England had now used up some of the tools in its policy arsenal; it had undertaken forward dollar obligations and raised the interest rate within close reach of its realistic maximum.

The speculators in this particular case had lost none of their original determination. Their continued forward sales of sterling moved the net arbitrage margin once more against London from point *C* to *D* in Figure 11-4. At this point the British authorities saw themselves forced to give up further defense of the spot rate and officially devalued sterling. Along with this devaluation, the bank rate was once more raised to the unprecedented level of 8 percent. These measures are shown in Figure 11-4 by the move from point *D* to point *E*. The net arbitrage margin was now heavily in favor of London, and the remaining move toward point *F* reflects the reaction of the U.S. Federal Reserve, i.e., an increase in the U.S. rate of interest.[12]

The final situation at point *F* was similar to that at *A* and *C*, but only in the sense that it indicated a zero (or near zero) net arbitrage margin. It differed in the crucial respect that the spot rate was different at point *F* from what it had been at both *A* and *C*. At point *F* speculators no longer expected devaluation of sterling and consequently refrained from further forward sales of sterling. The reason for this was, of course, the expectation that the devaluation would improve the U.K. balance of payments.

Some general observations may be made on the basis of the present example. The point of contention between the speculators and the authorities was the spot rate of exchange. The speculators pressed for devaluation, while the authorities attempted to defend the rate of its pegged level. The net arbitrage margin was useful in tracing the resulting movements and countermovements. The crucial background of this confrontation was the balance of payments deficit, which shaped specula-

---

[11]Normally, a higher rate of interest (i.e., tight money) is expected to slow down domestic economic activity, reduce upward pressure on prices, and reduce demand for imports. This may improve the overall balance of payments in the long run. See Chapter 13 below. In the case at hand, these effects did not become noticeable quickly enough.

[12]This was discussed in the previous example.

tive expectations. As long as these expectations persisted, official alterations of the net arbitrage margin were only temporarily successful in
defending the spot rate.

REVALUATION OF THE GERMAN MARK

Our next example represents in some ways the opposite of the two
previous examples. West Germany has had a rather chronic balance of
payments surplus for a number of years. This has led to several official
revaluations of the German mark (DM) during the last decade. We are
interested in the role of the net arbitrage margin and short-term capital
flows during the "crisis" periods preceding each official revaluation.
Rather than describing any one of these events specifically, we will
summarize the typical features of these situations.

Let us begin at point A in Figure 11-5 with a zero net arbitrage margin
and a large overall surplus in the German balance of payments. This
surplus tended to have inflationary effects on the German economy, which
typically operated under conditions of high-capacity utilization. The

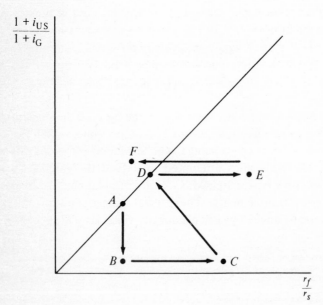

Figure 11-5

surplus made foreign exchange available to German exporters. When converted into marks these foreign funds became additional domestic purchasing power with inflationary impact on a fully employed economy. The German Bundesbank, responsible for resisting inflation, would now use an increase in the interest rate i_G for this purpose.[13] But this anti-inflationary policy had international implications. Figure 11-5 shows the resulting movement of the net arbitrage margin from A to B in favor of Germany.

At point B short-term capital inflows were compounding the overall surplus in the German balance of payments. Speculators, who may already have expected revaluation at point A, would now become even more determined. In this situation they would expect the future spot rate ($/DM) to be higher than the forward rate $(\$/DM)_f$ and accordingly buy forward marks. The resulting upward pressure on the forward rate would move the net arbitrage margin further in Germany's favor to point C in Figure 11-5.

The Bundesbank now faced a conflict between policy objectives as far as its use of the interest rate was concerned. At point C the inflationary domestic situation called for tight money policy, i.e., a higher rate of interest. But this would have given further impetus to short-term capital inflows and inflation via the balance of payments surplus. In other words, the balance of payments called for a low interest rate, while the domestic situation called for a high interest rate. Faced with this conflict, the Bundesbank has on several occasions reduced the interest rate, thus giving priority to the balance of payments. In addition, the Bundesbank would attempt to reduce the forward rate.[14] Figure 11-5 shows the combination of these two policy measures as the movement from C to D.

We may view point D as the end of the first round in the confrontation between the Bundesbank and the speculators.[15] Continued speculative pressure on the forward rate depends on the speculators' expectations at point D. If the overall balance of payments surplus remains large, and inflation remains an urgent issue, speculative forward purchases of

[13]The Bundesbank is the German equivalent of the U.S. Federal Reserve and the Bank of England.

[14]Rather than intervening directly in the forward market and buying forward marks, the Bundesbank offered a special forward rate of its own to those German commercial banks who would be willing to invest foreign exchange funds abroad. This amounted to offering these banks a net arbitrage margin favoring lending abroad, even though the actual net arbitrage margin favored Germany. In this way the Bundesbank hoped to "recycle" some of the short-term capital inflow and relieve the balance of payments pressure.

[15]Many situations involving speculation and large short-term capital flows have ended here. Speculators may have become convinced of the authorities' determination and ability to continue defending the spot rate. In this respect point D in Figure 11-5 is similar to point C in Figure 11-4.

marks might move the net arbitrage margin from D to E in Figure 11-5. It was usually a situation of this type which made it necessary to revalue, i.e., raise r_s and thereby move the net arbitrage margin toward point F.

In this example we once more find the authorities using the interest rate as well as the forward rate in order to defend the fixed spot rate. Again we observe the crucial role played by the overall balance of payments situation, which tends to shape speculators' expectations. Again we conclude that the discussed policy measures meet with temporary success only as long as the overall balance of payments disequilibrium remains large and speculators' expectations cannot be changed.

SPECULATION AND STABILITY

When discussing the foreign exchange market in Chapter 9, we observed how a balance of payments deficit puts downward pressure on the spot rate of exchange. Under a system of pegged rates, this pressure first takes the form of official reserve losses and eventually leads to official devaluation as these reserves are exhausted. A surplus, on the other hand, leads to upward pressure on the spot rate. Pressure for revaluation may result from the inflationary effect of the surplus on the domestic economy, as we have seen in the German example.

These tendencies are part of the basic link between the balance of payments and the foreign exchange market. We may now ask ourselves how this link is affected by speculation. For example, is speculation consistent with this basic link, or does its effect run counter to this link? Putting it differently, suppose a country has a deficit and its (overvalued) currency is therefore under devaluation pressure; will speculation add to this pressure, or will it tend to abate this pressure? Our case studies above would lead us to see speculation as adding to this pressure and therefore as strengthening the link between the balance of payments and the foreign exchange market. This effect of speculation may be considered stabilizing in the sense that it supports the basic market tendencies according to which an overvalued currency should decline and an undervalued currency should rise.[16]

But our case studies were individual examples, and it would be wrong

---

[16]A more general and quite different view of speculation sees it as destabilizing if it tends to amplify fluctuations in the exchange rate and as stabilizing if it tends to smooth out such fluctuations. This approach to speculation does not utilize the link between the balance of payments and the foreign exchange market and is disregarded in our discussion here.

to draw general conclusions from specific examples. There is no simple way to predict how speculators, as a group, will react to any particular situation. Speculators make mistakes in their expectations. They may expect the spot rate to fall when in fact it may rise, and vice versa. If this did not occur with some regularity, there would be no risk in speculation.

Let us briefly look into this possibility of false (and unprofitable) speculative expectations. Suppose the overall balance of payments is in equilibrium. Speculators, however, expect a deterioration and sell domestic currency forward because they expect the future spot rate to fall below the forward rate. But now let us assume that the overall balance of payments improves and removes all pressure from the spot rate in spite of the fact that the speculative forward sales have moved the net arbitrage margin against the domestic country. The speculators will eventually have to buy the domestic currency they have contracted to deliver at a higher price than they can sell it. They therefore incur losses. The effect of this type of speculation may be considered destabilizing in the sense that it has run counter to the basic link between the balance of payments and the foreign exchange market. Speculative forward sales have caused capital outflows and brought downward pressure on the spot rate even though the overall balance of payments was actually improving.

This leads us to the hypothetical situation where the overall balance of payments remains in equilibrium except for short-term capital flows caused by speculation. In this case, there will be a deficit if speculators expect a deficit and a surplus if they expect a surplus.[17] It is theoretically conceivable under such circumstances that a currency might be forced into devaluation or revaluation for no other reason than speculation. Exchange rates would no longer reflect international relationships between basic economic factors such as costs of production and demand, but speculative expectations. This situation would be undesirable from the point of view of international division of labor, allocation of the world's resources, and the administration of the international monetary system.

It is difficult to judge whether or not speculation, on balance, tends to be destabilizing. Much has been said and written about the undesirable effect of speculation in connection with the devaluation of sterling and the revaluations of the German mark. In both cases short-term capital flows

---

[17]The volume of speculative funds is of great importance here. If many billions of dollars are available for sudden speculative attacks and if official reserves are relatively small, the case described here may become a real possibility. Some observers have viewed the increasing volume of short-term funds and their rising volatility with concern for this reason.

were extremely large and difficult for the authorities to contend with. It does not appear, however, that speculation was destabilizing in either case.

In fact, these cases were chosen as examples because they illustrate a rather less complicated approach to speculation than most other situations. The U.K. balance of payments, for example, had been in deficit for many years. Each year the pressure on sterling increased. There was very little doubt that sterling was overvalued. The Bank of England, in 1967, was looking back on a succession of fights for the fixed sterling rate. Most experts in Britain as well as elsewhere considered devaluation, when it finally came in 1967, as long overdue. In a situation of this special type, speculators' expectations are not hard to predict. Their added pressure to devalue sterling was stabilizing even though it was certainly not welcomed by those who wished sterling to remain at $2.80.

If there is a conclusion to be drawn from this discussion, we must be careful to keep it within the framework of our examples covered. It appears that in a system of pegged exchange rates, speculative pressure will make it more difficult for the authorities to defend a given spot rate in the face of extensive and persistent disequilibrium in the balance of payments.

SUMMARY

During the normal conduct of their business exporters and importers find themselves with foreign exchange receivable or payable at some future date. Such positions involve uncertainty with regard to changes in the spot rate of exchange. The forward exchange market enables exporters and importers to hedge against this exchange risk.

The forward exchange rate is the rate at which the buyer and the seller agree at present to exchange domestic currency for foreign exchange at a future date.

The forward rate is determined by supply and demand for forward exchange. The forward rate may differ from the spot rate to the extent that supply and demand for forward exchange differs from the supply and demand for spot exchange.

Speculators take exchange risks by buying or selling forward exchange. Their profits or losses depend on the relationship between the (known) forward rate and the (as yet unknown) spot rate on the day the forward contract comes due.

Interest arbitrageurs are hedgers like exporters and importers; they use the forward market to hedge against the exchange risk.

The interest arbitrage operation depends on a constellation of the interest rate differential, the spot rate, and the forward rate of exchange, which may be referred to as the net arbitrage margin.

The net arbitrage margin can be used to predict the direction of short-term capital flows.

Speculation may cause short-term capital flows between international financial centers by changing the net arbitrage margin through the forward exchange rate.

Monetary authorities can affect short-term capital flows by changing the net arbitrage margin. If the interest rate is used for this purpose, the authorities may face conflicts between economic objectives, since the interest rate is an important factor in the domestic economy.

Stabilizing speculation is consistent with the basic link between the balance of payments and the foreign exchange market. It increases the downward pressure on the overvalued currency and the upward pressure on an undervalued currency.

Speculation and the resulting capital flows may become extremely heavy in situations where the monetary authorities attempt to defend the spot rate in the face of persistent and extensive balance of payments disequilibrium.

SUGGESTED FURTHER READINGS

Most texts deal with foreign exchange, forward exchange, and the net arbitrage margin in one and the same chapter. For comparison, see Leland B. Yeager, *International Monetary Relations* (Harper & Row, Publishers, Incorporated, New York, 1966), chap. 2. This book also contains useful and interesting case studies in Part II. See also Charles P. Kindleberger, *International Economics*, 5th ed. (Richard D. Irwin, Inc., Homewood, Ill., 1973), chap. 17; and Ingo Walter, *International Economics* (The Ronald Press Company, New York, 1966), chap. 10. For in-depth studies of forward exchange and arbitrage, see Paul Einzig, *A Dynamic Theory of Forward Exchange* (Macmillan, London, 1961); Herbert G. Grubel, *Forward Exchange, Speculation and the International Flow of Capital* (Stanford University Press, Stanford, Calif., 1966).

Chapter 12

The Balance of Payments and the Domestic Economy

The last four chapters were all devoted to various aspects of the balance of payments. In those chapters we viewed the balance of payments as the reflection of a country's external position in trade and finance. Our preoccupation with the external position does not mean, however, that external and internal economics are to be viewed as separate entities. On the contrary, the balance of payments is closely linked to the level of internal or domestic economic activity. In fact, no theory of domestic economic activity can claim validity without taking into account the external aspects of the economy. Similarly, no theory of the balance of payments exists which does not involve in a major way the level of domestic economic activity.

In the present chapter we will study some of the links between internal and external activity. Our discussion will focus on the relationships between the balance of payments and three basic domestic variables: the price level, the level of income, and the level of employment.

235

THE DOMESTIC PRICE LEVEL AND
THE BALANCE OF PAYMENTS

Just as prices of individual goods are determined by supply and demand, it is conceivable that the general price level depends on the interaction between aggregate supply and aggregate demand. By aggregate supply we mean total production in an economy, while aggregate demand may be defined as the sum of all goods and services demanded. For example, the general price level will tend to rise if aggregate demand exceeds production and tend to decline if aggregate demand falls short of production.[1]

The balance of payments $(X - M)$ reacts to changes in the domestic price level in a predictable way.[2] If the domestic price level rises, exports will become more expensive and therefore less attractive to foreign buyers. Imports, on the other hand, will now compare more favorably with domestic goods, and increased substitution of foreign goods for domestic goods will take place.[3] Accordingly, the balance of payments can be expected to deteriorate if domestic prices rise. A decline in domestic price level will have the opposite effect, i.e., exports will rise and imports will fall.

This simple proposition is shown in Figure 12-1. If we start, for example, at point A with balance of payments equilibrium $(X - M = O)$, an increase in the price level to point B leads to a deficit $(X - M < O)$, and a price level decrease to point C produces a surplus $(X - M > O)$.

Figure 12-1 has countless applications in the real world. For instance, deterioration of the U.S. balance of payments in the early 1970s has been viewed by many as a consequence of inflation in the United States.[4] On the other hand, until recently the German surplus has often been linked to Germany's ability to hold inflation down relative to her major trading partners.

From this straightforward and generally accepted proposition, let us now turn to a somewhat more complex question. Granting that the balance of payments depends on the domestic price level, is it also conceivable that the domestic price level, in turn, depends on the balance of payments?

---

[1]For the time being, we will disregard "structural" or "cost-push" inflation, which may occur independently of the state of aggregate demand. For more detail see the following chapter.

[2]For the purposes of the present chapter, the balance of payments will consist of exports and imports only. This restriction will be relaxed in the following chapter.

[3]We are assuming here that the domestic price levels in all foreign countries remain constant.

[4]This view is supported by the fact that the trade accounts $(X - M)$ in the U.S. balance of payments deteriorated during this time, while earlier these accounts had shown a surplus in spite of the overall deficit.

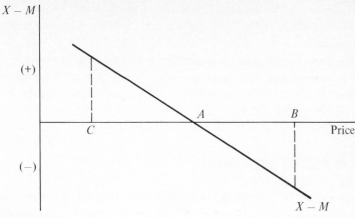

Figure 12-1

To find an answer we must once more return to the determination of the price level. In particular, we must consider the role played by exports and imports in this context. Let us recall from above that inflation results from excessive aggregate demand because supply and production are insufficient to satisfy all of this demand at constant prices.

Exports can be viewed as foreign demand for domestic supply or production. Assume, for example, that domestic aggregate demand is just equal to domestic production and the price level is therefore constant. Now add to this domestic demand the foreign demand for exports. Total aggregate demand now exceeds domestic production, and the domestic price level must rise. By including exports in aggregate demand, we can view them as a factor in the determination of the domestic price level. An increase in exports in this way tends to be inflationary, while a decrease tends to be deflationary.

Turning now to imports, let us again recall our general framework of price determination. Aggregate demand determines the price level because it represents demands on domestic productive resources. Imports, however, reflect domestic demands on foreign, rather than domestic, resources. Assume once more that aggregate demand exactly equals domestic production at constant prices. Now assume further that part of this aggregate demand is for foreign products, i.e., imports. This means that demand for domestic products is reduced by the amount of imports. Aggregate demand for domestic products is now smaller than domestic production, and prices must fall. We conclude that imports must be subtracted from aggregate demand for domestic production. An increase in imports consequently tends to be deflationary, while a decrease tends to be inflationary.

We have now established an important two-way link between the balance of payments and the domestic price level. Not only do price changes affect the balance of payments, but changes in the balance of payments also affect the price level.

ADJUSTMENT VERSUS SETTLEMENT

The above-described interaction between domestic economic activity and the balance of payments brings us to the important topic of balance of payments adjustment. Before we discuss the technical aspects of this topic, let us briefly consider its meaning and its relation to our previous discussions of the balance of payments. Much of the material in Chapters 8, 9, and 10 was devoted to various methods by which disequilibrium in the balance of payments can be settled. Settlement, as we know, simply means making or receiving payment in cash or credit for a deficit or a surplus. Settlement does not affect the *causes* of balance of payments disequilibrium.

Adjustment, on the other hand, refers to the interaction of various economic variables by which balance of payments equilibrium is reestablished. What sets this process into motion is the disequilibrium of the balance of payments itself, and in this sense we may speak of automatic adjustment mechanisms.

We have already studied one such mechanism, i.e., a system of freely flexible exchange rates. Here an original disequilibrium in the balance of payments causes a change in the exchange rate, which in turn reestablishes equilibrium in the balance of payments. The present chapter is devoted to adjustment mechanisms which operate in spite of an exchange rate which is fixed by pegging or an exchange rate which is held at a given level by controlled floating.

If the exchange rate as the adjusting variable is ruled out, this function is taken over by other variables such as the level of domestic prices and income. However, these variables are key aspects of the domestic economy apart from their role in balance of payments adjustment. Analyzing balance of payments adjustment by price and income effects, therefore, requires some knowledge about the determination of these variables, i.e., aggregate economic concepts. Once we have studied these concepts, we will understand not only the adjustment mechanisms but also the basic relationships between the domestic economy and the balance of payments.

BALANCE OF PAYMENTS ADJUSTMENT BY PRICE EFFECT

Let us first consider price as the adjusting variable and use an example for this purpose. This takes us back into the eighteenth century and the economic strategies of great trading nations such as England, Spain, Portugal, Holland, and France. The national gold stock during this era of *mercantilism* was accorded sufficient importance to make a balance of payments surplus a matter of high strategic priority. Mercantilism, in other words, involved great emphasis on foreign trade as a source of gold for national treasuries.[5]

Typical mercantilist strategy consisted of import restriction and export subsidies. It was in this era of mercantilism that the English economist David Hume (1711–1776) sought to demonstrate its futility by using our two-way link between the balance of payments and the domestic price level. Hume's argument is outlined in Figure 12-2. Starting at point *A* and assuming that the mercantilist policy—for example, the imposition of an import tariff—is successful, the balance of payments function will shift upward, a surplus (*AB*) will be achieved, and the desired gold inflow will indeed materialize.

But this gold inflow will increase spending, if the gold stock is closely linked to the money supply. The result is a rising domestic price level, which reduces exports and increases imports. This process must continue as long as the inflationary gold inflows continue—in other words, as long as there is a balance of payments surplus. Only at point *C*, where the balance of payments is once more in equilibrium, will the inflationary gold inflow stop. In Hume's view, therefore, the result of mercantilist policy designed to produce external surpluses (at point *B*) would eventually be nothing but internal inflation (at point *C*).

Figure 12-2 shows how a surplus will generate inflation which, in

---

[5]We are obviously assuming the existence of a gold standard as the underlying system of international settlement.

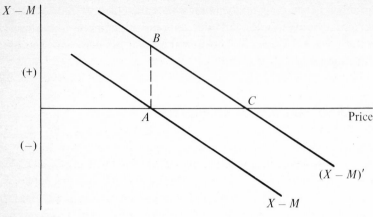

Figure 12-2

turn, will eliminate the surplus. The balance of payments, in other words, has returned to equilibrium after the original equilibrium (at point *A*) was disturbed. This adjustment occurred automatically through the two-way link between the balance of payments and the domestic price level. It is easy to visualize the opposite case in which a deficit leads to deflation which in turn eliminates the deficit.[6] This leads us to the conclusion that the balance of payments will automatically tend to move toward equilibrium regardless of whether it is originally in surplus or in deficit. This tendency is known as the *price adjustment mechanism* of the balance of payments.

SOME QUALIFICATIONS

The applicability of this analysis to real-world situations depends on its assumptions. The price adjustment mechanism will be applicable to the extent that the assumptions we have used in deriving it are reasonably realistic. Let us therefore examine our basic framework of price determination for the realism of its assumptions.

We recall that an excess of aggregate demand over production resulted in inflation, while deficient aggregate demand resulted in defla-

[6]Using Figure 12-2, we need only to consider point *C* as the starting point. The $(X - M)'$ function now shifts down to $(X - M)$, and point *A* is the eventual outcome.

tion. Underlying this approach is evidently the assumption that supply or production is constant. How realistic is this assumption? It is conceivable, for example, that an excess of aggregate demand over production results in an increase of production rather than inflation. Deficient aggregate demand, similarly, could lead to a decline in production rather than prices. Instead of price changes, in other words, we might consider changes in production or—the same thing—in real national income.[7]

This distinction between price changes and income changes is anything but a fine point of economic theory. Consider the following example: Aggregate demand is equal to production, and there is consequently no reason for either prices or income (production) to change. Now a sudden decline of aggregate demand occurs. Let us use this sudden change to compare the implications of price versus income changes.

The price mechanism as discussed above would suggest deflation as a result of declining aggregate demand. Production and real income remain constant, which means that the economy continues to enjoy—at a lower general price level—the same physical amount of products. Real income remains unchanged.

Now consider an alternative suggesting that production and real income, rather than prices, adjust to the decline in aggregate demand. This means a reduced real national income along with a reduced level of employment. What was a purely monetary phenomenon with price adjustment has turned into a real reduction of income and employment.

The implication of this alternative for the balance of payments is crucial. A sudden deficit by reducing aggregate demand creates unemployment. A surplus, on the other hand, stimulates employment in the domestic economy.

Most economists today would consider unrealistic the assumption that production is constant and that all adjustment therefore takes the form of price changes. However, this does not invalidate all aspects of the price adjustment mechanism. One obvious situation comes to mind immediately. While production may be variable, it cannot rise indefinitely. It will reach its limit when productive resources are fully employed. Whenever production is at this full employment level, an excess of aggregate demand leaves inflation as the only possibility.

---

[7]The assumption of constant production is actually not just an assumption but a basic conclusion derived by economists of the classical school (of which Hume, incidentally, was a member). Production, according to this school of thought, will always be at the full employment level as long as prices and wages are flexible enough to clear all markets. Regardless of the level of aggregate demand, therefore, the economy would always produce its capacity output. Changes in demand could affect the price level at which this output would sell, but not its physical quantity.

Our framework of economic activity must therefore provide for both price and income changes. Briefly stated, it provides for changes in income whenever income is below the full employment level and for price changes after income has reached its full employment level. The economist most prominently connected with the emphasis on variable real income and employment was John Maynard Keynes (1883–1946). In order to adapt our framework to this emphasis, we must develop some basic aspects of Keynesian economics.

THE DOMESTIC INCOME LEVEL
AND THE BALANCE OF PAYMENTS

Let us for the time being disregard the limiting case of full employment income and consider real income to be fully variable. The level of real income in the economy will then be determined by the level of aggregate demand.[8] A small addition to our terminology will serve to clarify this point. We have already identified aggregate output or production with real national income. To be more specific, output is identical to income earned if we measure the value of total output in terms of its cost of production. These costs of production can all be shown to be income payments to owners of factors of production such as labor, land, capital, managerial skills, etc. Total output and national income earned are, therefore, alternate ways of looking at the same thing.

Whether or not a particular level of output or income earned is actually an equilibrium level, in the sense that no forces exist which would move it to a different level, depends on the proportion of income earned which people are willing to spend, i.e., aggregate demand. Only if aggregate demand is exactly equal to income earned will national income be at an equilibrium level. If aggregate demand falls short of income earned, the equilibrium income level must decline. If aggregate demand exceeds income earned, equilibrium income must rise.

As far as exports are concerned, we now have established their connection with the equilibrium level of income, because we recall that exports are a component of aggregate demand. In order to place this connection in its proper context, we must consider the remaining components of aggregate demand. This leads us to the Keynesian consumption function. People's desire to spend on consumer goods, according to

---

[8]For the reader with a background in basic macroeconomics, the following passages will represent some repetition.

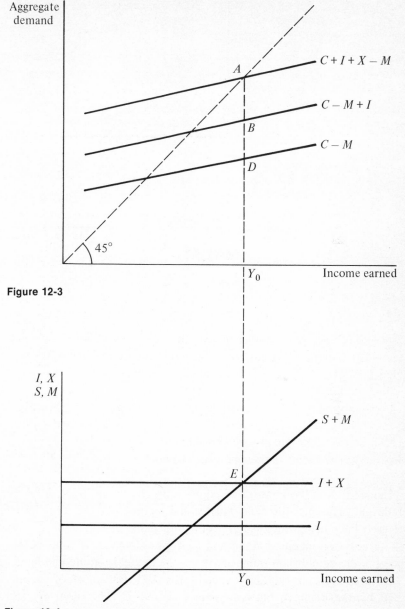

Figure 12-3

Figure 12-4

Keynes, is a function of their income earned. This behavioral proposition (C) is shown in Figure 12-3, which measures income earned on the horizontal axis and aggregate demand on the vertical axis. Since we are

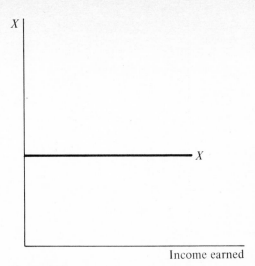

Figure 12-5

concerned in Figure 12-3 with consumption of domestic goods and services only, we must subtract consumption of foreign goods and services, i.e., imports, from the consumption function. The function labeled $C - M$ in Figure 12-3, consequently, shows aggregate consumer spending on domestic goods and services only.

Consumption is only one component of aggregate demand, however. The other components we are considering are investment (I) and exports (X).[9] These two components are consequently added to consumption in Figure 12-3. The result is the aggregate demand function ($C + I + X - M$).

Consider now the concept of equilibrium income in Figure 12-3. In equilibrium, aggregate demand must equal income earned. The dotted 45-degree line, being equidistant from both axes, is the locus of this equality between income earned and aggregate demand. It follows that point A is the equilibrium point and Y_0 is the equilibrium income level.

At point A consumption expenditures DY_0 fall short of income earned by the distance between points A and D. This deficiency in consumption spending is explained by the fact that out of this income earned people not only consume but also save (S) and import (M). This is shown in Figure 12-4 by the distance EY_0. Saving plus imports (EY_0) at

---

[9]A further component of aggregate demand, i.e., government spending on goods and services, is disregarded here because it is not essential to our analysis.

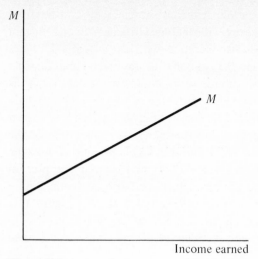

Figure 12-6

the equilibrium income level Y_0 are therefore equal to that amount of earned income AD which was withheld from consumption spending. If total spending or aggregate demand is nevertheless equal to income earned at point A in Figure 12-3, this is so because investment spending (I) and spending by foreigners (X) make up the difference.

We conclude that for income to be in equilibrium, investment plus exports must equal savings plus imports:

$$I + X = S + M$$

Figure 12-4 was added on to Figure 12-3 to make this equilibrium condition explicit. Point E in Figure 12-4 is the equilibrium point by the same reasoning which led us to point A in Figure 12-3.

Now that we have shown how the balance of payments affects national income, let us find out how national income affects the balance of payments. The basic elements of this link are already contained in the analysis above. All we have to do is to bring them into clearer focus. In Figures 12-3 and 12-4 exports were added to aggregate demand as a constant independent of national income. Figure 12-5 therefore shows the export function as a horizontal line.[10]

Imports, on the other hand, increase with income earned. If con-

---

[10]Exports are a function of foreign, rather than domestic, income earned.

sumers' spending on domestic goods, which is shown by the consumption function in Figure 12-3, increases with income, it stands to reason that their spending on foreign goods also increases with income earned. Figure 12-6 shows this import function.[11] If exports do not change, but imports rise as income increases, the balance of payments must deteriorate as income increases. This is graphically expressed in Figure 12-7, in which the import function of Figure 12-6 is simply subtracted from the export function of Figure 12-5. The resulting function shows the state of the balance of payments as a function of different levels of national income.

Note the similarity between Figures 12-7 and 12-1. While at present we are concerned with income effects on the balance of payments, Figure 12-1 served to show the price effects. Recall also that in Figure 12-1 equilibrium of the price level and the balance of payments was established at the intersection between the balance of payments function and the horizontal axis.

This, however, is not the case in Figure 12-7. Balance of payments equilibrium and income equilibrium do not necessarily occur simultaneously. A look at the condition for income equilibrium $(I + X = S + M)$ derived above explains the reason. If X equals M, the two sides of the condition are still unequal as long as I differs from S. We can rewrite the condition to emphasize this point:

$$X - M = S - I$$

[11]This function was already contained in Figure 12-4, where imports were added to saving.

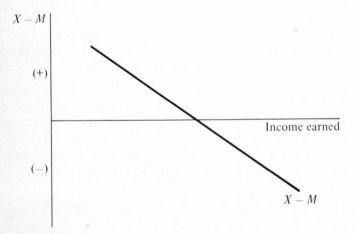

Figure 12-7

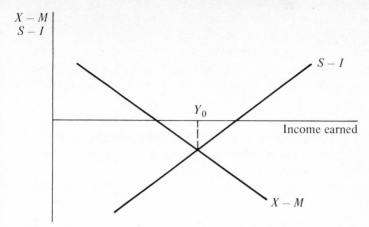

Figure 12-8

This version of the income equilibrium condition shows that any state of the balance of payments is consistent with income equilibrium as long as the difference between exports and imports is exactly compensated by the difference between savings and investment.

Let us clarify this by using an example. Suppose income earned is $100 billion. We are interested in finding out whether or not this $100 billion represents an equilibrium level of income. If it is, it will not change after the recipients of this income have made their spending decisions. If it is not, it must either decrease or increase. Let us assume that consumers wish to spend $85 billion on domestic goods, to spend $5 billion on imports, and to save the remaining $10 billion. Investors intend to spend $12 billion on domestic investment goods, and exporters plan to sell $3 billion worth of exports. We find that aggregate demand $(C + I + X)$ is equal to income earned and that our $100 billion is therefore an equilibrium level. This is consistent with the equilibrium condition.

$$X - M = S - I$$

$$3 - 5 = 10 - 12$$

The balance of payments deficit of $2 billion is compensated by the excess of investment spending over savings. The net deduction from aggregate demand in the foreign sector is balanced by the net addition in the domestic sector.

We may now go one step further and present the equilibrium

condition in diagrammatic form. Figure 12-7 already contains the left half
of this condition. To this we must add a function expressing the
relationship between income earned and the difference between savings
and investment. Investment, as we know from Figure 12-4, is independent
of income, i.e., a constant. Saving, however, increases with income. The S
$- I$ function must therefore have a positive slope.

Figure 12-8 allows us to determine not only equilibrium income but
also the state of the balance of payments. The figure is drawn here in such
a way as to illustrate the example given above. The balance of payments
is in deficit at the equilibrium income level.

BALANCE OF PAYMENTS ADJUSTMENT
BY INCOME EFFECT

Figure 12-8 is useful in demonstrating the income adjustment mechanism
of the balance of payments. Let us recall what we mean by balance of
payments adjustment. Suppose the balance of payments is in equilibrium,
and now a sudden shift in exports or imports occurs. Will the balance of
payments adjust to the change by once more moving back toward
equilibrium?

In Figure 12-9 a sudden increase in exports (ΔX) shifts the balance of
payments function $X - M$ upward. At the original equilibrium income

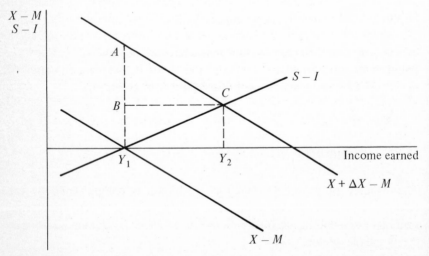

Figure 12-9

level Y_1 a surplus measured by the distance between points A and Y_1 opens up. But Y_1 no longer remains an equilibrium income, because we now have more expenditures or aggregate demand in our economy. Income must rise to Y_2, where aggregate demand is once again equal to earned income, i.e., $X + \Delta X - M = S - I$. At point C the balance of payments is still in surplus (CY_2), but this surplus is smaller than the original surplus (AY_1 or ΔX). The original surplus, in other words, has been at least partially adjusted.

The explanation of this result follows directly from the Keynesian framework we are using: An increase in exports upsets the old equilibrium position Y_1 and leads to a higher income. Income therefore rises in response to the increase in exports. But imports also rise in response to the increase in income. The rise in imports consequently offsets part of the original shift in exports, thus reducing the original surplus.[12]

It is easy to visualize the opposite case, in which the balance of payments function shifts downward and the resulting deficit causes income to fall. But since imports will fall with income, this deficit will be partially adjusted. The construction of the proper diagram is left to the reader as a useful exercise.

We conclude that income effects will tend to move the balance of payments back toward, if not completely to, equilibrium in case this equilibrium has been disturbed by a sudden shift of the balance of payments function. This tendency is known as the *income adjustment mechanism* of the balance of payments.

OTHER SHIFTS

The income adjustment mechanism contains a two-way link between the balance of payment and national income: While the balance of payments affects income because it is a component of aggregate demand, income also affects the balance of payments because imports vary with income.

It is not necessary for both parts of this link to be present in every situation. A change in income, for example, can be caused by a sudden shift in consumption, savings, or investment rather than exports or

---

[12]Given a rise in income of BC in Figure 12-9, imports rise by AB. Note that $AY_1 - AB = BY_1 = CY_2$. The final balance of payments surplus at Y_2 (CY_2) is therefore equal to the original surplus at Y_1 (AY_1) minus the income-induced increase in imports (AB). Note also that the final surplus CY_2 is exactly equal to the increase in saving induced by the rise in income (Y_1Y_2). This increase in saving is the reason why the original surplus does not adjust completely back to equilibrium. The smaller this increase in saving (the flatter the $S - I$ function), the smaller will be the final surplus, i.e., the more completely will the balance of payments adjust.

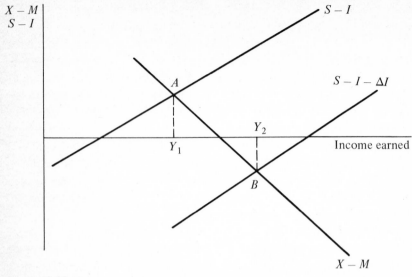

Figure 12-10

imports. A change in income, in other words, may be caused by a shift of the $S - I$ function rather than a shift of the $X - M$ function. In Figure 12-10 we present such a sudden increase in investment by a downward shift of the $S - I$ function. Income increases from Y_1 to Y_2. The balance of payments, having been in surplus (AY_1) at Y_1, moves into deficit (BY_2) at Y_2. This change in the balance of payments is income-induced. The described situation therefore includes only one-half of the two-way link involved in the income adjustment mechanism of the balance of payments.

The discussion of Figure 12-10 leads to a very significant general conclusion. What we have shown is that virtually no domestic economic event which affects national income will remain without effect on the balance of payments. Any shift in any domestic component of aggregate demand will also have external effects. This will obviously be an important consideration in the discussion of national economic policy, which is reserved for the next chapter.

PRICE AND INCOME EFFECTS COMBINED

Our final task in this chapter is to include both price and income effects in the same general framework. The problem we are facing here is to decide which changes in aggregate demand lead to price changes and which lead to income changes. Realistically, we might even expect both types of effects from the same change in aggregate demand. We may use two sets of assumptions concerning combinations of price and income changes.

First, we might assume that prices are flexible only in the upward direction. Any increase in aggregate demand in this case will lead to inflation, while any decrease in aggregate demand will lead to a decline of real income and employment. This assumption attempts in a simplistic way to take account of situations in which declining aggregate demand fails to stop inflation while at the same time increasing unemployment.[13] In a situation of this type the balance of payments tends to react to a decline in aggregate demand primarily through the income mechanism and to an increase through the price mechanism. It will improve in response to a decline in aggregate demand and deteriorate in response to an increase in aggregate demand.[14]

The second set of assumptions we may use centers on the notion that

---

[13]Suppose, for example, that inflation already exists in the economy for reasons other than excess aggregate demand. The absence of a price effect of declining aggregate demand will then make it impossible to fight inflation with declining aggregate demand. The presence of the income effect, however, will increase unemployment. A situation of this nature could be found in the United States in 1970–1971, for example.

[14]To the extent, of course, that the decline in aggregate demand is accompanied by both a decrease in income and inflation, the income and the price effects will work against each other in the balance of payments. Rising U.S. deficits during 1970–1971, for example, suggest that the price effect outweighed the income effect.

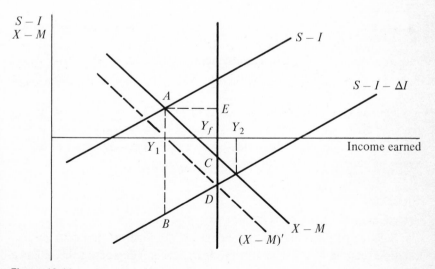

Figure 12-11

there is an upper limit to income variability, i.e., full-employment income. Any shift in aggregate demand which would lead to an equilibrium income above the full-employment level would necessarily cause inflation. On the other hand, as long as income variation remains below the full-employment level, prices remain constant.

Consider Figure 12-11, where Y_f indicates the maximum real income attainable under full employment. Originally, income is in equilibrium at Y_1. The balance of payments is in surplus (AY_1). Now we assume a sudden increase in investment spending $(\Delta I$ or $AB)$, which shifts the $S - I$ function down. If income were fully variable, it would rise to Y_2. But this income level exceeds the physical maximum of Y_f. Real income can rise only as far as Y_f. After this level is reached, the still-remaining excess of aggregate demand (CD) causes inflation. As we know from the discussion of the price mechanism, however, inflation deteriorates the balance of payments. This we show in Figure 12-11 by a price-induced downward shift of the $X - M$ function to the position labeled $(X - M)'$. At point D income is in equilibrium at full employment, since aggregate demand equals income earned:

$$S - I - \Delta I = (X - M)'$$

The balance of payments has moved from original surplus (AY_1) into deficit (DY_f). The total deterioration may be measured by ED. This represents a combination of the income effect CE (the movement along the $X - M$ function) and the price effect CD (the shift of the $X - M$ function).

Figure 12-11, in short, describes a shift in aggregate demand which causes both income and price changes. The increase in investment not only picks up the slack in employment existing at Y_1 but also causes inflation. The balance of payments reacts negatively to both these changes.

The general framework of Figure 12-11 obviously lends itself to the analysis of a great variety of situations. Rather than doing this in the hypothetical manner of this chapter, we will apply this framework to issues of economic policy in the following chapter.

SUMMARY

The balance of payments is dependent on the level of domestic prices. Inflation relative to other countries' price levels will worsen the balance of payments, while deflation will improve it.

The domestic price level, in turn, is also dependent on the balance of payments. A sudden improvement in the balance of payments will raise the domestic price level. A sudden deterioration of the balance of payments will cause a decline in prices.

The price adjustment mechanism of the balance of payments is based on both parts of this two-way link between the balance of payments and the domestic price level.

The price adjustment mechanism must be qualified to the extent that shifts in aggregate demand may have effects other than price changes.

The balance of payments is also dependent on the level of domestic national income. An increase in income will raise imports and thereby worsen the balance of payments. A decline in income will reduce imports.

The level of domestic national income, in turn, is also dependent on the balance of payments. A sudden improvement in the balance of payments will raise national income, while a deterioration will reduce national income.

The income adjustment mechanism of the balance of payments combines both parts of this two-way link between the balance of payments and the level of domestic national income.

Most situations involve both price and income effects. The problem here is to decide which changes in aggregate demand lead to price changes and which ones lead to income changes.

SUGGESTED FURTHER READINGS

The discussion in this chapter was deliberately brief and simplified. For more extensive coverage, see Ingo Walter, *International Economics, Theory and Policy* (The Ronald Press Company, New York, 1968), chaps. 13 and 14; also Charles P. Kindleberger, *International Economics,* 5th ed. (Richard D. Irwin, Inc., Homewood, Ill., 1973), chaps. 15 and 20. Students with no background in macroeconomic principles may wish to consult a principles textbook such as Paul A. Samuelson, *Economics,* 9th ed. (McGraw-Hill Book Company, New York, 1973), chaps. 11 and 12.

International Economic Policy

We have now arrived at the important juncture in our study of international economics where it is possible to discuss both the internal and the external aspects of economic policy. We begin with a very broad concept of economic policy.

AGGREGATE DEMAND POLICY

The previous chapter described the crucial role of aggregate demand in the determination of equilibrium income. For the time being we will define economic policy as an activity of the government by which aggregate demand is adjusted for the purpose of attaining certain objectives. Such objectives or policy targets generally include full employment, price stability, and balance of payments equilibrium. The policy tools used by the government consist basically of monetary and fiscal policy.

Monetary policy affects aggregate demand through changes in the national money supply and changes in interest rates. For example, an easy money policy, by making more money available to the public and by permitting interest rates to drop, will stimulate spending, aggregate demand, and, therefore, income and employment. Tight money, on the other hand, will make credit harder to obtain and more expensive. Borrowing and spending will drop, and aggregate demand will thus be restricted.

Fiscal policy affects aggregate demand directly by government spending, i.e., the government's demand for goods and services, and by taxation. In order to stimulate aggregate demand, the government consequently increases its spending or decreases taxes, or both. To restrict aggregate demand government spending would have to be reduced, or taxes would have to be raised, or both.

Deciding which type of policy—expansionary or contractive—the government should pursue appears to be easy. If, compared with the full-employment level of income earned, aggregate demand is deficient, an expansionary fiscal or monetary policy is called for.[1] If aggregate demand is excessive, i.e., exceeds the full-employment mark, restriction would be the proper policy. The logic of this proposition is straightforward: Since the authorities, through fiscal and monetary policy, have the means to raise and lower aggregate demand, they can be expected to adjust aggregate demand in such a way as to generate income equilibrium at the full-employment mark.

Let us state this in terms of a diagram. In Figure 13-1 the heavy vertical line indicates the full-employment level of income earned. Now consider the lowest one of the three aggregate demand functions ($C + I + G_1$) drawn in Figure 13-1.[2] This demand function is deficient because it generates an income equilibrium Y_1 which is below the full-employment mark. This means that the combined spending of consumers (C), investors (I), and government (G_1) amounts to less than full-employment income earned (Y_f). The government should therefore increase its spending from G_1 to G_2, thereby shifting the aggregate demand function into position $C + I + G_2$ and attaining equilibrium at full employment (Y_f).

Should the aggregate demand function be originally in position $C + I$

---

[1] This answer is easy because for the time being we are regarding full employment as the only target of economic policy.

[2] Note by the absence of $X - M$ from these functions that we are dealing with a closed economy at this point. Also, government spending on goods and services (G), as a component of aggregate demand, was disregarded in Chapter 12 and is newly introduced here.

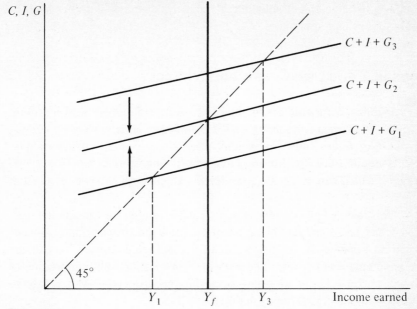

Figure 13-1

$+ G_3$, we know that this is an inflationary level. The income level Y_3 is not attainable in real terms, since it exceeds the full-employment mark. The government should reduce its spending from G_3 to G_2.

Figure 13-1 defines clearly the simplified relationship between employment and the price level which we are using at present. The increase in government spending from G_1 to G_2 raises employment, but not the price level. The decrease from G_3 to G_2 reduces the price level, but not employment. Inflation, in other words, does not occur in this model unless and until the full-employment mark is exceeded. This simplifying assumption holds a special consequence for our policy analysis: Full employment and price stability can be considered as one and the same policy target because they can be simultaneously achieved by the proper adjustment of aggregate demand. We will qualify this very important assumption later on.

While the use of government spending (G) makes the exposition of Figure 13-1 simple, the same general principle applies to taxation and monetary policy. Taxation will affect consumer spending and thus shift aggregate demand by way of its C component. Monetary policy is geared

primarily to investment spending (I) and to consumer durables such as
automobiles and appliances (C).

EXTERNAL EQUILIBRIUM AS A POLICY TARGET

Let us reflect for a moment on the basic policy framework set forth here.
We regard fiscal and monetary policy as tools for achieving policy targets.
These targets are full employment, price stability, and balance of payments equilibrium. So far we have talked only about the former two
targets, which can in fact be considered a single target, as we recall from
above.

This leaves balance of payments equilibrium as the remaining target
and leads us to the following question: Can the proper application of
fiscal or monetary policy bring about full employment as well as balance
of payments equilibrium? The answer is of considerable importance to
policy makers. It has on many occasions been decisive with regard to
choices among actual policy actions.

In order to see this question as clearly as possible, let us now
concentrate on external equilibrium as a target, disregarding for the
moment the domestic target of full employment at stable prices. What
type of economic policy is needed to achieve balance of payments
equilibrium? We know from the last chapter that the balance of payments,
in the Keynesian model, is a function of national income. In terms of
Figure 13-2 this means the following. If a deficit (at point A) is to be

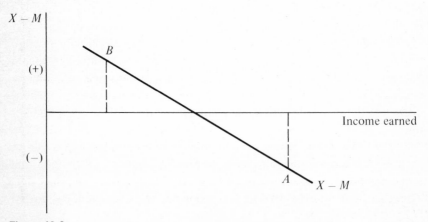

Figure 13-2

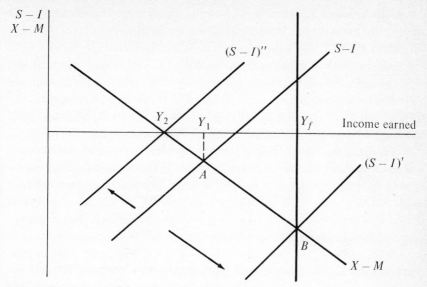

Figure 13-3

adjusted, income has to be reduced by restrictive fiscal or monetary policy. If a surplus (at point *B*) is to be adjusted, income must be increased by expansionary policy. It will be recalled that the basis of this is the Keynesian proposition, according to which imports rise and fall with income while exports remain unaffected by changes in domestic income.

INTERNAL VERSUS EXTERNAL TARGETS

Having discussed each target separately, we are now ready to discuss them together. This is necessary because a country's economic situation at any one time consists of a certain state of aggregate demand as well as the balance of payments.

Consider the following situation: Aggregate demand is deficient, and the economy is consequently operating below the full-employment level. At the same time the balance of payments shows a deficit. The internal target of full employment, therefore, calls for expansionary policy, while the external target of balance of payments equilibrium calls for contractionary policy.

Figure 13-3 pictures this situation. The original equilibrium position at point A, where $S - I = X - M$, shows an equilibrium income Y_1 well below full-employment income, Y_f. The balance of payments at point A is in deficit by AY_1. The government can attain the full-employment target by shifting the $S - I$ function into position $(S - I)'$. This could be done, for example, by expansionary monetary policy, which would stimulate investment through increased availability of credit and a reduction in the rate of interest.[3] At point B, full employment is achieved, but only at the expense of a greatly increased balance of payments deficit, BY_f.

On the other hand, priority might have been given to the external target of balance of payments equilibrium. In this case restrictive policy would have been used, and the $S - I$ function would have been shifted into position $(S - I)''$. Equilibrium income Y_2 would have involved balance of payments equilibrium, but only at the expense of even higher unemployment than in the original position, Y_1.

We conclude that in a position of deficient aggregate demand and external deficit, the government cannot simultaneously attain both the internal and the external target with the same economic policy. Full employment can be reached only at the expense of a larger deficit, and balance of payments equilibrium can be reached only at the expense of increased unemployment.

For example, the situation in Great Britain prior to sterling devaluation in 1967 offers some evidence that a policy conflict of the nature described here in fact existed. It appears that the external target had priority since the persistent deficit was repeatedly attacked with so-called "belt-tightening" or austerity programs. These programs combined various fiscal and monetary measures designed to contract aggregate demand with the explicit purpose of improving the balance of payments. It was by no means clear that the domestic employment situation required restrictive economic policy. One might speculate that the failure of this policy, as evidenced by the persistence of the deficit and the eventual need to devalue sterling, was caused by the unwillingness of the domestic sector to accept the austerity forced upon it for the sake of external equilibrium.

The United States in the early 1960s may similarly be viewed in terms of the framework above. Employment was considered well below the desirable level. The Kennedy administration was contemplating a wide-ranging tax cut, expecting to stimulate aggregate demand and employ-

---

[3]A downward shift of $S - I$ in Figure 13-3, where I is measured negatively is equivalent to an upward shift of the aggregate demand function in Figure 13-1.

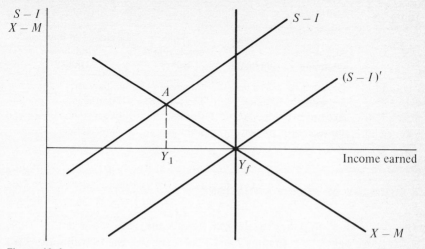

Figure 13-4

ment. The U.S. balance of payments, however, was in deficit. The conflict became apparent when Federal Reserve officials pointed to the potentially harmful effects of expansionary policy on the balance of payments. Priority was eventually given to the internal target, and the tax cut was put into effect in 1964.

Let us pursue the discussion of external and internal targets a little further by way of another example. Consider a situation with deficient aggregate demand and a balance of payments surplus. In Figure 13-4 the original equilibrium is shown at point A. Income (Y_1) falls short of the full-employment mark, and the balance of payments is in surplus (AY_1). It is immediately evident that expansionary policy, shown by the shift of the $S - I$ function into position $(S - I)'$, works toward attainment of both full employment and balance of payments equilibrium.[4] The balance of payments, in other words, does not present a constraint on the government's ability to stimulate employment in this case, nor does potential unemployment act as a constraint on the pursuit of external equilibrium.

_____

[4]Note that the $X - M$ function in Figure 13-4 intersects the income axis at Y_f. This was done to make simultaneous attainment of full employment and external balance possible. This is, however, a special case. The $X - M$ function could intersect the income axis anywhere to the right of Y_1. In general, therefore, a downward shift of the $S - I$ function represents a movement toward rather than actual attainment of both targets.

Table 13-1

	Aggregate demand	Balance of payments	Full-employment policy	Balance of payments equilibrium policy
Figure 13-4	Deficient	Surplus	Expansion	Expansion
Figure 13-3	Deficient	Deficit	Expansion	Contraction
Figure 13-5	Excessive	Surplus	Contraction	Expansion
Figure 13-6	Excessive	Deficit	Contraction	Contraction

A SUMMARY OF POLICY SITUATIONS

The discussion of policy tools and targets may be conveniently summarized by Table 13-1. In lines 2 and 1 we recognize the two situations we have just discussed. Line 3 indicates another type of conflict situation, one involving excessive aggregate demand and a balance of payments surplus. The conflict here is found in the need for contraction to control inflation and the need for expansion to adjust the external surplus. Figure 13-5 illustrates this situation. The original position at point A indicates an income level characterized by inflation and external surplus. If the government wishes to fight inflation, it will contract aggregate demand and shift the $S - I$ function into position $(S - I)'$. The new equilibrium

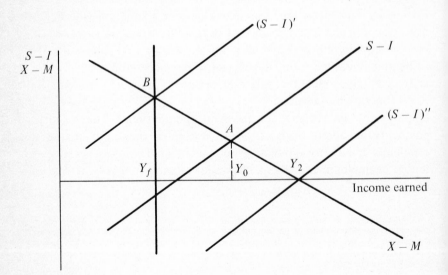

Figure 13-5

point, B, involves price stability, but the surplus has increased to BY_f. The external target may be reached at Y_2, but only at the expense of even greater inflation.

This type of conflict has existed in Germany, for example, on various occasions. Anti-inflationary measures (i.e., contraction of aggregate demand) in that country, with its chronic balance of payments surplus, have had the tendency of increasing this surplus even further. The surplus, however, has not always been viewed as an unmixed blessing by the German authorities, not to mention those countries where this surplus inevitably showed up as a deficit. The reader will recall from the discussion in Chapter 11 that large and volatile capital flows tend to occur in situations like this. In the German case these capital flows provide the banks abundantly with the very liquidity which the authorities seek to reduce by way of contractionary policy.

Monetary contraction, in other words, may lead to inflation if it aggravates the problems associated in any case with a large balance of payments surplus. This explains policy decisions by the German authorities which would normally be difficult to understand, such as the sudden switch in 1961 from tight to easy money policy at the height of an inflationary boom. This reversal was the consequence of priority shifting from the internal to the external target.

Line 4 in Table 13-1 finally describes another situation in which no conflict arises. Figure 13-6 corresponds to this case and requires no further discussion.

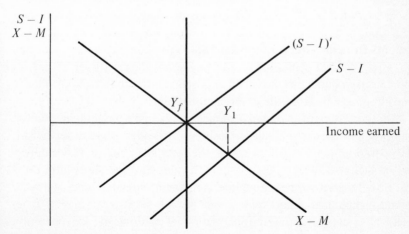

Figure 13-6

We may look at the midsixties in the United States for an example of this situation. The Johnson administration's massive spending in connection with the war in Vietnam and its simultaneous maintenance of domestic programs had pushed aggregate demand to excessive levels, while the balance of payments further deteriorated. Most observers agreed that monetary and fiscal constraints were the proper policy recommendations on both fronts.

At this point it may be helpful to the reader to summarize for himself the discussion centering on Table 13-1. For each line of the table the corresponding diagram should be reviewed, and one or several real-world examples should be found. Even though this framework represents a somewhat mechanistic approach to problems which too often defy simple analysis, it provides a good basis for the following discussion.

CONFLICT ABATEMENT BY SUPPLEMENTAL POLICIES

In summarizing Table 13-1, the following observation may be made with regard to all four situations: Two targets—full employment and external equilibrium—are being pursued with only one policy, i.e., variation of aggregate demand. The government resembles a marksman who must hit two targets with one shot. This is possible only if the targets are lined up, as indeed they are in lines 1 and 4 of Table 13-1. A problem arises in lines 2 and 3, where the targets are not lined up. In these cases, two separate policies must be employed in order to attain both targets.

A country with an external deficit and unemployment, for example, may be expected to go ahead with expansion of aggregate demand, while at the same time looking for a policy which will protect the balance of payments from the effects of this internal expansion. In a situation of this type, direct control of the balance of payments suggests itself. Many an import tariff or quota has thus been imposed in order to free expansionary domestic programs from the external constraint.

Another attempt to match policy tools with targets in conflict situations has been the Federal Reserve's so-called "operation twist." This operation consists in "twisting" the term structure of U.S. interest rates in such a way as to keep long-term rates low and short-term rates high. Low long-term rates stimulate investment spending and aggregate demand, while high short-term rates attract short-term capital from abroad, thus counteracting the income effect of domestic expansion on the balance of payments.

The capital account has often attracted the attention of policy makers in such conflict situations. The German Bundesbank, for example, has often sought to control the surplus, when it interfered with restriction of aggregate demand, by curbing short-term capital inflows. In Italy, similarly, the authorities keep a close watch over the short-term foreign borrowing and lending of the banks with the explicit purpose of freeing domestic policy from the balance of payments constraint.

There is of course another side to the story of the external constraint. The negative reaction of the balance of payments to domestic expansion has traditionally been regarded as a kind of insurance against irresponsible government finance. Thus, the traditional "rules of the game" of the system of fixed exchange rates very much encompassed "balance of payments discipline." This view is particularly plausible in the classical economic model, where any governmental net addition to aggregate demand had to cause inflation since full employment was the natural state of affairs. In the modern Keynesian world, however, where expansion of aggregate demand may be an entirely legitimate concern of the government, it is often difficult to distinguish between responsible and irresponsible government finance.

CONFLICT RESOLUTION BY EXCHANGE RATE POLICY

The search for additional policy tools to match the targets described above has not always met with success, especially in cases of persistent external disequilibria. If the conflict prevails, in spite of the described policies, a country must consider devaluation or revaluation of its currency.

At point A in Figure 13-7 we have unemployment and external deficit. To combat unemployment, aggregate demand is expanded to $(S - I)'$. In the absence of any further action this would bring less unemployment but a larger deficit at point B.

Now let the country in question devalue its currency. We recall that devaluation makes exports cheaper and imports more expensive. It will therefore shift the $X - M$ function upward.[5] Ideally, assuming that it is

---

[5]Actually, devaluation may not improve the balance of payments. Although the volume of exports will rise, each unit will sell at a lower price in terms of foreign currency. Export revenue, therefore, *could* fall. The volume of imports will fall, but since each unit now costs more in terms of domestic currency, total import expenditure *could* rise. The actual outcome therefore depends on the nature of the demand for exports and imports. In assuming here that devaluation will improve the balance of payments, we are following the practical expectations in most cases.

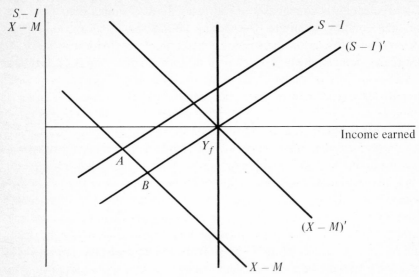

Figure 13-7

possible to shift each function by precisely the correct amount, point Y_f may be reached, implying full employment and external equilibrium. Two targets have been reached by a combination of two policies.[6]

The treatment of the remaining conflict situation involving excessive aggregate demand and external surplus is symmetric to the foregoing case. Currency appreciation (i.e., revaluation) may be employed in combination with contraction of aggregate demand. The reader may refer to Figure 13-5 and show how this policy combination shifts both functions to the left.

DEVALUATION AND FULL EMPLOYMENT

It is possible to refine the basic framework presented here in several ways. One of the situations which has not yet been covered but which has received much attention involves a large external deficit at, or close to, the full-employment level of national income. A country in this situation

[6]Under special circumstances devaluation alone might have reached both targets. Suppose the $S - I$ function in Figure 13-7 happens to pass through point Y_f to begin with. In this case, point B describes the original situation, and devaluation alone will move us to point Y_f.

appears to have a problem only as far as its balance of payments is concerned, and one policy (e.g., devaluation) should suffice. It turns out, however, that the situation is not quite so simple. In Figure 13-8 equilibrium income is exactly at the full-employment mark. The upward shift of the $X - M$ function, reflecting devaluation, leads to equilibrium at point B. This income level, however, is not obtainable because it exceeds the maximum or full-employment income at Y_f. The inevitably following inflation will make exports more expensive and imports relatively cheaper. In this way inflation will cancel the effect of the original devaluation and shift the $X - M$ function back down again.

Let us review this result in practical terms. The fact that we have full employment at the outset means that no idle resources are left in the economy. Devaluation, however, by offering to sell more exports, requires additional resources to produce these additional exports. Furthermore, if imports are to be reduced, more domestic resources will be needed to produce domestic substitutes for the forgone imports. In short, devaluation will require additional domestic resources.[7] If all domestic

[7]These employment-creating aspects of devaluation were well recognized by many countries during the worldwide Great Depression of the early 1930s. Whole series of competitive devaluations took place for the purpose of stimulating depressed economies. Of course, the multilateral scope of these devaluations made the whole sequence futile.

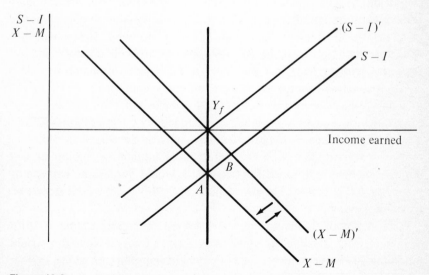

Figure 13-8

resources are already employed, however, producers of exports and of import substitutes must bid resources away from their present employments. This can only be done at higher wages and prices. The resulting inflation, then, eats into the margin of price advantage which the devaluation had opened up to the exporters.

How then can a country with a fully employed economy correct a serious external deficit? The answer emerges from Figure 13-8. It must contract aggregate demand in order to free the resources required by devaluation. In Figure 13-8 this is reflected by the upward shift of the $S - I$ function. The eventual result of contraction and devaluation could be full employment and external equilibrium at Y_f.

CONFLICT PREVENTION—FLEXIBLE EXCHANGE RATES

On a number of occasions now we have discussed situations in which the state of the balance of payments has had significant effects on the conduct of domestic economic policy. Recall, for example, the German reversal from tight to easy money policy in response to external pressures, or the British austerity programs designed explicitly to maintain sterling at $2.80 per pound.

Situations of this sort raise some basic questions about the organization of our Western world economy. Take the British case, for example: If devaluation is initially ruled out, and if the target of external balance is given priority over the internal target of full employment, British workers must lose their jobs and the general standard of living must decline (or grow at a slower pace) for the sake of the balance of payments. The external constraint on the domestic economy seems formidable.

As we have seen, this constraint has been felt even in the United States, whose economy is much less dependent on international trade than the British one. A hypothetical case may be envisaged in which an expansionary program with the potential of adding $20 billion to real national income is dropped for fear that it would burden the balance of payments by $1 billion. The proverbial tail, in this case, would indeed be wagging the dog.

Examples of this nature are perhaps the strongest arguments for a system of freely flexible exchange rates. Since a freely flexible rate would automatically bring about balance of payments equilibrium, such a system would free policy makers from the external constraint. Each country, in other words, would be free to gear the level of aggregate demand exclusively to the domestic target of full employment without concern about the external consequences, such as changes in the international value of its currency.

This freedom from the external constraint will gain added importance in the section below, where we introduce price stability as a target which is largely independent of full employment.

CONTROLLED FLOATING AND THE CONFLICT

In the sections above we have discussed the role of exchange rate policy and flexible rates in situations where domestic and external objectives call for aggregate demand to be moved in opposite directions by economic policy. Controlled floating amounts to a compromise measure between fixed rates subject to devaluation and revaluation on the one hand, and freely flexible rates on the other. To the extent that the rate is allowed to float in response to market pressures, the country in question would be free to aim for full employment without being constrained by external disequilibrium. However, to the extent that the authorities decide to once more engage in pegging operations in order to control the floating, the rate becomes fixed and the external constraint may emerge again. The crucial point is, therefore, where the otherwise floating rate will be controlled. Our discussion suggests that this may depend on the actual impact of the external constraint in each particular case.

Consider the example of a country with considerable unemployment. We assume the exchange rate is subject to controlled floating. As the target of full employment is pursued with expansionary policies, the exchange rate will float downward.[8] It may be necessary for the exchange rate to drop substantially in response to the expanding national income. A large decline, however, may not be acceptable to the authorities, who have some notion as to a limit beyond which the exchange rate should not be allowed to fall. If this notion leads to pegging at a point where the income effect on the balance of payments remains strong, a considerable balance of payments deficit may once more be the result.

The authorities' decision where to control the floating rate is subject

---

[8]If the rate were fixed, a deficit would develop in the balance of payments. This is prevented by downward movement of the exchange rate, which is defined here as the price per unit of domestic currency in terms of foreign currency.

to two opposing factors. On the one hand, the exchange rate can be used to eliminate the external constraint on the pursuit of full employment. For this purpose the rate should be allowed to float as freely as possible. On the other hand, large changes in the exchange rate may carry the stigma of instability and might be expected to disrupt orderly trade relations.[9] The authorities will therefore aim at control points which remove as much as possible the external constraint on domestic policy while at the same time maintaining an acceptable level of stability. This compromise is not always easy to achieve.

INFLATION AND UNEMPLOYMENT

It is time now to come to grips with what seems to be a fact of modern industrial life, the simultaneous occurrence of inflation and unemployment. In our discussion so far, inflation occurred only after aggregate demand had surpassed the full-employment mark. Let us name this more conventional type of inflation "demand-pull" inflation. Demand-pull inflation and unemployment are mutually exclusive under this definition.

This model, however, does not correspond well to reality in the United States, for example, where substantial unemployment and inflation have existed side by side for a number of years. Let us refer to that kind of inflation, which seems to be largely independent of aggregate demand, as "structural" or "cost-push" inflation. With structural inflation in the picture, it is no longer possible to view full employment and price stability as one and the same target.

Although this problem has existed for some time, it has haunted the Nixon administration in particular. Elected on a pledge to reduce inflation, President Nixon found it difficult to do so by contraction of aggregate demand without also aggravating the unemployment problem. The institution of the New Economic Policy (NEP) in August 1971 with its Pay Board and Price Commission was based on the realization that price stability and full employment represent two targets requiring two policies. NEP was the second policy, geared toward holding wages and

---

[9]Note that instability here simply means large and perhaps sudden changes in the exchange rate. Recall from Chapter 11 a different meaning of instability.

prices down and thus removing the (structural) inflation constraint from expansive aggregate demand policy designed to achieve full employment.[10]

Where does all this leave us with regard to balance of payments adjustment? Let us try to incorporate both demand-pull and structural inflation into our policy framework. We will assume now that prices will always rise in response to expansion of aggregate demand, even before full employment is reached. In addition, contraction of aggregate demand will bring no drop in prices but will leave unchanged whatever rate of inflation exists.

Armed with these qualifications, let us briefly review Table 13-1 once more. As far as external adjustment is concerned, the situation in line 1 seems to benefit from our new assumptions. The surplus will adjust more quickly, since expansion of aggregate demand mobilizes not only the previous income effect but now also a price effect. The domestic situation, of course, will pose the problems discussed above, as lower unemployment rates can only be achieved at the expense of increasing inflation.

Line 2, we recall, presents a conflict situation. Our new assumptions tend to heighten this conflict. If the domestic target is given priority and aggregate demand is expanded, the external deficit will be further burdened by the resulting inflation. If the external target prevails, contraction of aggregate demand will be less effective in adjusting the external deficit since inflationary pressures continue to exist.

In line 3, also a conflict situation, our new assumptions have a different effect. If the domestic target is pursued and aggregate demand is contracted, the external surplus may nevertheless be adjusted by continuing inflation. In this sense, the existence of structural inflation tends to weaken the conflict between internal and external targets.[11] If the external target has priority, the new assumptions have little effect, because expansion of aggregate demand from an already excessive level would increase inflation in any case.

The situation in line 4, finally, is aggravated by structural inflation. The deficit will be slow to adjust if contraction of aggregate demand is

---

[10]The problem of inflation and unemployment occurring simultaneously has plagued virtually every Western industrial economy. Policies such as price or wage controls, designed to attack this problem, come under the general heading of *incomes policy*.

[11]Note, however, the following section on a country's relative position.

accompanied by unmitigated inflation. This seems to have been the case in the United States in 1971.

We may conclude that the existence of structural inflation adds to the problems of external adjustment where it is most crucial, i.e., in cases of balance of payments deficits. This includes the problem associated with devaluation at full employment which we discussed in a special section above.

THE RELATIVE POSITION

The entire discussion so far has been conducted in absolute terms. It was implicitly assumed, in other words, that the policy actions undertaken by the country in question were the only changes to be considered. Everything abroad was assumed to remain constant. This is not the case, of course, and it is easy to see that what matters is expansion or contraction relative to the economies abroad, rather than in absolute terms. Inflation, in absolute terms, also becomes quite meaningless in this context. Only the difference between inflation at home and abroad will affect the balance of payments.

In a world of seemingly universal inflation, this is important to keep in mind. Let us try, at least conceptually, to isolate the two types of inflation we have discussed in their effects on balance of payments adjustment. We could assume, for example, that structural inflation exists throughout the Western industrial world at roughly comparable rates. If this is indeed the case, structural inflation has little effect on the short-term changes in differential inflation rates which tend to dominate balance of payments adjustment. These changes may then be explained primarily by variation in aggregate demand, thus restoring somewhat more analytical power to our basic framework of Table 13-1.

SUMMARY

The principal form of economic policy is the control of aggregate demand with the objective of achieving full employment at stable prices.

An expansionary policy tends to deteriorate the balance of payments, while a restrictive policy tends to improve the balance of payments.

Balance of payments equilibrium as a policy target may or may not be consistent with the other targets, depending on the situation.

Deficient aggregate demand with external surplus and excessive aggregate demand with external deficit are situations in which one policy alone will make it possible to approach both the internal and the external target.

Deficient aggregate demand with external deficit and excessive aggregate demand with external surplus are conflict situations which do not permit the pursuit of both targets with one policy.

Supplemental policies, such as tariffs or special incentives and restrictions aimed at the capital account, can be used to abate the conflict.

If such supplemental policies fail and the conflict persists, an official alteration of the exchange rate may be the only remaining way to resolve the conflict.

Devaluation in a fully employed economy will lead to inflation unless the resources required for the additional exports and import substitutes are released by restriction of aggregate demand.

A system of freely flexible exchange rates would free policy makers from the external constraint.

Structural inflation makes it necessary to view price stability as a target by itself, i.e., separately from the target of full employment. This makes balance of payments adjustment more difficult in cases of a deficit.

A country's economic position, i.e., the state of aggregate demand and the rate of inflation, must be regarded in relative rather than absolute terms.

SUGGESTED FURTHER READINGS

A very thorough treatment of conflicts between internal and external goals is provided by James E. Meade, *The Balance of Payments* (Oxford University Press, London 1951), chaps. 7–10. See also Charles P. Kindleberger, *International Economics*, 5th ed. (Richard D. Irwin, Homewood, Ill. 1973), chap. 22; and Ingo Walter, *International Economics, Theory and Policy* (The Ronald Press Company, New York, 1966), chap. 17. For an interesting concept which treats monetary and fiscal policy as separate weapons, see Robert A. Mundell, "The Appropriate Use of Monetary and Fiscal Policy for Internal and External Stability," *IMF Staff Papers*, March 1962.

Chapter 14

The International Monetary System Before World War II

In our study so far, the balance of payments has been a focal point of considerable importance. This is as it should be. The balance of payments is, after all, the economic link between nations, measuring economic interaction on a broad scale. Up to this point, however, we have approached the balance of payments from the individual country's point of view. We have studied, for example, how the balance of payments affects the value of a country's currency (Chapter 9), and what implications for domestic economic policy the balance of payments contains (Chapter 13).

In the remaining two chapters we shall shift our viewpoint to the global picture. How are different countries' balances of payments reconciled with each other? How does the individual country fit into the global picture? This approach leads us into a discussion of the international monetary system. The discussion is organized in historical sequence. This form of presentation, however, should not be viewed as an abbreviated history of international monetary relations. Rather, it attempts to trace, very selectively, the background of those issues which are particularly relevant to the contemporary international monetary debate.

THE INTERNATIONAL MONETARY SYSTEM

By an international monetary system, in general, we mean any form of prevalent order according to which exchange and trade take place between nations.

The basic purpose of any such system is to make possible an efficient allocation of the world's real resources and to facilitate efficient trade in real goods and services. An international monetary system, in other words, must do for international division of labor and exchange what a national monetary system does for domestic division of labor and exchange. Actually, at this stage of our study we come to the all-important link between the pure theory of trade discussed in Chapters 1 through 4 and the aggregate monetary approach we used in Chapters 8 through 13. The aggregate monetary discussion describes the monetary arrangements—such as the balance of payments and the foreign exchange market—which make it possible to obtain the real gains from trade which we discussed in the earlier chapters.

The point is worth repeating: The ultimate rationale of any international monetary system must be its subordination to the basic principles of international division of labor and trade.

Very broadly speaking, an international monetary system can serve this purpose in two alternate ways. First, it can leave the determination of exchange rates completely to free market forces, resulting in a system of freely flexible exchange rates. As we recall from Chapter 9, the balance of payments would fade into the background in such a system since it would at all times be instantaneously adjusted by changes in the exchange rate.

Secondly, an international monetary system may be based on fixed exchange rates, with the attendant problems of adjusting balances of payments by means other than exchange rate fluctuations.

INTERNATIONAL LIQUIDITY

On the whole, the system of fixed exchange rates has prevailed. Our discussion will consequently be focused on the various problems associated with a fixed-rate system. The most obvious aspect here is the need for international liquidity, i.e., the monetary means of settling balance of payments disequilibrium.

We recall from Chapter 9 that the balance of payments will be in deficit or surplus whenever the exchange rate is fixed at a level which fails to clear the foreign exchange market. The authorities will then have to step in, adding to supply or demand in such a way as to clear the market at the desirable rate. For these pegging operations the authorities will need international reserves whenever a deficit is involved. The availability of international liquidity, therefore, which may be defined as the sum total of all countries' international reserves, is a crucial aspect of a fixed exchange rate system.

Economic conditions are constantly changing, so that while fixed exchange rates presumably remain constant for long periods, it cannot be expected that fixed rates will remain equal to market-clearing equilibrium rates. Balance of payments disequilibrium is therefore the logical consequence of a system of fixed exchange rates. In order to remain rational, i.e., to facilitate free trade, such a system must solve the following problem: It must maintain the flow of goods and capital free of restrictions, even though this flow may result in balance of payments disequilibrium. If exchange rate variation is ruled out, a deficit country, for example, may feel forced into direct trade restrictions such as tariffs, quotas, or exchange controls, in case its stock of international reserves is insufficient to support the fixed exchange rate.

The availability of reserves to each individual country is obviously dependent on the size of the stock of overall international liquidity. We may ask ourselves, therefore, how much international liquidity is required to maintain the system. Although this question cannot be answered precisely, we can envisage certain upper and lower limits. Is it desirable, for example, that each country have unlimited international reserves? The likely result would be for each country to attempt running prolonged deficits. However, this would be impossible to do, since one country's deficit must be another's surplus. No country would want to have a surplus, since everyone already has ample reserves. The situation would soon deteriorate into worldwide skyrocketing of demand for imports while no one would remain willing for long to sell exports. The inevitable result would be runaway inflation on a global scale. This outcome is analogous to the effect of an excessive domestic money supply on the domestic price level.

Clearly, there must be some upper limit to each country's stock of reserves and, therefore, to international liquidity.

Coming now to the lower limit of an adequate supply of international liquidity, we recall from Chapters 12 and 13 the way in which a country can remove a deficit by adjustments of price and income levels while holding the exchange rate constant. A declining stock of limited international reserves under a system of fixed exchange rates serves as a signal for such adjustment to be initiated.[1] But here again, extremes are possible. An insufficient level of reserves could precipitate such adjustment of price and income levels. If deficit countries are forced into precipitous deflationary adjustment by their lack of reserves, the resulting decline in their demand for other countries' exports may transfer some of the deflationary forces to other countries. Such deflationary chain reactions can have disastrous worldwide consequences in terms of employment and production, as we shall see further below.

Let us conclude, therefore, that a system of fixed exchange rates requires an overall volume of international liquidity large enough to avoid worldwide deflation and small enough to avoid worldwide inflation. Once more we may invoke the analogy to a domestic monetary system. Too much money in relation to a given volume of real transactions means inflation; not enough money means deflation and unemployment. This general principle has long been recognized by national monetary authorities, whose primary responsibility it is to control the national money supply within the proper limits.

THE CONTROL OF INTERNATIONAL LIQUIDITY

This analogy, while emphasizing the need for a proper level of international liquidity, falls short in one important respect: National money supplies are managed by officials who derive their authority from national governments. International liquidity cannot be managed with the same degree of authority, because there is no international government.

We are consequently faced with the following question. How can a system function which requires a proper level of liquidity but apparently lacks the authority to create and control liquidity? This must be answered

---

[1] Such adjustment mechanisms may be automatic ones of the type we studied in Chapter 12, or they may result from policy action as we have seen in Chapter 13.

on several different levels, some of which will concern us throughout this and the following chapter.

First, it has been suggested that the system has not functioned properly for precisely the reason given above. But this suggestion is very difficult to judge in the absence of actual alternatives with which the existing system could be compared. Looking at the period from 1945 to the present for example, one might cite the numerous currency crises as evidence for the failure of the system. On the other hand, using our basic rationale of an international monetary system, we may observe that world trade has never been seriously disrupted during this period. On the contrary, the volume of trade has expanded more rapidly than overall world production. The same cannot be said, however, for the period between the two world wars.

Secondly, and perhaps more to the point, we have not yet defined international liquidity in terms of its actual components. Whether or not international liquidity can be controlled within certain limits may depend on the nature of the various assets which are generally in use as international reserves. If certain national currencies, for example, are widely used as international reserves, the authorities in charge of these currencies will have a certain amount of control over international liquidity. In addition, international liquidity can be managed by more or less formal agreement between different countries.[2]

THE CLASSICAL GOLD STANDARD, 1870–1914

Our present international monetary system is a fascinating product of evolution as well as deliberate planning. In order to understand its background and some of the notions currently associated with it, let us trace the broad outline of its history.

We pick up the story during 1870–1914, which is considered the classical period of the gold standard.[3] The dominant center of international trade and finance was London. Sterling and the other major currencies were freely convertible at given ratios into gold, which was thus the basis of their convertibility at fixed rates into each other. There was no major currency crisis during this period, and no major currency had to be

[2]Such cooperative management of liquidity will be discussed in Chapter 15.

[3]For the technical discussion concerning the functioning of a gold standard the reader may wish to consult Chapter 9.

devalued or revalued. International trade and finance flourished. Perhaps the most visible achievement of this period was the great freedom with which goods and capital moved across national borders. Direct trade restrictions, while not altogether unknown, were not generally used for the purpose of balance of payments adjustment.

This task was left to the "rules of the game," which prescribed the classical reaction of an economy to external disequilibrium. Deficits were to be adjusted by prompt, if not precipitous, internal deflation. Surpluses, similarly, were to be removed by internal inflation. It was presumably the willingness of all countries to adhere to these "rules of the game" which kept the classical gold standard working so successfully.

And yet, having just discussed the basic aspects of international liquidity, we may feel some lingering doubts. If gold, exclusively, constituted international liquidity, a question arises with regard to the adequacy of the total gold stock. It is difficult to believe that the world's stock of gold available for monetary use just happened to be neither too large nor too small and to have remained "correct" for fifty years. Even if gold had been available in sufficient volume, and even if mining of new gold had in some way kept up with the rising trend in the volume of international trade and hence the payments imbalances to be settled, the question of control would remain. Was it possible to gear the size of the world's gold stock to the necessarily changing requirements of the system? The only way in which this could have been achieved would have been periodic changes in the price of gold in terms of sterling and other major currencies. But this did not occur between 1870 and 1914.

STERLING AS RESERVE CURRENCY

The answer to our dilemma rests with the role of sterling as a reserve currency during this period. Sterling was acceptable as an international reserve asset to virtually all gold standard countries. Sterling balances, consequently, were widely used in the settlement of balance of payments disequilibrium. They therefore constituted an important component of international liquidity. Sterling balances could be acquired by countries outside Great Britain through various forms of loans from Britain or, of course, by way of a balance of payments surplus. Britain's position as an international investor facilitated the flow of sterling into even the remotest corners of the world. Never before or since has any country invested a comparable share of its savings abroad.[4]

This key position of sterling goes a long way toward answering our question about the control of international liquidity. Whoever controlled the availability of sterling balances controlled an important component of international liquidity. We are, of course, referring to the Bank of England, whose dominance in international monetary affairs was almost legendary during this classical period of the gold standard. The bank's principal tool for controlling the availability of sterling reserves to foreigners was the British rate of interest. If this interest rate, called the "bank rate," was raised, sterling funds would flow into Britain from abroad in order to take advantage of the increased yield on short-term investments. If the rate was lowered, sterling funds would flow out.

Finding the Bank of England thus in charge of international liquidity raises yet another question. How responsive can a single national central bank be to the liquidity needs of the world at large? Or, to put it differently, how consistent is the task of maintaining international liquidity at proper levels with the domestic task of a central bank, i.e., the maintenance of domestic monetary order and prosperity? It may well be that the success of the gold standard during 1870–1914 is ultimately explained by the fact that these two tasks were, on the whole, consistent with each other as far as the Bank of England was concerned. Domestic prosperity in Britain was closely linked with economic stability abroad by virtue of her enormous and far-flung overseas investments. It is no coincidence that the decline in Britain's monetary leadership was accompanied by large losses in her foreign investments.

POSTWAR ADJUSTMENTS

World War I dealt a blow to the British leadership position from which it would never recover. The war effort forced Britain into the sale of parts of her foreign investments. New capital was badly needed at home to revitalize exhausted domestic industries, and it was therefore no longer

---

[4]Leland B. Yeager, *International Monetary Relations*, Harper & Row, Publishers, Incorporated, New York, 1966, p. 256. According to Yeager, about 40 percent of British savings during the forty years before 1914 were invested overseas. In percentage terms this would be more than ten times the current U.S. foreign investment position.

available for overseas investment. Generally speaking, the concentration of all efforts on the war had left little time and resources to look after overseas economic interests. Many countries which were formerly dependent on British products and capital developed their own industries and turned elsewhere—mostly to the United States.

France and Germany, as the most directly involved combatants, were literally depleted and would require much time and outside help to rebuild their economies. Only the United States emerged in a greatly strengthened position. United States products had been in great demand during the war, which resulted in a large U.S. balance of payments surplus. When the United States later entered the war, it became a source of massive aid to its allies, some of which was in the form of loans repayable after the war.

In short, the world economy had undergone a fundamental shock which would require major realignments in the relative positions of most countries. During the first half-decade after the war, the international monetary situation remained too unsettled to suggest even the existence of a monetary system. Although most countries were resigned to letting their currencies fluctuate more or less freely in response to market forces, this situation cannot be viewed as a *system* of flexible exchange rates. The general view of the postwar period was one of temporary transition. Exchange rates had to float because no one knew just how to stabilize them in the face of the great upheaval the world had just witnessed.

GERMAN WAR REPARATIONS

One example of the great strain to which the international economy was subjected as a consequence of the war was the problem of German war reparations. As a result of the Treaty of Versailles (1919) and a subsequent Allied ultimatum, Germany was obliged to pay a very large sum of war reparations. The exact amount of these reparations was never really determined, since it was repeatedly revised as subsequent events showed the difficulties in transferring such massive sums internationally in terms of real purchasing power.

Let us consider for a moment the general problem of such transfers. Suppose, for example, that this debt had been payable in German marks. In terms of prewar gold marks, a debt of $31.5 billion would have been 132 billion marks at 4.2 marks per dollar. By the end of 1921, however, the dollar was worth about 300 marks. Germany, therefore, could easily have paid her debt of 132 billion marks in 1921, paying in fact only $0.44 billion. Hyperinflation of the German mark was rapidly making it useless. By the end of 1923 the mark had inflated to 1.4 trillion times its prewar level.[5] The rate of exchange was bound, of course, to reflect this hyperinflation.

It was for these reasons that the reparations were set in dollars rather than German marks. Even though this fixed the real value of the transfer, a problem still remained with regard to Germany's ability to pay. In other words, how was it possible for Germany to acquire the dollar funds it owed? Our study of the balance of payments and the foreign exchange market suggests that Germany would have had to run up balance of trade surpluses equivalent to its reparation debt.

This, however, was not a realistic possibility in view of the general disarray of the international scene and the depleted state of Germany's economy. Even if they had been possible to achieve, persistent large surpluses by one of the major countries would have caused a severe strain on the other countries. Because of these problems, and primarily at France's insistence, German reparations were set in goods, mainly coal. In order to ensure Germany's willingness and ability to make these payments in kind, the French occupied the German coalfields in 1923. Disregarding the politics of this move, the resulting situation was hardly indicative of free trade under a rational monetary system!

The terms on which this problem was eventually resolved reflect the emerging leadership role of the United States and the U.S. dollar. Under the successive Dawes and Young plans, Germany received large dollar loans underwriting her ability to pay, while at the same time the amount of the debt outstanding was significantly pared down.

THE REESTABLISHMENT OF THE GOLD STANDARD

The mid-1920s saw a concerted effort by all major nations to reestablish the gold standard in essentially its old form. Most notably Britain stabilized sterling at its prewar gold parity in 1925. The United States had returned to gold as early as 1919. France and Italy joined the gold standard after devaluing their currencies. Germany and Russia, whose old currencies had been destroyed by hyperinflation, adopted new gold-

[5]Leland B. Yeager, op. cit., p. 271.

backed currency units. Switzerland and the Netherlands returned to their prewar gold parities.

In spite of all these efforts, however, only the external form and not the real functioning of the gold standard was reestablished. The basic flaw in the new system was that Britain's real economic position was no longer the same as before 1914. The prewar gold parity for sterling had been made unrealistic by subsequent events. Sterling was now over-valued.

The price of maintaining a currency at a fundamentally overvalued . level in a system of fixed exchange rates is painful domestic deflation and unemployment. The British economy paid this price in full during the middle and late twenties. No longer were the policy goals of the Bank of England consistent with the maintenance of adequate international liquid-ity. On the contrary, its main concern seemed to have been the support of sterling at an overvalued rate. The use of bank rate policy for this purpose meant high interest rates in Britain, which tend to have a deflationary effect on international liquidity, as we have seen above.

Faced with constant concern over her balance of payments, Britain furthermore began to gradually erode her time-honored policy of free trade and capital movement. All this could not help but impair foreign confidence in sterling as a reserve asset.

The question of international liquidity, in other words, was far from settled during these years. The U.S. dollar, although it had gained considerably on sterling during and after World War I, was not yet in a position to take the place of sterling as a principal source of international liquidity. Two of the most tragic events in modern times, the Great Depression and World War II, would have to run their course before the dollar would take on this role.

THE COLLAPSE OF THE INTERNATIONAL ECONOMY

The reestablished gold standard of the midtwenties soon proved to be untenable. Although few economists would point to the international monetary situation of the twenties as the cause of the Great Depression, many agree that a deflationary bias of global proportions existed. This deflationary bias not only intensified the collapse but also added to the problems of recovery.

International liquidity was in short supply after sterling had lost some of its prewar luster. Fixed exchange rates at overvalued levels on the one hand and insufficient international liquidity on the other leave individual deficit countries with two alternatives, i.e., domestic deflation or various types of trade restriction. As we approach the late twenties, evidence of both alternatives becomes more and more widespread.

In addition to these basically ominous signs, short-term capital movements played an important part in precipitating pressure on overvalued currencies and spreading a crisis from one currency to others. In Chapter 11 we have discussed the technical aspects of such capital flows. It will be recalled that rumors of impending devaluation tend to cause large outflows of what came to be called "hot money." Such outflows made support of the exchange rate by the authorities more difficult. In addition, as devaluation rumors with respect to one currency are spreading, speculators may try to anticipate the effect of this devaluation on other currencies. A devaluation of the German mark, for example, means an upward revaluation of sterling against the mark. Speculators may ask themselves what the chances will be for the British balance of payments to withstand this increase in the price of sterling. If that balance of payments is in deficit to begin with, a run on the mark may be quickly followed by a run on sterling.

This type of chain reaction occurred again and again during 1931–1932. Sterling came under heavy pressure after a crisis originating in Austria had pushed both Austria and Germany off the gold standard in 1931. When the British government suspended the convertibility of sterling into gold in September 1931, the gold standard came to an end amidst nervous foreign exchange markets and failing economic activity in general on a worldwide scale.

DEFLATION IN THE UNITED STATES

Even surplus countries with basically strong currencies and ample gold reserves were not immune to the general atmosphere of financial panic. After sterling had been left floating by the run of September 1931, the U.S. dollar came under attack. By now there was no major currency left in favor of which one could speculate against the dollar. So the run on the dollar took the form of massive gold purchases, primarily by foreigners with dollar holdings. In spite of the fact that U.S. gold supplies were ample, this gold drain had its effect on the U.S. economy.

In 1931 the U.S. economy was in the midst of its most severe depression on record. Most economists today are inclined to agree that an expansionary monetary policy should have been the order of the day.[6] United States monetary authorities at the time, however, did not take a decisive view of the matter. It appears that fear of inflationary consequences of monetary expansion loomed large. In this situation, the external gold drain served as a warning sign for those who advocated monetary caution. The "rules of the game" of the old gold standard, after all, prescribed deflation (i.e., monetary contraction) as the correct response to a gold outflow.

In this way the U.S. economy was denied an expansionary monetary policy, which, as hindsight tells us, might have alleviated the worst of the Great Depression.

Partly in order to sever this deflationary link between foreign gold purchases and the domestic economy, President Roosevelt, with the approval of Congress, took the United States off the gold standard in the spring of 1933.

MONETARY ARRANGEMENTS OF THE THIRTIES

Although no longer tied to gold since 1931, sterling did not float with complete freedom. An Exchange Equalization Account was established for the purpose of avoiding extreme exchange rate fluctuations. The account would buy and sell sterling on the foreign exchange market as any particular situation required.

A number of countries continued to maintain their international reserves in terms of sterling despite the abandonment of the gold link by Britain. These countries, mainly the members of the British Empire and Scandinavia, formed the *sterling area*, with exchange rates pegged to sterling and thus fixed between each other.

The United States enacted the Gold Reserve Act of 1934, which once more linked the dollar to gold. The price per fine ounce of gold was set at $35, where it remained until November 1971. By virtue of this act, the U.S. government undertook to buy all gold at this price and sell gold at this price to foreign central banks and other official institutions.

---

[6]See for example, Milton Friedman, *Capitalism and Freedom*, University of Chicago Press, 1963, p. 50.

Germany attempted to maintain the pre-depression gold parity of the mark. As this parity became more and more unrealistic, the German government resorted to exchange control on a broad scale. Exchange control, in essence, makes the purchase of foreign currencies for unauthorized purposes illegal. However, authorization was given only to the extent that demand for foreign exchange remained in line with the desired exchange rate. The official exchange rate thus becomes completely divorced from actual market forces. The effect is in many ways comparable with direct trade restrictions such as tariffs or quotas.

France and a number of other European countries (such as Switzerland, Italy, and Belgium) did not leave the gold standard. They formed the *gold bloc* in 1933, promising each other assistance in defending fixed parities based on gold. But most of their currencies eventually proved to be overvalued, and a great deal of internal deflation as well as direct trade restriction was required to maintain their parities. In the end the leading gold bloc country, France, saw itself forced to devalue.

The circumstances surrounding this devaluation of the franc in 1936 introduced a new element to the international financial scene. In the so-called Tripartite Monetary Agreement, France received assurances from the United States and Great Britain that the devaluation of the franc would not be countered by competitive devaluation, exchange controls, or direct trade restrictions.[7] This agreement showed that cooperation between major countries was necessary and possible. Not until after World War II, however, would cooperation become a major cornerstone of the international monetary system.

THE FAILURE OF THE SYSTEM IN RETROSPECT

What sort of conclusions can be drawn from this historical outline? One might perhaps be tempted to conclude that in turbulent times, such as the period between the two world wars, no international monetary system could have worked. Any international system, monetary or otherwise, requires a minimum of agreement on certain ground rules, at least by its principal members. The period of turbulence was also the period of

---

[7]Sterling, of course, could not be devalued in the normal sense of the word since it was floating at the time. We recall, however, that the British Exchange Equalization Account kept a tight rein on the exchange rate and could presumably have lowered the rate of sterling in retaliation to the franc devaluation.

transition from international order and relative peace under British leadership to an era of extreme nationalism.

The old "rules of the game" were essentially international (rather than nationalistic) in their orientation. Balance of payments adjustment was to be given priority over internal goals. Although there is some doubt about the acceptance enjoyed by these rules even in the classical gold standard period, there is little doubt that the balance between internal and external goals shifted toward the internal ones.

Part of the turbulence on the international economic scene was evidently caused by the world's prolonged adherence to a monetary system which no longer fitted the underlying economic conditions. Much of the speculative panic in 1931–1932 was compounded by the authorities' refusal to part with overvalued parities. And, what is worse, trade restrictions designed to protect overvalued currencies contributed to the worldwide failure of production and employment.

A SYSTEM OF FLEXIBLE RATES?

Finally, we might ask ourselves how a system of flexible exchange rates might have fared under similar circumstances. Is it possible, for example, that such a system would have insulated different economies from the spread of deflation and unemployment, since deflationary reaction to overvalued parities would not have been necessary? Actually, we have seen that after World War I and again in the early thirties many currencies did indeed float. Do these experiences give us indications about a flexible rate system?

This question is difficult to answer. A distinction must be made between an international monetary system based on freely flexible rates and the experience of some countries with a flexible rate. An example will clarify this point. Suppose country A's currency is completely flexible while country B operates a fixed-rate system. How, then, is the exchange rate between A and B determined? Since B pegs its rate at some level deemed desirable, it is B whose policy actions determine A's exchange rate with regard to B. This would give B a good deal of influence over A's external as well as internal affairs. The exchange rate, after all, affects prices of imports and exports, and changes in this rate may cause far-reaching changes in production and consumption patterns in A.

While A may be willing to accept such changes as results of free market forces, it will almost certainly refuse to accept them as a consequence (perhaps even intended result) of B's pegging operations. A, therefore, will probably reserve the right to intervene in the foreign exchange market to cancel such policy-induced effects on its currency. Most countries with floating exchange rates, in fact, have intervened in the exchange market from time to time. Britain's Exchange Equalization Account is an example of such a floating rate situation which is nevertheless subjected to official market intervention.

Once official intervention is established in principle, it becomes difficult to judge the purpose of each case of intervention. This problem arises not only in a situation where some currencies are fixed and some float, as in our example above, but also in a system where all currencies float.

It appears, therefore, that a workable system of flexible rates must either rule out all official intervention or establish generally acceptable principles on the basis of which intervention may occur. Either one of these alternatives requires international agreement on certain ground rules. In terms of the necessity for such agreement, then, there is no great difference between fixed and flexible rates.

SUMMARY

The purpose of an international monetary system is to facilitate unrestricted trade in real goods and services.

Just as a national economy requires a proper level of its money supply, the international economy requires a proper level of international liquidity. An excessive level of international liquidity will cause worldwide inflation, while a deficient level will lead to deflation and unemployment.

The proper level of international liquidity will not establish itself automatically. Some degree of control is necessary.

During the period of the classical gold standard, the Bank of England exercised some control over sterling balances held abroad, which functioned as an important component of international liquidity. The policy instrument used for this purpose by the Bank of England was its bank rate.

Immediately after World War I all major currencies were floating, but this state of affairs was generally considered temporary.

German war reparation payments posed a problem for the international monetary system. It was difficult to make the transfer in real, rather than in monetary terms.

During the mid-twenties a concerted international effort was made to reestablish the gold standard in its old form. Many currencies were overvalued at their prewar gold parities. Painful internal deflation was required, especially in Great Britain, to maintain such overvalued parities.

The reestablished gold standard showed a deflationary bias because sterling no longer functioned as reserve currency to the same extent as it had before 1914.

The deflationary bias of the international monetary system in the late twenties contributed to the depth and duration of the Great Depression. Financial panic in 1931–1932 attacked one currency after another by way of speculative short-term capital flows.

The international system contributed to the Great Depression in the United States in the sense that an expansionary monetary policy might have been followed in 1931 if Federal Reserve officials had not been concerned with gold outflows.

A system of flexible exchange rates would require international agreement on the conditions under which exchange market intervention could take place. Even a system in which all official intervention is ruled out would require agreement and cooperation on just this point.

SUGGESTED FURTHER READINGS

On the classical gold standard, see R. G. Hawtrey, *The Gold Standard in Theory and Practice,* 5th ed. (Longmans, Green, London, 1947); also Arthur I. Bloomfield, *Monetary Policy Under the International Gold Standard: 1880-1914* (Federal Reserve Bank of New York, 1959), and his "Short-Term Capital Movements under the Pre-1914 Gold Standard," *Princeton Studies in International Finance,* July 1963. A celebrated discussion of post-World War I conditions may be found in John Maynard Keynes, *The Economic Consequences of the Peace* (Harcourt, Brace & World, Inc., New York, 1920). A very useful and detailed survey up to World War II may be found in Leland B. Yeager, *International Monetary Relations* (Harper & Row, Publishers, Incorporated, New York, 1966), chaps. 14 to 18.

Chapter 15

The International Monetary System since World War II

The Second World War brought an end to whatever order the international-
al monetary situation may have had regained by 1939. Too great was the
strain on the world's resources to speak of monetary order during the
conflict. Once more the world underwent a fundamental shock to its
economic structure, the result of which would have to be a realignment of
economic relations between nations.

The clearest aspect of this realignment was the emergence of the
United States as the undisputed leader of the Western world. United
States shipments of armaments and essential consumer goods during the
war had been the material backbone of the Allied war effort. After the war
only the U.S. economy was able to provide essential reconstruction aid,
since all of the European economies had been largely exhausted or
destroyed.

But there were differences between international reaction to this
situation and the aftermath of World War I. The memory of monetary

turmoil in the twenties and thirties was still fresh, and concern about a possible recurrence was widespread. These memories and concerns prompted the major Western nations to convene at Bretton Woods, New Hampshire, in 1944, in order to design a workable international monetary system.

THE BRETTON WOODS SYSTEM

The result of this conference was a comprehensive blueprint of an international monetary system which sought to combine certain features of the old gold standard with a greater degree of flexibility and some measure of control over international liquidity.

First and foremost, the principle that the international monetary system must facilitate unrestricted trade and investment was reaffirmed.

Secondly, national currencies would be defined in terms of gold parities, and exchange rates would therefore be fixed. Only in case of *fundamental* disequilibrium in its balance of payments would a country be expected to change its exchange rate.

Thirdly, international liquidity would be made available in sufficient amounts to tide countries over periods of temporary (rather than fundamental) balance of payments deficits.

The role of assisting countries in temporary balance of payments difficulties fell to the International Monetary Fund (IMF). The principal feature of its organization was to create a fund or a pool of many different currencies on which individual countries would be able to draw in times of need. We recall from Chapter 9 that the support of its currency by a deficit country requires the sale of foreign currencies on the foreign exchange market by the authorities. Let us see how the IMF can increase a country's access to foreign currency funds needed for such pegging purposes.

Each country deposits its *quota* with the IMF, 25 percent of which must be deposited in gold while the remaining 75 percent is in the country's own currency.[1] Equipped with these deposits of gold and all members' currencies, the fund can begin its operation, which consists basically of selling and buying currencies. More specifically, the IMF will

---

[1]The size of each country's quota was set according to its international trade volume, stock of reserves, and other measures of relative economic importance.

sell a particular foreign currency to a country which needs that currency for its pegging operations in the foreign exchange market. The buying country pays with its own currency. In fact, these purchases are more properly viewed as foreign currency loans, since the buying country is expected to sell these foreign funds back to the IMF within a reasonable period.[2]

In addition, there are limits to such borrowing. Any country may automatically borrow up to 25 percent of its quota. This automatic drawing right is called a country's *gold tranche.*[3] Borrowing in excess of the gold tranche is possible, but no longer automatic. Such borrowing falls into a country's *credit tranche.* In order to make credit tranche loans, the IMF will have to be persuaded that the borrowing country is taking appropriate measures to adjust its balance of payments deficit, such as anti-inflationary monetary and fiscal policy, etc. This persuasion will become more difficult as the credit tranche percentage increases.[4] When the IMF's holding of a country's currency has reached 200 percent of its quota, this country has reached the limits of its credit tranche.[5]

THE IMF AND INTERNATIONAL LIQUIDITY

How do these arrangements affect international liquidity? To begin with, the original depositing of each country's quota does not affect liquidity. Each country deposits 25 percent of its quota in gold. This will reduce its gold reserves, but increase reserves under the gold tranche category.

Next we consider borrowing up to the gold tranche limit. The borrowing country counts the foreign currency funds obtained as reserves, but its gold tranche is reduced by an equivalent amount. The country whose currency is being borrowed, on the other hand, obtains an increase in its gold tranche equal to the amount borrowed. International liquidity has therefore increased by the amount borrowed.

Borrowing under the credit tranche increases international reserves of the borrowing country as well as the country whose currency is being

---

[2]A period of up to three to five years was considered reasonable.

[3]The name results from the fact that these 25 percent are equal to the percentage of the quota which had to be deposited in gold.

[4]In addition, the IMF collects a "service charge" on all drawings. This charge rises with the percentage of its quota a country wishes to borrow *and* with the length of time a drawing has been outstanding.

[5]Actually, the so-called "first credit tranche," i.e., 25 percent in excess of the gold tranche, has been treated as all but automatic.

borrowed. The former adds the borrowed foreign exchange to its reserves, and the latter receives an increase in its gold tranche.

It is important to note that these IMF operations in no case generate a *permanent* addition to international liquidity, since all borrowed reserves must be repaid.[6] Such repayment occurs when the borrower country buys its own currency back from the IMF.

We may conclude, then, that the IMF was given considerable power in the area of borrowed reserves or temporary liquidity. *Temporary* balance of payments disequilibria and *temporary* liquidity creation—these concepts seemed well coordinated by the Bretton Woods planners. The cure for fundamental disequilibrium, after all, was to be currency devaluation or revaluation. The function of the IMF must thus be seen in the light of the overall design of the Bretton Woods system.

The twenties and thirties had demonstrated the weakness of rigidly fixed exchange rates in terms of deflationary pressure on deficit countries with overvalued currencies. Floating rates, on the other hand, and general uncertainty about the future course they would take, had given rise to speculative runs, competitive devaluation, and much disruption of trade in general. The founders of the Bretton Woods system intended to avoid the disadvantages of both rigidly fixed and uncooperatively flexible rates. They sought to combine the best features of a fixed-rate system (i.e., stability and orderliness of trade) with the best features of a flexible-rate system (i.e., balance of payments adjustment by exchange rate changes).

The result was a system in which exchange rates were to remain fixed unless fundamental disequilibrium occurred. Such fundamental disequilibrium was to be adjusted *not* by internal deflation or inflation, but by exchange rate alteration. International liquidity in this new system would be needed to finance temporary rather than fundamental balance of payments disequilibrium.[7] It was in this context that the IMF, with its powers to control temporary additions to liquidity, was to add flexibility and resiliency to the Bretton Woods system. Before we discuss the performance of this system, let us turn to some related postwar developments.

---

[6]This statement may be qualified in two ways. First, if the IMF should relax its lending standards across the board so that *at any time* more drawings will be outstanding, the increase in liquidity is in a sense permanent. Secondly, Special Drawing Rights (SDRs) are permanent additions to liquidity. They will be discussed below.

[7]The general IMF rule, that foreign currency drawings should be repaid in three to five years, may serve as some notion as to the time period after which a temporary disequilibrium would be considered a fundamental one.

STERLING CONVERTIBILITY AND DEVALUATION IN 1949

One of the goals of the Bretton Woods convention had been the return to normal trade relations free of restriction as soon as possible. This, however, proved to be a difficult and lengthy process. At the end of the war all currencies except the U.S. dollar were subject to stringent exchange controls by their national authorities. It was illegal, in other words, to purchase foreign exchange for unauthorized purposes. Such controls reflected the inability or unwillingness of various countries to either peg the exchange rates at some given level or to allow its determination by market forces.

Most of these exchange controls were deemed necessary in the face of extreme dollar shortage in Europe. The demand for dollars was as great as the need for imports from the United States. By comparison, the supply of dollars was all but nonexistent, since no European country was able yet to produce significant exports for the U.S. market. The resulting dollar shortage was so acute that only exchange controls were considered capable of preventing the collapse of various European currencies.

The first country to reintroduce convertibility of its currency into dollars was Great Britain in 1947. Armed with a large dollar loan from the United States (which would enable the Bank of England to support sterling by selling dollars in the foreign exchange market), Britain removed all exchange controls at $4.03 per pound sterling. This move was not successful, however. Foreign owners of sterling balances rushed to exchange these funds into dollars.[8] They apparently felt that $4 per pound sterling was a bargain price. They were right, as subsequent events soon showed. The dollar loan was quickly exhausted, and Britain was forced to retreat into exchange control.

But the long-range goal of sterling convertibility was not abandoned. Whenever conditions permitted, controls were relaxed in various ways. Unofficial markets for sterling developed overseas, and traders found ways to circumvent official exchange controls. This gradual revival of market forces tended to show sterling as overvalued at $4.03. Official recognition of this fact came in 1949, when sterling was devalued by no less than 30 percent to $2.80. Even after this sharp increase in the price of

---

[8]The existence of about $3.5 billion worth of sterling balances in foreign hands was the legacy of sterling's rule as a reserve currency. Britain had financed part of her wartime imports in terms of "domestic balances due foreigners." Compare Chapter 8 for the mechanics of such financing.

the U.S. dollar, exchange controls would not be abandoned altogether for another six to eight years.

EUROPEAN BILATERALISM

The sterling devaluation of 1949 could not be ignored by other countries. If the point of this devaluation was to make sterling cheaper in terms of dollars, but not other currencies, then other countries would have to follow Britain's lead and devalue their currencies also. This is what happened without delay. Virtually all major Western countries, except of course the United States, devalued shortly after Britain. This result indicated the basic strength of the U.S. dollar with regard to the rest of the world. The problem of realignment was, therefore, basically one between the United States and Western Europe.

The problem among European countries themselves was not so much one of realignment as it was the task of dismantling the maze of exchange controls and trade restrictions. Trade in postwar Europe was largely based on bilateral arrangements, which tend to be a corollary of strict exchange control. Let us consider for a moment the basic implications of bilateralism.

A country conducting trade through bilateral agreements attempts to balance its payments with regard to each trading partner separately rather than with regard to all trading partners as a group. Great Britain, for example, might have a deficit with the United States but a surplus with France. Britain's total balance of payments is in equilibrium only if her liabilities to the United States can be cleared against her claims on France. This clearing mechanism, however, requires convertibility of all three currencies into each other: Britain must be able, for example, to pay off the United States with French francs or sterling. France must be able to acquire dollars if she chooses to pay her debt to Britain in dollars, etc.

Multilateralism, i.e., the clearing of a surplus with one country against a deficit with another, requires convertibility. Inconvertibility and exchange control, on the other hand, often lead to bilateral balancing. Let us use a greatly oversimplified example to show the shortcomings of bilateral trade.

Suppose basic economic conditions are such that America exports wheat to Britain and imports wine from France. Britain exports textiles to France and imports wheat from America. France, consequently, exports wine to America and imports textiles from Britain. Without exchange control, such triangular trade would result in efficient resource allocation in the sense that the production of wine, wheat, and textiles would take place wherever the resource endowment is best suited to such production. Given appropriate exchange rates, the three balances of payments could be in equilibrium through multilateral clearing.

Now consider the consequences of bilateralism in this example. Britain has no wine to export to America, and trade between Britain and America ceases, since it cannot be bilaterally balanced. France has no wheat to export to Britain, and America has no textiles to export to France. Trade, in other words, ceases altogether in this simplified example.

In reality, of course, some product can usually be found which can be exchanged. But the exchange will be severely constrained by bilateralism. France may export wheat to Britain not because she is an efficient producer of wheat, but because Britain has some unused bilateral claim on France. The implications of bilateralism, then, are twofold. First, it leads to misallocation of resources, and secondly it tends to reduce the volume of trade.

THE EUROPEAN PAYMENTS UNION

In order to gradually relax and finally dismantle bilateralism, the European Payments Union (EUP) was established in 1950. In essence, the EPU operated as a clearing house between Western European countries. Bilateral claims and liabilities were converted into positions with the EPU. In this way each country ended up with one position vis-à-vis the EPU, rather than with a host of bilateral positions. This transition to intra-European multilateralism was carefully managed by the EPU through the extent to which individual countries were allowed to build up net debtor positions with the EPU. Such net debtor positions, of course, reflected balance of payments deficits with the other European countries.

As the EPU gradually succeeded, exchange controls were abandoned step by step. At the same time this process enabled the Organization of European Economic Cooperation (OEEC) to work toward reduction of direct trade restrictions on a broad scale. By 1958 it was apparent that economic conditions in Europe had improved sufficiently to formally abandon most controls. The EPU was terminated, and all major currencies became convertible into each other and, most importantly, into the U.S. dollar. Europe, in other words, was ready to join the international economy under the general IMF provisions discussed above.

THE GOLD–DOLLAR STANDARD

The year 1958 marks an important junction in our discussion. The preceding years may be considered a period of reconstruction and reorganization required by the ravages of World War II. But now in 1958 conditions came into line with what had been viewed at Bretton Woods as eventually desirable. Exchange controls were phased out, exchange rates were fixed, direct trade restrictions were being reduced, and a general spirit of international cooperation prevailed.

The system which actually emerged, however, did not conform in all respects to the Bretton Woods design. The shortage of U.S. dollars, for example, continued to present a problem for IMF operations. According to IMF rules, loans extended under the gold or credit tranche had to be repaid in gold or any convertible currency, regardless of which currency had been borrowed. It was therefore conceivable that loans in semiconvertible or soft currencies would have to be repaid in convertible or hard ones.[9] In order to avoid such possibilities, most countries borrowed dollars in the first place. In the first four years of IMF operations, 85 percent of all drawings were in U.S. dollars. The IMF's automatic access to dollars, however, was limited to 75 percent of the U.S. quota, as we have seen above. The effectiveness of the IMF was therefore limited by this concentration of demand on the U.S. dollar. If IMF drawings had been more evenly distributed over several currencies, as perhaps envisaged in its original design, the IMF would have had a larger effective pool of liquidity.[10]

The preference for U.S. dollars over other currencies was widespread. Even the EPU's basic unit of account for its clearing purposes had been the U.S. dollar. Since only the dollar, furthermore, was actually convertible into gold, its standing as an international reserve asset became

---

[9] An overvalued currency may be viewed as a soft one in the sense that it is likely to drop in relative value. In the postwar period many countries tried to prevent such declines by exchange controls, i.e., by limiting their currency's convertibility. In this way the concepts of "soft" and "inconvertible" become related.

[10] Large amounts of dollar reserves were nevertheless acquired abroad. This process did not involve the IMF but was based directly on U.S. balance of payments deficits, which began in the early fifties. We will discuss the problems of this liquidity source in greater detail below.

equal to that of gold. With the advent of convertibility in 1958, the system of fixed exchange rates was working in the following way: Formally, and in keeping with the Bretton Woods design, exchange rates were fixed on the basis of each currency's gold parity. In practice, however, the gold link existed only for the dollar. All other currencies were pegged to the dollar, rather than to gold.[11] This arrangement was called the gold-exchange standard or, perhaps more aptly, the gold–dollar standard. Needless to say, the dollar–gold equivalence is a crucial aspect of such a system.

CONDITIONS IN THE EARLY SIXTIES

Convertibility had come to stay. In fact, it ushered in a period of rapidly growing trade volume and general prosperity on both sides of the Atlantic. Very broadly speaking, therefore, one might say that the gold-exchange standard worked well.

The sixties, however, were not without their strains and stresses on the international monetary scene. With the benefit of hindsight, some of these strains can be viewed as early signs of some basic inconsistencies in the system. The U.S. dollar became the major source of international liquidity. Between 1958 and 1968, foreign countries were thus able to add some $30 billion to their stock of reserve assets, most of which were in the form of dollars.[12] The principal channel through which those dollars found their way abroad was of course the U.S. balance of payments deficit.[13]

This deficit had already been a factor in 1958 when it made the transition to convertibility easier for European currencies than would have been the case otherwise. Now, during the sixties, the U.S. deficit became a more or less permanent feature of the international monetary system. The Bretton Woods system, in other words, which counted heavily on adjustment of fundamental deficits, ended up relying on just such a deficit to obtain its international liquidity.

Initially, to be sure, there seemed to be little reason to adjust the U.S. deficit. The world was starved for dollars. Foreign central banks were eager to replenish their reserves with dollars. At its fixed gold parity the dollar was as sound a reserve asset as gold. In fact, dollar funds could be

---

[11]Some countries of the sterling area continued to peg to sterling.
[12]Bank for International Settlements, 42d Annual Report, Basel, 1972, p. 14.
[13]Recall from Chapter 8 the role of "domestic balances due foreigners."

invested in short-term U.S. Treasury bills, while gold had to be stored and guarded and earned no return.

We recall from Chapter 14 that the U.S. commitment to maintain the dollar's gold parity at $35 per ounce was qualified by the provision that gold sales would be restricted to foreign central banks and other official institutions. The possibility therefore arose that private markets for gold would develop abroad.[14] If the price of private gold were to exceed $35, confidence in the gold-exchange standard might suffer, since such a price differential might be taken as evidence for overvaluation of the dollar.

In order to prevent such problems, the *London gold pool* was established in 1960. The purpose of this pool was to provide the Bank of England, as agent for the gold pool, with a buffer stock of gold which could be used for intervention in the private gold market.[15] In this way, the price of private gold was kept in line with its official dollar parity throughout most of the sixties.

THE EURO-DOLLAR MARKET

An important element in the actual functioning of the gold-exchange standard, besides official willingness to hold dollars, was the international use of the dollar in the private sector. A large portion of all international trade was invoiced and paid for in U.S. dollars, regardless of whether or not the United States was a party to this trade. This meant that exporters and importers everywhere maintained transactions balances in dollars which tended to rise with the volume of world trade.[16]

In addition, this private use of the dollar in trade gave rise to its use in financing operations. Not all of this dollar financing remained based in the United States. A large market for dollar financing developed in Europe after 1958. This so-called *Euro-dollar market* was centered in London, where the international banking establishment shifted from its earlier sterling financing to increasing use of the dollar.

On the demand side of the Euro-dollar market were users of short-term dollar loans, and on the supply side were owners of dollars who were looking for better returns on their funds than were available in

---

[14]Private markets for monetary gold are illegal in the United States.

[15]The members of the gold pool were Belgium, Italy, the Netherlands, Switzerland, Germany, Britain, and the United States. Although all members contributed gold to the pool, the heaviest burden fell on the United States.

[16]It may be recalled from Chapter 10 that these privately held dollars gave rise to a debate over the definition of the U.S. deficit.

the form of U.S. interest rates. What evolved was a network in which a given dollar balance could be lent out again and again to traders, for example, who needed dollar financing. In this way the Euro-dollar market economized on international liquidity by increasing the turnover of dollar balances.

THE PERSISTENCE OF FUNDAMENTAL DISEQUILIBRIUM

As we have seen above, the U.S. deficit, although inconsistent with Bretton Woods principles, nevertheless contributed much to the actual functioning of the system. The same cannot be said for other countries' external disequilibria, especially when it became evident that they were fundamental and persistent rather than temporary. Two examples of such disequilibrium positions in the sixties were Britain's deficit and Germany's surplus.

In the case of Great Britain, we must recall her earlier position of dominance. The pound sterling was still a reserve currency in the sterling area and in certain other countries. This accounted for the fact that British short-term liabilities to foreigners, i.e., foreign-owned sterling balances, were several times larger than British reserves of gold, dollars, and other convertible currencies. This "overhang" inherited from the past compounded a situation which came to be characterized by persistent deficits in Britain's balance of payments.

Britain was reluctant to devalue, in part because such devaluation would cause large losses to all foreign holders of sterling balances. The sixties consequently saw a number of sterling crises caused by the chronic deficit and intensified by the large volume of sterling in foreign hands. These crises have been compared to runs on a bank whose liquid liabilities far exceed its liquid assets. Such a position is entirely normal for a commercial bank, unless of course doubts arise among its depositors about the solvency of the bank.

Great Britain's resistance to devaluation throughout a series of such crises made great liquidity demands on the Bretton Woods system. The IMF, although cooperating fully, did not have sufficient resources. Most of the funds needed for the defense of sterling came from joint assistance operations of the other major countries.[17]

On the whole, Britain's experience was not entirely in keeping with

[17]We will discuss operations such as the General Arrangements to Borrow and "swap facilities" below.

the Bretton Woods design. Again and again defense of sterling was enacted in terms of domestic austerity programs. This, however, was precisely the deflationary reaction to external deficit which had been so notorious during the Great Depression. Apart from such gloomy associations with the past, deflationary programs for external purposes were becoming increasingly unacceptable and unsuccessful in modern industrial economies. As a consequence, Britain saw herself forced on various occasions during the sixties to resort to direct trade restrictions such as surcharges on imports. When sterling devaluation finally came in 1967, it was as a last resort after all other measures had failed.

The German case was one of persistent surplus. Domestic monetary reform in 1948 and subsequent recovery—which has been called an "economic miracle" by some—were gradually being reflected in external surpluses. The hyperinflation of the twenties had left the Germans with an intense aversion to inflation of any kind. Relatively docile labor unions and specific government programs favoring export industries are also often cited in connection with Germany's surplus.

What interests us here is Germany's reluctance to adjust this surplus, which by all signs proved to be fundamental. In terms of real welfare, after all, a persistent surplus means that a nation is giving up a larger share of its total output to foreigners in the form of exports than it receives back as imports. Currency revaluation could remove this gap by making foreign products cheaper to domestic consumers and domestic products more expensive to foreigners.

Resistance to revaluation typically comes from the export industries, who see their position in foreign markets eroding.[18] These industries are usually quick to point out that they would have to curtail employment in the event of revaluation.[19] While these arguments do not alter our observation about the real-welfare effect of a fundamental surplus, they usually have sufficient political backing to make revaluation very difficult for a government.[20]

ADDITIONAL FINANCING ARRANGEMENTS

We have discussed the cases of Great Britain and Germany as examples of persistent disequilibrium which was not anticipated at Bretton Woods

---

[18]In the case of Germany, the politically powerful farm sector also opposed revaluation because it meant lower prices for agricultural imports. Compare the EEC farming problem in Chapter 5.

[19]During the crisis of 1969 (which eventually resulted in revaluation) German workers demonstrated under slogans such as: "Revaluation—Betrayal of the German Worker."

[20]The German mark was revalued in 1961, 1969, 1971, and 1973, but both the size and frequency of these revaluations were widely regarded as insufficient.

and which would eventually contribute to the failure of the system. In the meantime much thought and energy went into the design of mechanisms by which exchange rates could be supported even when such exchange rates reflected fundamental disequilibrium. The liquidity requirements of the system in the sixties were correspondingly large and growing. On occasion they were far in excess of regular IMF capability.

To remedy this situation the General Arrangements to Borrow were formed in 1962 among the so-called *Group of Ten*.[21] Under this agreement the members of the group would lend their own currencies to any member who faced balance of payments problems beyond the scope of IMF assistance. A total of $6 billion was committed to this purpose by the Group of Ten. Funds under this agreement were mobilized repeatedly during massive currency crises, such as the sterling crisis of 1967 or the run on the French franc in 1968.

Another such mechanism of mutual assistance consisted of so-called *reciprocal credit facilities* between individual central banks largely within the Group of Ten. Under this program, also known as *swap agreements*, two central banks would be prepared to exchange a given amount of their currencies at a given rate for a given period of time. For example, a country whose currency was under speculative attack could obtain the foreign currency needed for its pegging operations at the fixed rate of exchange. After the crisis had passed—perhaps because enough foreign exchange had been made available to prove speculators' expectations wrong—these foreign funds could be repaid at the originally agreed-upon rate of exchange.[22] In essence, these swaps amounted to foreign currency loans without interest or exchange risk to the borrower.

Generally speaking, we may view the sixties as a period of cooperation and mutual assistance between the major Western central banks. But this cooperation was concerned almost exclusively with just one problem; how to meet currency crises. Very little was accomplished in finding ways to eliminate the underlying causes of these crises. While the means of financing balance of payments disequilibria, in other words, were expanded and improved, little was done about improving the balance of payments adjustment mechanism.

Critics of the system went further and contended that it was precisely the ease with which disequilibrium could be maintained which prevented

[21]The members are: Belgium, Canada, France, Germany, Italy, Japan, the Netherlands, Sweden, Britain, and the United States.

[22]Actually, these swaps were purchases of spot foreign exchange coupled with simultaneous forward sale. The forward rate, however, was not the free market rate but one agreed upon by the authorities. It was usually equal to the spot rate. For the technical details on forward operations, recall Chapter 11.

the adjustment mechanism (i.e., more frequent exchange rate changes) from working properly.

THE TWO-TIER SYSTEM IN 1968

Even though the currency crises of the sixties cannot be considered minor events without implications, they did not amount to frontal attacks on the system directly. The U.S. dollar as the center of the gold-exchange standard continued in its role of reserve currency, and its link to gold was maintained by the United States officially and by the gold pool in the private markets.

Gold, however, was gradually draining out of U.S. reserves, as foreign central banks redeemed at least part of their dollar holdings. This gold drain, combined with rapidly increasing dollar liabilities to official as well·as private foreigners, caused mounting concern about the ability of the United States to adhere to the official gold price of $35. Speculators were beginning to view the price of gold as a one-way proposition. Buying gold in the London gold pool at about $35 seemed to involve no risk, since the United States would certainly not *lower* the officially supported gold price.

Early in 1968 private gold purchases in London and elsewhere were building up to massive proportions. Faced with staggering daily gold losses, the authorities decided to close and then to abolish the gold pool altogether. The resulting arrangement became known as the *two-tier system.* The private price of gold was now free to follow private supply and demand. The dollar's gold parity, which had been an important component of the system, now became somewhat artificial, even though the United States remained prepared to sell gold at $35 to foreign central banks and official institutions until August 1971.[23]

THE EUROPEAN VERSUS THE U.S. VIEW

The closing of the London gold pool was the first serious crack in the Bretton Woods system. It seemed inevitable now that further large

---

[23]The private gold price oscillated around $40 for the remainder of 1968 and throughout the first half of 1969. In the following ten months it remained close to $35, occasionally even falling slightly below. Beginning in September 1970 it began an upward move, which accelerated in May 1972. By the end of 1972 the price was around $70, and by June 1973 it had reached $127.

increases in foreign dollar holdings would undermine the position of the dollar as a reserve currency. Already the United States was using political persuasion to limit gold purchases by foreign central banks. This meant that foreign central banks had to be persuaded to hold more dollars than they desired. If, in addition, we recall that the source of these no longer entirely welcome dollars was a continuing U.S. balance of payments deficit, we have the makings of a tense situation.

There were marked differences between the European and the American perception of this situation.[24] In the European view, the key to the problem was the U.S. balance of payments deficit. In particular, the Europeans pointed to inflation in the United States, which was associated with the war in Vietnam. This inflation, they claimed, not only deepened the U.S. deficit and thus forced even larger dollar funds on European central banks, but also eroded the real value of these dollar reserves. In the European view, accordingly, the United States was to "put its house in order" in the interest of the international monetary system. Translated into our terminology, this means that the Europeans expected the United States to attempt balance of payment adjustment by deflationary internal policies.

The United States took a different view of the matter. Was it, asked U.S. spokesmen, entirely consistent on the part of the Europeans to decry their swelling dollar reserves on the one hand but to insist on their balance of payments surpluses on the other? The U.S. deficit, after all, was the European surplus. The Europeans could therefore achieve their objective of reducing the U.S. deficit by reducing their own surpluses. This could be done without undue reliance on internal adjustment (i.e., inflation) by revaluation of European currencies against the dollar.

In short, while the existence of fundamental disequilibrium was acknowledged on both sides of the Atlantic, the task of adjustment was suggested by each side to the other. The resulting impasse would not be resolved for some time.

SPECIAL DRAWING RIGHTS

In the meantime, agreement was reached on the need to create an international reserve asset which would take some of the burden of

---

[24]To speak of one single European viewpoint is, of course, an oversimplification. French, German, and British views of monetary reform, for example, differ widely. Nevertheless, when we describe a single viewpoint, we refer to those issues in which there was something like a European consensus.

expanding international liquidity from the U.S. dollar. This new asset took the form of Special Drawing Rights (SDRs) under the sponsorship of the IMF.

SDRs are automatic rights to draw on the IMF over and above all other drawing facilities. They are allocated to each country in proportion to its IMF quota. The country receiving this allocation is not required to deposit gold or its own currency in exchange. Neither do drawings of SDRs have to be paid back, as do all other drawings on the IMF. Therefore, SDRs constitute a permanent net addition to international liquidity.

It was expected that SDRs would be acceptable to all member countries just as gold or convertible currencies would be.[25] A deficit country could thus use SDRs for settling purposes by exchanging SDRs for whatever currency it requires.

The decision to issue SDRs must be approved by an 85 percent majority of the IMF membership.[26] The IMF was empowered in this way to distribute among its members $3.5 billion of SDRs in 1970 and $3 billion each in 1971 and 1972.

THE DOLLAR CRISIS OF 1971

The creation of SDRs was undoubtedly an impressive achievement of international cooperation. Never before had an international institution been given the power to create a monetary asset of its own. The world seemed a step closer to a system in which international liquidity could be managed independently of the vagaries of Russian or South African gold sales or the U.S. deficit.

And yet, the achievement was in the area of balance of payments *financing* rather than *adjustment.* By early 1971, it became clear that the impasse on adjustment between American and European views had, if anything, intensified. Several factors brought the situation to a head in August 1971.

First, the U.S. balance of payments showed deficits in 1970 and 1971 which were enormous if compared with those of previous years. Particu-

---

[25]Clearly, the success of the SDR scheme rests largely on this question of acceptability.

[26]IMF voting does not proceed in terms of one vote per country. A country's votes are proportionate to its *quota*. Since both the United States and the EEC have more than 15 percent of the total vote, they each could veto further issuing of SDRs.

lar concern was caused by the fact that the *trade balance,* which is widely regarded as a basic measure of international competitiveness, turned into deficit for the first time.[27]

Secondly, monetary policies in the United States and in Germany were in opposite phases. The United States was in the midst of monetary expansion to facilitate recovery from the recession of the late sixties. Germany was fighting inflation by restrictive monetary measures. The result of this disparity was large short-term capital flows into Germany.

Finally, heavy speculative inflows reflected spreading belief that the German mark would have to be revalued. The Germans, swamped by these inflows, decided not to revalue officially but to float the mark in May. At the same time, Switzerland revalued by 7 percent in order to forestall similar inflows. So far the crisis had revolved mainly around these two currencies.

But by August a massive flight from the dollar into various European currencies set in. European central banks saw their dollar reserves increase rapidly and did not hesitate to present large sums to the United States for redemption into gold and other reserve assets.[28] The United States, accordingly, lost $3 billion of its reserves and drew to the extent of another $2.4 billion on its official swap facilities in the first eight months of 1971.

On August 15 President Nixon announced that the United States would no longer redeem the dollar by selling gold or other reserve assets. The immediate effect of this announcement was the closing of all European exchange markets. When they reopened a week later, all European currencies were floating.[29]

This left the Japanese yen as the only major currency still pegged to the dollar at its precrisis level. The Bank of Japan was immediately obliged to buy huge sums of dollars at the yen's upper intervention point. About $4 billion had to be absorbed within two weeks, before the Japanese government found it impossible to stem this tide and allowed the yen to float.

What followed was a period of very intense international bargaining. The generally accepted premise in these negotiations was that fixed

---

[27]For a detailed presentation of the U.S. balance of payments, see Chapter 10.

[28]By other reserve assets we mean convertible currencies other than dollars.

[29]France introduced a distinction between the "commercial" franc, i.e., francs used for trade and other current account transactions, and the "financial" franc. The former remained pegged, and the latter was allowed to float.

exchange rates should be restored as soon as possible and that a basic realignment of parities was necessary. But beyond this premise remained substantial disagreement as to how these goals should be achieved.

Together with the suspension of the dollar's gold link the United States had also announced a 10 percent surcharge on all imports. This surcharge caused great concern abroad. The possibility, for example, of EEC retaliation with a surcharge of its own raised fears that an era of global trade restriction was impending.

THE SMITHSONIAN AGREEMENT OF DECEMBER 1971

In retrospect it appears that the U.S. surcharge was meant primarily as a bargaining card in the ensuing negotiations. The basic U.S. objective in these negotiations was substantial revaluation of European currencies and the yen. The U.S. import surcharge would presumably induce other countries to let their floating currencies appreciate substantially against the dollar, since the eventual removal of the surcharge would weaken the dollar beyond the point of general realignment established by floating *with* the surcharge.[30] In this way the United States sought to make large appreciations against the dollar an accomplished fact by the time realignment of fixed rates would take place.

Europe and Japan took a different view. First and foremost they insisted that the dollar be devalued. A deficit country, they argued, should devalue its currency rather than expect the rest of the world to revalue.[31]

Devaluation of the dollar had special implications. As we have already seen, all other countries' currencies under the gold-exchange standard were pegged to the dollar. Changes in other countries' exchange rates, therefore, were normally expressed in terms relative to the dollar. A dollar devaluation obviously could not take this form. Rather, the dollar's gold parity would have to be changed. The United States resisted this course initially, in part because it seemed probable that many countries (other than European countries and Japan) would follow such a devaluation and thereby cancel part of its effect.

A compromise was reached in December 1971 and formalized as the

[30]As we might have expected, few currencies actually floated *freely*. Several European and the Japanese Central Bank bought dollars from time to time in order to avoid what they felt would be excessive appreciation of their currencies against the dollar. Recall our remarks on a system of freely flexible rates in Chapter 14.

[31]By this time the Europeans had given up their view that the U.S. deficit should be adjusted only by internal deflation.

Smithsonian Agreement. The provisions of this agreement were as follows:

Table 15-1 Smithsonian Currency Realignment

Currency	Change against gold, percent	Change against U.S. dollar, percent	New rate per U.S. dollar
Japanese yen	+7.7	+16.9	308.00
Swiss franc	+7.1	+13.9	3.84
Austrian schilling	+5.1	+11.6	23.30
German mark	+4.6	+13.6	3.2225
Belgian franc	+2.8	+11.6	44.8159
Dutch guilder	+2.8	+11.6	3.2447
Pound sterling	0	+8.6	2.60571*
French franc	0	+8.6	5.1157
Italian lira	−1.0	+7.5	581.50
Swedish krona	−1.0	+7.5	4.8129
U.S. dollar	−7.9		

*Dollars per pound sterling.
Source: Bank for International Settlements, 42d Annual Report, Basel, June 1972, p. 30.

The structure of exchange rates was realigned by changing the gold parities of most currencies, *including* that of the dollar. While the gold parity of the dollar was decreased, that of most other currencies was raised. In this way the dollar was devalued against all European currencies and the Japanese yen. Table 15-1 gives the details of this realignment.

In addition to this realignment, the margins between the new parities and their upper and lower intervention points were raised from 1 to 2.25 percent, thus allowing a total margin of 4.5 percent.[32]

Finally, the United States removed the import surcharge, and all parties agreed that more basic changes were necessary in the international monetary system.

Plans for monetary reform were to be prepared by the *Committee of Twenty,* which was appointed at the annual IMF meeting in September 1972. This committee was broadly representative of IMF membership. It was charged with presenting a preliminary report to the 1973 annual meeting.

[32]For details on this margin, recall Chapter 9.

Table 15-2   Some dates in Postwar International Finance

1944	Bretton Woods Conference, IMF
1947	Sterling temporarily convertible at $4.03
1949	Sterling devalued to $2.80
1950	EPU established
1958	General convertibility—EPU discontinued
1960	London gold pool begins operations
1962	General Arrangements to Borrow—Group of Ten
1967	Sterling devalued to $2.40
1968	London gold pool closed down
1970	First SDR allocation
1971	May: German mark floats
	August: Dollar crisis—U.S. off gold—all currencies float
	December: Smithsonian Agreement
1972	September: Committee of Twenty established
	December: U.S. trade deficit $6.4 billion
1973	February: Dollar devalued
	March: Joint European float against the dollar—yen, Swiss franc, sterling, lira continue to float independently
	June: Gold price at $127

DOLLAR DEVALUATION OF 1973

President Nixon had praised the Smithsonian Agreement as "the most significant monetary agreement in the history of the world." Insofar as it involved drastic realignment of all major currencies by negotiations, it had indeed been unprecedented. But subsequent events would show that it failed to achieve its objectives.

Most notably, the U.S. balance of payments continued to deteriorate in spite of the dollar devaluation. The balance of trade alone showed a record deficit of $6.4 billion for 1972. Forecasts for 1973 predicted a trade deficit of $4 to $5 billion. It may have been too early in 1972 to expect the devaluation of December 1971 to be effective. The effect of devaluation is generally believed to be a matter of several years.

In addition, the U.S. economy was expanding relatively fast during 1972. The income effect of this surge in aggregate demand may have helped to offset the price effect of devaluation.

THE 1973 CRISIS

The 1973 crisis began in its by now familiar form, i.e., heavy speculative sales of dollars for German marks. Only the volume of these sales was unprecedented. The German central bank was reported to have absorbed $6 billion over a ten-day period, with a record of $2 billion on a single day. Once more, the authorities of Germany and other European countries were faced with intense pressure to resort to unpopular revaluation.

U.S. reaction to this crisis was swift and generally welcomed by Europe and Japan. After hurried consultation in European capitals and Tokyo, the dollar was devalued by 10 percent on February 14. But the Smithsonian Agreement did not survive. Several major currencies, such as the yen, the pound sterling, and the Swiss franc emerged from the crisis floating. In addition, while the crisis itself revived general momentum for thorough reform of the monetary system, the threat of global trade restrictions was also resurrected. The U.S. government, for example, was preparing to ask Congress for broad powers in this area, and the possibility of retaliation arose in Europe and Japan.

In March 1973 six members of the EEC, joined later by Norway and Sweden, settled upon fixed exchange rates among themselves within a narrow 2.25 percent margin and agreed to float as a bloc against all other currencies, notably, of course, the U.S. dollar.[33] This arrangement formalized the international monetary problem as one existing primarily between Western Continental Europe and the United States. The members of the joint float would intervene only if their currencies approached the support limits in terms of member currencies. They no longer bought or sold dollars as a matter of official policy.

The Federal Reserve Bank of New York, normally in charge of official U.S. foreign exchange market operations, similarly stayed out of the market during early 1973. The dollar thus floated with relative freedom during this period. Its rate promptly fell to levels which caused surprise among U.S. experts, who at this time began to predict improvement in the U.S. balance of payments.

THE SYSTEM IN THE SEVENTIES

What conclusions can be drawn from these recent developments? First and foremost, we must not draw parallels to the 1930s too readily. Although considerable monetary unrest has plagued the postwar system, international trade and investment have never been seriously interrupted.

[33]Sterling and the Italian lira as well as the yen and the Swiss franc continued to float independently.

Neither can it be said that the postwar system has interfered with general prosperity in the Western industrial world.

While these basic facts should put some perspective on current developments, they are no cause for complacency. The system seems to have deteriorated to a point where thorough reform or massive trade restriction may remain the only alternatives for the seventies.

The Bretton Woods system, preoccupied as it was with insuring against the deflationary bias of the prewar period, may have guarded insufficiently against the opposite extreme, i.e., an inflationary bias. As we have seen, the system proved incapable of eliminating chronic disequilibrium in several major balances of payments. Instead, it provided ample liquidity to finance these disequilibria, an approach which in turn compounded the U.S. deficit. When the method of providing this liquidity, i.e., the U.S. deficit, eventually compromised the dollar as a reserve asset, the system was in serious difficulties. This situation, although developing throughout the sixties, was precipitated by recent internal inflation in the United States and the attendant deficits in its balance of trade. The European countries and Japan contributed to these difficulties by insisting on their surpluses and, by implication, on the U.S. deficit.

The need to reform the system is universally recognized, and each new crisis cannot help but add momentum to this project. There is no lack of reform proposals. But a detailed survey in this area would go beyond our scope. Let us simply outline some of the practical elements which are considered important.

Above all, recent events have shown that a workable balance of payments adjustment mechanism is needed. Since it is no longer realistic to expect countries to deflate internally in response to a deficit, this adjustment mechanism will have to be provided by greater and more frequent flexibility of exchange rates. A practical measure of success in this area would be that countries can no longer maintain semipermanent surpluses or deficits. This flexibility will have to be achieved within the framework of a system, since uncoordinated floating, as we have seen, tends to encourage *ad hoc* intervention in the exchange market with potentially disruptive effects.

Secondly, the heavy reliance on the dollar as a reserve currency will have to be reduced. Success in this area will further facilitate the adjustment of the U.S. deficit. The creation of SDRs may be regarded as a step in this direction. Its effectiveness so far seems to have been overshadowed by the large size of recent U.S. deficits.

Thirdly, changes in the volume of international liquidity will have to be controlled, not by a single country, but through cooperative international arrangements. This again points to SDRs as an important component of monetary reform.

The three elements listed here are, of course, interdependent in various ways. For example, to the extent that greater exchange rate flexibility improves the adjustment process, liquidity needs will be reduced. If, on the other hand, liquidity is expanded too rapidly and ample financing of disequilibria is made available, the adjustment process will once more become sluggish. Or, looking at the second element, if reliance on the dollar as a source of international liquidity cannot be reduced, a U.S. deficit (and surpluses elsewhere) will be required, and the adjustment process will suffer.

In conclusion, let us once more recall that the basic rationale of any monetary system is to facilitate real trade and investment. The success of a system can therefore be measured by the absence of trade restrictions and exchange controls, with the possible exception of controls against speculative short-term capital flows. If the world allows itself to drift into a situation where import surcharges and quotas become the means by which a monetary system is kept in existence, it is making concessions to irrationality. Such a situation is faced by the captain who throws his passengers overboard in order to keep his ship afloat. He is confusing means and ends. The seventies will be crucial for international trade, since the Western world seems to be facing a choice of this nature.

SUMMARY

Under the Bretton Woods system, exchange rates are fixed unless fundamental disequilibrium occurs.

The IMF represents a pool of national currencies and gold on which member countries can draw in proportion to their quotas.

The IMF does not add permanently to international liquidity. SDRs are an exception to this rule.

Sterling was the first European currency to return to dollar convertibility after World II. But this proved premature and ended in devaluation and renewed exchange controls in 1949.

Bilateralism leads to misallocation of resources and reduces the volume of trade. The EPU was a clearing institution designed to dismantle European bilateralism and exchange controls.

The U.S. dollar's initial shortage abroad and its convertibility into gold made it an international reserve asset. Exchange rates, although formally defined in terms of relative gold parities, were actually pegged to the dollar under the gold-exchange or gold–dollar standard.

The U.S. balance of payments deficit became the largest single source of international liquidity. In a sense, therefore, the liquidity needs of the postwar system forced a deficit on the United States.

Perhaps the most important flaw in the Bretton Woods system was the persistence of disequilibria which were clearly fundamental. Britain's deficit and Germany's surplus are examples of such disequilibria.

The General Arrangements to Borrow and the Reciprocal Credit Facilities (swaps) were devices for mutual assistance between the central banks of the Group of Ten.

The closing of the London gold pool in 1968 and the resulting two-tier system significantly reduced dollar convertibility into gold.

While the need to adjust the U.S. balance of payments deficit as well as the European surpluses was recognized on both sides of the Atlantic, each side suggested the other do most of the adjusting.

SDRs are permanent additions to international liquidity. Their creation requires the approval of an 85 percent IMF majority.

The dollar crisis of 1971 eventually led to the Smithsonian Agreement of December 1971. This agreement provided for currency realignments including a dollar devaluation and revaluations of most European currencies and the Japanese yen. In addition, the margin between intervention points was extended to 4.5 percent.

Fourteen months after the Smithsonian Agreement the dollar was once more devalued, and several major currencies were allowed to float.

Reform of the international monetary system will have to deal with the basic adjustment mechanism, the heavy reliance on the U.S. dollar for international liquidity, and the problem of providing liquidity in a controlled manner.

It appears that the seventies will present a choice between thorough monetary reform or increasing worldwide trade restrictions.

SUGGESTED FURTHER READINGS

A detailed survey of international monetary conditions up to about 1963 is provided in Leland B. Yeager, *International Monetary Relations* (Harper & Row, Publishers, Incorporated, New York, 1966), chaps. 19 to 28.

Students interested in keeping up with recent developments will find the following publications useful: *Federal Reserve Bulletin,* Board of Governors, The Federal Reserve System, Washington, D.C.; *Monthly Review,* Federal Reserve Bank of New York; *The Annual Report* of the Bank for International Settlements, Basel; *Quarterly Bulletin,* Bank of England, London; *Monthly Report* and *Annual Report* of the Deutsche Bundesbank, Frankfurt.

The literature on various international monetary issues is extremely large. For a good sampling see R. A. Mundell and A. K. Swoboda (eds.), *Monetary Problems of the International Economy* (University of Chicago Press, 1969). See also *The International Monetary System in Transition,* a symposium (Federal Reserve Bank of Chicago, 1972), and Lawrence H. Officer, "International Monetary Reform: A Review Article," *Journal of Economic Issues,* March 1972.

Index